INTERNATIONAL CONFLICT
AND
BEHAVIORAL SCIENCE

INTERNATIONAL CONFLICT AND BEHAVIORAL SCIENCE

The Craigville Papers

ROGER FISHER, EDITOR

BASIC BOOKS, INC.

Publishers

NEW YORK

Foreword

Physical scientists today play a prominent role in the world-wide effort to reduce the risk of nuclear disaster. It may be only natural that, as nations threaten one another with nuclear weapons, the nuclear physicist is called on for advice. Yet, if a woman threatens to hit her husband with pots and pans, it would never occur to us in seeking to preserve the peace to ask the advice of an aluminum expert. We would turn to those who have studied problems of human behavior. It is no derogation of the physical scientist to suggest that the training and knowledge of the behavioral scientist may have greater relevance than his to the problem of achieving a less dangerous way of handling international conflict. It was Einstein who pointed out: "The unleashed power of the atom has changed everything except our way of thinking." The problem of changing our way of thinking is a problem of human behavior.

A physiologist myself, and hence no expert in the field, I have been struck by the persistence of the ways of thinking which underlie group conflict. Our habits of thought in relation to aggressive nationalism seem deeply ingrained. A man's particular in-group—be it family, clan, city, religion, political ideology, class, or nation—is concerned with status, position, property. He regards the group into which he has been accidentally born as superior to other groups and calls on his gods for assurance and support. Like many other animals—bees, ants, baboons, and yaks—he is prepared to fight and die for his group. One fights and dies for his territory, whether one is a Siamese fighting-fish, bird, rat, lion, seal, Athenian/Spartan, Roman/Carthaginian, or an American/Russian in the nuclear age. These aggressive aspects of people in groups are products of millions of years of biological evolution.

The beliefs we hold so strongly are mostly established by accidents of birth and of what we learn, hit or miss, before we are seven years old. Emotionally charged prejudices—as well as high ideals—are propagated from generation to generation by parental and adult prestige and by myths and symbols. The strongest beliefs one holds often bear little relation to the realities of life as related to the common good.

How have men in the past preserved their ideals but transcended their group distrusts, fears, and hates of one another? Despite the strength of our parochial hates, they have always had an ephemeral quality. Catholics and Protestants no longer want to kill each other; the seventeenth century's theological issues have lost their urgency. What factors bring about changes of this sort? As a layman, I think of communication; transportation; trade; and exchange of students, scientists, artists, athletes, writers, and professional and business people as solvents for current group tensions. But these are obviously neither necessary nor sufficient conditions. We need understanding, and we need theory. Today, as never before, we feel an urgent need to hasten the dissolution of the hates between East and West, since there will be nothing ephemeral about the results of a nuclear war. How can these threatening international-conflict situations be resolved, or, if that is asking too much, how can they be successfully coped with? What alternatives are there to mutually suicidal nuclear war?

This book deals with approaches to peace by a group of behavioral scientists concerned with answers to these questions. The project itself grew from the beliefs that the most difficult problems are not those concerned with the disposition of weaponry and hardware, but those of human conduct, and that behavioral scientists should have something to contribute.

As always, for those seeking to bring about a change, the initial question is: Where do the choices lie? On this, as on other questions, this book presents no single answer. It is not a polemic presenting us with an either/or choice between salvation and doom. None of the authors purports to have the answer. The intentional diversity of their interests and views was designed, not to produce a single answer, but to illuminate the kinds of contribution which behavioral science can make.

Here is a primer on the most pressing problem of the day. This book breaks ground in exploring alternative ways in which our knowledge of human behavior may improve the chance of human survival.

Boston, Massachusetts
March 1964

HUDSON HOAGLAND
President, American Academy
of Arts and Sciences

Acknowledgments

Contributions from many sources were instrumental in organizing the conference of which this book is the final result.

On behalf of the American Academy of Arts and Sciences, I would like to acknowledge a debt of gratitude to the Carnegie Corporation and to the New Hope Foundation for financial support which made the project possible and to express appreciation to the Massachusetts Congregational Christian Conference, which graciously arranged living quarters for the conference at the Craigville Inn.

On behalf of the authors, I would like to thank the Academy itself, in its many manifestations, for undertaking the project, supporting it with whatever service was required, and letting us see what such an experiment could produce. In particular, acknowledgment is due Hudson Hoagland, president of the Academy, for his lively interest and perseverance, and Carl Binger, Stanley Cobb, and Lawrence Frank, who served on the ad hoc Academy committee overseeing the project. Erik Erikson, also on that committee, gave so much of himself in working on ideas as to some of which he was quite skeptical that he deserves our special appreciation. Geno Ballotti and Ralph Burhoe, assisted by the staff of the Academy, especially Judith Andrews, Patricia Flaherty, Nancy Howell, Sandra Katz, and Catherine Wilder, handled the administration of the project, earning the praise and gratitude of us all.

On behalf of the editorial committee, I would like to thank Babette Spiegel, Marian Poverman, and Barbara Mello of Cambridge Editorial Research, Inc., who relieved us of the bulk of the onerous aspects of an editor's task, and to thank our fellow authors for bearing with us during the long process of converting "The Craigville Papers" into a book.

For myself, as chairman of the editorial committee, I would like to acknowledge the substantial editorial work of my colleagues, Kenneth Boulding, Morton Deutsch, and Lester Grinspoon. Finally, it should be noted that, to the extent that one man deserves credit for this cooperative venture, he is Lester Grinspoon who, as instigator and director, was its guiding spirit from beginning to end.

Cambridge, Massachusetts   ROGER FISHER
February 1964

The Authors

KENNETH E. BOULDING, M.A. (Oxon.): co-director, Center for Research on Conflict Resolution; professor of economics, University of Michigan; author of several books including *Conflict and Defense* (1962), *The Image* (1956), *Economic Analysis* (3rd ed., 1955), *The Economics of Peace* (1945).

URIE BRONFENBRENNER, PH.D.: professor of psychology and child development and family relationships, Cornell University; fellow, Center for Advanced Study in the Behavioral Sciences, Stanford, California, 1955–1956.

MORTON DEUTSCH, PH.D.: professor of psychology and education and director of the Laboratory of Social Psychology, Teachers College, Columbia University; co-author of *Interracial Housing* (1951) and *Research Methods in Social Relations* (1959); co-editor of *Preventing World War III, Some Proposals* (1962).

AMITAI ETZIONI, PH.D.: associate professor of sociology and staff member of Institute of War and Peace Studies, Columbia University; author of *A Comparative Analysis of Complex Organizations* (1961), *The Hard Way to Peace* (1962), and *Winning without War* (1964).

ROGER FISHER, A.B., LL.B.: professor of law, Harvard Law School; author of "Constructing Rules That Affect Governments," in *Arms Control, Disarmament and National Security* (1961), and other articles on international law; consultant, Department of Defense.

WILLIAM A. GAMSON, PH.D. (social psychology): assistant professor of sociology, University of Michigan, and staff member of the Center for Research on Conflict Resolution; articles on coalition formation, community conflict, and international conflict.

KATHLEEN GOUGH, PH.D.: research associate in anthropology, University of Oregon; author of articles on South Indian caste and kinship; co-author with David M. Schneider of *Matrilineal Kinship* (1961).

LESTER GRINSPOON, M.D.: senior research psychiatrist, Massachusetts Mental
Health Center, Boston; instructor in psychiatry, Harvard Medical
School; publications in social psychiatry, group therapy, psycho-
pharmacology, and medicine.

E. JAMES LIEBERMAN, M.D., M.P.H.: psychiatrist, Bethesda, Maryland; publications on psychological aspects of nonviolence, psychochemical
weapons, and international communication.

ELLIOT G. MISHLER, PH.D. (social psychology): director of psychological
research, Massachusetts Mental Health Center, Boston; clinical associate in psychology, department of psychiatry, Harvard Medical
School; publications in social psychiatry, epidemiology, and social
organization.

ANATOL RAPOPORT, PH.D.: professor, Mental Health Research Institute, University of Michigan; fellow, Center for Advanced Study in the Behavioral Sciences, Stanford, California, 1954–1955; author of *Science
and the Goals of Man* (1950), *Operational Philosophy* (1953), *Fights,
Games, and Debates* (1960), *Strategy and Conscience* (1963).

JAMES A. ROBINSON, PH.D.: associate professor of political science and senior
member, International Relations Program, Northwestern University;
author of *Congress and Foreign Policy Making* (1962), *The House
Rules Committee* (1963).

ARTHUR WASKOW, PH.D. (history): Peace Research Institute fellow, the
Institute for Policy Studies, Washington, D.C.; author of *The Limits
of Defense* (1962) and *The Worried Man's Guide to World Peace*
(1963).

Contents

PART V: Influencing National Action, 255

INTERNATIONAL
CONFLICT
AND
BEHAVIORAL
SCIENCE

Introduction

ROGER FISHER

No one, it may be assumed, is happy with the present method of coping with international conflict. It is dangerous and it is costly in both economic and human terms. Yet when one seeks alternative ways of handling international conflict, the question of where to begin appears overwhelming. There is no single correct way of looking at conflict. Certainly there is no single answer to the question of what ought to be done. This book grew from the premise that the most difficult problems are not those of the physical or natural sciences but those of human behavior. If peace is primarily a problem of people, not of hardware, behavioral scientists should have something to contribute. But what?

Under the sponsorship of the American Academy of Arts and Sciences, thirteen of us met and considered "alternatives to the use of force as a means of settling international problems." We were four social psychologists, a mathematical psychologist, two psychiatrists, a sociologist, an anthropologist, a political scientist, an economist, an historian, and an international lawyer. Even among these limited disciplines, the group was hardly a representative selection. Although our degrees of experience in international affairs varied, we were all biased by an immediate concern for the state of the world and a skepticism about the way governments are now behaving.

We accepted the working assumption that conflict is an inevitable feature of social life and that in international relations, as in other areas of human interaction, there are constructive as well as destructive ways of handling it. Each of us was asked to consider some aspect of the system of influences working upon, or the operating assumptions of, decision-makers in international conflict situations; to formulate propositions as to changes which ought to be made in the way international conflict is handled; and to suggest how such changes might be brought about.

At Craigville, on Cape Cod, we lived and worked together for five weeks during the summer of 1962. We had expected that, like the blind men who each grasped a different part of the elephant, our various perceptions of the problem would be diverse and often seemingly unrelated. Our expectations were fulfilled. We were confronted with preliminary working papers which discussed different aspects of the international conflict process from different points of view, papers which were often concerned with methodological questions, papers which were written at different levels of generality, and papers giving different advice to different audiences. Working together we not only learned a good deal about the difficulties of cross-disciplinary communication but developed some sense of the "elephant problem," as jointly perceived by this particular group of blind, or at least nearsighted, academicians. Although we had no Soviet behavioral scientist in the group, we needed none to stir up controversy and lively discussion. Often, the nearest we could come to a joint perception was agreeing as to where we disagreed.

Half the papers here bear almost no relation to the preliminary working papers written before the conference. Some are the product of the kind of examination of first principles that comes when candid and persuasive colleagues question the value not only of one's latest idea but also of one's entire approach. For many of us, the intensive interchange across disciplinary lines provided experience which we should derive from our universities but too often do not. Although the papers remain the output and responsibility of their respective authors, none of us came through the summer unaffected by his colleagues. This introduction must serve as a joint and mutual acknowledgment.

Perhaps more important than the individual papers, the volume as a whole suggests the relationship of various intellectual efforts in the peace field to each other. Anyone following at all closely current discussion of the problems of war and peace is aware of the welter of suggestions and prescriptions for the world's ills. The mass of published material is exceeded by the informal, mimeographed, and oral outpourings of conferences, panels, round tables, newsletters, and programs of organizations and individuals actively concerned with saving the world from nuclear destruction. If peace research is to be a serious academic pursuit, there will have to be more than a large quantity of unrelated projects and proposals. We will need to develop some understanding of the whole problem and how the various efforts being made are intellectually related to each other.

By and large, the ideas in this volume are cumulative rather than inconsistent; the critical ways in which they differ from each other are implicit rather than explicit. Before turning to differences of subject matter, we can point to three large variables which go far toward reconciling differences in approach and make it possible to establish contact between different ideas and different disciplines. These variables, cutting across everything in this volume and other research efforts as well, may be roughly labeled "academic scale," "time scale," and "what is taken as given."

DIFFERENCES IN ACADEMIC SCALE

A great difference among us and among others working in peace research lies in our conception of what we are trying to do. The papers here run the gamut from modest and cautious conclusions to wild and imaginative suggestions. At one end of the scale are those who emphasize scientific method. They feel at home designing or executing a research project, carefully analyzing properly selected data, and drawing sound and limited conclusions. We all recognized that our summer institute would not offer an opportunity for carrying on research of that kind. Except for papers drawing on research previously undertaken, this volume contains little that resembles the reports of a social scientist's research project—the well-considered and cautious conclusions of a scholar, footnoted, documented, and prepared to be defended against all comers.

Most of these papers fall near the other end of the scale. They are intended to suggest hypotheses and approaches, to stimulate thinking in different directions, to propose new ways of looking at a problem. This is not accidental. Our project was the first of a proposed several-year effort by the American Academy of Arts and Sciences to apply behavioral science to problems of war and peace. Each of us was asked to say what he wanted to say but was encouraged to let his reach exceed his grasp, to be suggestive rather than exhaustive.

In seeking to develop theories and hypotheses, we took a cue from the physical sciences. In peace studies even more than in physical science, it seemed to some of us, theory and suggestion must precede proof. A leap forward in man's ability to control his future will require a great many ideas, some of which will prove to be without merit. A credible theory can be as useful as a well-documented conclusion. Not only may it open the way for further investigation and reflection, it may also begin immediately to compete with the equally unverified theories upon which those who are handling international conflict are now proceeding. To produce untested ideas was one of the tasks we set ourselves.

What I call academic scale underlies much of the difficulty we had in working across disciplinary lines. A lawyer or doctor, secure in his well-defined and well-established profession, may be quite willing to produce a half-baked theory or idea on a matter clearly outside his professional domain. In fact, it sometimes seems that those who have the highest competence within a specific professional field produce the least reliable views on international affairs. On the other hand, a social psychologist may be less willing to suggest a broad proposition on the kind of problems under discussion here for two reasons: (1) he is better aware of the complexities, and (2) the problem lies within an area in which his professional reputation is at stake. He may fear that if he abandons his scientific methodology, he may have little more to offer than a newspaper columnist.

Such different perceptions of what one is trying to do often lead to frustration, even after one understands a colleague's approach. For example, I was particularly interested in the consequences of threatening a government and thought that an expert in small-group behavior might provide some useful analogies. It seemed likely to me that when a group is threatened, each member is more concerned about his own standing in the eyes of his fellows than he is about the consequences to the group as a whole. Putting the problem to an expert, I received not the off-the-cuff answer for which I hoped, but a tentative design for a research project which might, in time, provide information bearing on the point.

Conflicts in methodology and objective were frequent. The fact that different academic tasks were being pursued should be kept in mind as these papers are read; in that variety lies much of their value.

DIFFERENCES IN TIME SCALE

The Craigville institute, like most projects concerned with avoiding nuclear war, started with the assumption that some action could and should be taken. Looking toward a better way of handling international conflict, it asked: What should be done? All of the papers here are designed to help answer that question. There is no necessary agreement, however, on the time period with respect to the question. The man who proposes a teletype between the White House and the Kremlin and the man who proposes world government may be differing only because they are answering different questions: "What should be done next week?" as opposed to "What should be done over the next generation?"

The time period which each writer is considering is usually not made explicit. In some cases it may be unimportant, or a paper may have some implications for the immediate future and others for a later period. There are no doubt criteria by which a person outside the government should choose the time scale for his recommendations if he wishes them to be effective. The criteria might depend on subject matter and the kind of decision involved. A goal or target situation may be of maximum use if it is sufficiently far in the future to provide perspective on immediate issues but not so remote as to appear unrelated to them. The papers demonstrate how significant a variable time may be. Others working out suggestions in peace studies may well want to ask themselves explicitly what period of the future they wish to consider—and why.

WHAT IS TAKEN AS GIVEN

The most critical variable explaining differences in approach among these papers, and among the proposals of others, lies in what each author takes as determined and what each assumes is subject to change. Independent of time, we each have a notion of what falls within the realm of the possible. If a person takes everything as determined, he can watch the world as a pure spectator sport, confident that nothing he can do will affect anything. If he operates on the assumption that there are no limits on his power, he is certainly wrong and is likely to be ineffective. Between these two extremes, each of us, explicitly or implicitly, takes some forces and conditions in the world as given and focuses on an area in which he believes a change can be made. In suggesting how things might be altered for the better, each assumes that certain changes can be brought about and that such changes might significantly affect the way international conflict is handled. Many, if not all, of our differences can be understood in terms of a different assessment of which handle is the easiest to grasp, a different assessment of where the greatest chance of bringing about significant improvement lies.

More accurately, each has focused, in these papers, on one or more variables while holding the others constant. There is no necessary inconsistency as to assumptions about what is possible. The papers suggest, rather, that different people can best study different problems. The fact that one change is possible does not mean that another is not. Nevertheless, there were large differences among us as to what should be taken as given and at which points change should be attempted. The papers invite an explicit study of the criteria by which one should define the changes considered to be within the realm of the possible.

TWO MAJOR DIVISIONS

The subject matter of bringing about alternative ways to handle international conflict—the problem of avoiding war—apparently divides into two major areas. The first is the task of devising the means by which conflict that is now carried on as intergovernmental conflict *ought* to be carried on. (What should the government do?) The second area covers problems involved in how to *cause* governments to carry on conflict properly. (How do we make the government do it?) This division of the peace problem seems basic and useful. In the first area, there are questions ranging from the theoretical—for example, how governments ought to behave and what the future world society ought to look like—to the distinctly practical—what the United States government ought to do in specific situations. Many of those outside the government, who nonetheless identify themselves with the administration, tend to look on the first area as the vital one. To them, the peace problem is primarily one of devising the theoretical guide lines or the practical policies which the government ought to follow.

To others devoting their energies toward peace, the major problem seems quite different. Those more alienated from the administration, as well as some within it, tend to believe that they know what the government ought to do and that the major problem is making it or allowing it to do so. They recognize that government officials operate under constraints and are subject to many influences. They see the peace problem as primarily one of altering these constraints or influencing governmental action. To a large extent, the peace movement in the United States today is directing its intellectual and political attention to this second area. Its workers are seeking to devise and implement ways of causing the government to do what they believe it ought to do.

This major division in subject matter between concern over how governments should cope with international conflict and concern over how to affect national decision-making often corresponds to a division between the audiences to whom such arguments are directed. Those working on the way in which international conflict ought to be handled are usually speaking to government decision-makers, though their material has relevance to others as well. Those working on the way to affect national decision-making are usually speaking to the peace movement and to others outside the government.

THE INTERNATIONAL PAPERS

Although the distinction between working on what governments ought to do and working on how to make them do it is a useful one, the papers in this volume do not fall neatly into one category or the other. The authors rightly felt no need to respect such boundaries. Nevertheless, the first ten papers are primarily relevant to devising wise national policies vis-à-vis other countries.

These international papers, in turn, fall into three groups. Some are concerned with trying to understand international conflict. Rapoport suggests that governmental policy is currently based on a misconception of the conflict between the Soviet Union and the United States. In *Perceiving the Cold War* he contends that the conflict between myths is far greater than actual differences. Gamson accepts the fact that Americans have differing perceptions of international affairs and asks how one can know which view is most plausible. In *Evaluating Beliefs about International Conflict,* he describes the way in which a person might determine that one set of underlying assumptions about East-West relations had greater validity than another, through a systematic examination of specific conflicts of the past.

These first two papers implicitly consider the Soviet-United States conflict as fundamental. Kathleen Gough, taking an anthropologist's look at the globe, identifies the primary long-range conflict as one between the unsatisfied peoples of the emerging nations and the rich, white, industrialized peoples. In *The Crisis of the Nation-State,* she questions whether the governments of existing nations can rapidly enough undertake the major changes required to cope with this basic conflict. Boulding backs still further away from immediate political issues, reflecting an economist's appreciation of the importance of theory. In his paper, *Toward a Theory of Peace,* he suggests that the principal danger to international stability lies in the attempt to organize an international system by threat and counterthreat, almost to the exclusion of other methods of social organization.

The first four papers are thus concerned with the assumptions a national decision-maker makes about the existing scheme of things. What is the structure and nature of the international conflict situation? With all its pitfalls, the analogy of a game may be useful. The first problem is to understand what game is being played. The questions of how best to play the game and how to change the game into a less dangerous one remain to be considered. The next two groups of papers deal with those questions.

During our discussions of international conflict at Craigville, we perceived that the danger of war arises when a nation has more at stake in a particular conflict than it has in the ongoing international community. To be willing to lose a particular conflict issue rather than fight, a country must perceive that its gains from existing and future international co-operation are greater than the loss that it may suffer on this particular occasion. Efforts to lessen the danger of war are designed to affect one or the other side of this scale—either to make particular conflicts less threatening to the nations involved or to develop the international community so that it has more to offer.

There are three papers on the handling of conflicts. My paper, *Fractionating Conflict*, proposes that a more conscious effort be made to keep the size of international issues under control. There are many advantages to considering a problem as a special case and not as a test case. Lieberman's paper, *Threat and Assurance in the Conduct of Conflict*, draws on his psychiatric training as well as his profound interest in Gandhian nonviolence. He suggests that conflict can be carried on in a manner that is constructive rather than destructive, that tends to be healing rather than divisive. In contrast, Waskow's paper, *Nonlethal Equivalents of War*, accepts the basic hostility between East and West and explores ways in which that conflict might be pursued vigorously and with a purpose of victory but without the use of military weapons. All of these papers concentrate on the process of conducting individual conflicts. All look toward ways of managing what may be considered units of conflict in a less threatening and less destructive way.

Three of the papers seem most relevant to the long-range problem of developing a more satisfactory international community. Morton Deutsch's paper, *Producing Change in an Adversary*, points out that to accept the assumption that another country is extremely hostile toward us does not mean that we should limit ourselves to reciprocal hostility. On the contrary, one of our purposes should be to turn the adversary into a friend. Deutsch explores some of the problems in pursuing such a policy. Bronfenbrenner considers one of the major hurdles to building international community—the difficulty of communicating between peoples who see international reality so differently—in his paper, *Allowing for Soviet Perceptions*. Etzioni's paper, *Atlantic Union, the Southern Continents and the United Nations*, concentrates on institutional aspects of building international community. Using proposals for an Atlantic community as a point of departure, he considers the conditions under which regional and bloc communities might gradually grow toward one in which the ultimate level of consensus would be the United Nations.

PAPERS ON INFLUENCING GOVERNMENT

The last six papers focus on the problem of how to cause a government to do what it ought to do. Here the problem of the handling of international conflict is not considered as a failure of knowledge or understanding about the policies which ought to be pursued. The problem is seen as the consequence of constraints or influences upon those who decide. Three papers explore psychological and institutional constraints on those making policy decisions. Rapoport's stinging *Critique of Strategic Thinking* attacks the superrational approach to human problems in which, explicitly or implicitly, affairs involving people in different countries are analogized to a game where the sole objective of each side is to have the other lose. He suggests that such an approach precludes reaching a successful international relationship as much as looking for a strategy to defeat one's spouse would preclude reaching a successful marriage relationship. Grinspoon looks at problems which may result from the life a responsible and busy decision-maker tends to lead. His paper, *Interpersonal Constraints and the Decision-Maker*, points out, among other aspects, the lack of critical feedback which so often exists when dealing with subordinates. My brief paper, *Defects in the Governmental Decision Process*, considers institutional features which may explain why able and informed officials sometimes make mistakes.

The papers in the final group bear on the problem of influencing the government from the outside. Mishler, in *The Peace Movement and the Foreign Policy Process*, suggests that those wishing to affect governmental policy should make a more careful study of the opportunities for exerting influence and the means which behavioral science indicates to be the most effective. In *The Social Scientist and Congress*, Robinson makes a modest proposal that colleagues who wish to be effective might be wise to work in areas where the government has need for their particular training and skills. Grinspoon's paper, *The Truth Is Not Enough*, received nation-wide notice when he presented a version of it at the annual meeting of the American Association for the Advancement of Science. He warns that anyone seeking to influence national decisions should be aware of the danger of tampering with the defense mechanisms which people who see no appropriate course of action use to protect themselves from unpleasant reality.

The problem of developing alternative ways of handling international conflict is obviously a large one. It is both a myriad of problems, a few of which are discussed in this volume, and a problem that can be looked at as a whole. By focusing light on various specific issues in the peace field simultaneously, efforts that are seemingly diverse help illuminate the large problem. Rather than providing the answer to the problem of international conflict, this book suggests that no single answer exists and that progressive improvement in the handling of international conflict will require many answers from many people. Rather than reporting on a task completed, this book suggests how much remains to be done.

PART I

The Nature of
International Conflict

1

ANATOL RAPOPORT

Perceiving the Cold War

The distinction between the issues and the causes of a conflict is a useful one. The issues are overtly stated claims, grievances or positions. They may be explicit and precise—for example, the presence of allied troops in West Berlin or the operations of guerrillas in South Vietnam. Or, issues may be vague and general—the triumph of democracy, or the victory of socialism. When major conflicts are examined in retrospect, it often becomes apparent that the issues were not the underlying bases of the conflicts but only the symptoms. The conflicts had deeper "causes," which were not overtly expressed either because they would compromise the conflicting parties or because the conflicting parties were not aware of them. For example, it has been maintained that a struggle for the control of markets, not a concern for democracy or *kultur,* was the "real cause" of World War I. Some, like Thucydides and Lewis F. Richardson, have maintained that mutually stimulated fears, nourished by mutually stimulating arms races, are the most important causes of wars. Others, notably psychiatrists, have maintained that aggressive, destructive drives are the underlying causes of major conflicts, including wars.

We have put the word "causes" in quotation marks to indicate that arguments concerning the sources of conflicts, particularly wars, cannot be supported on scientific grounds. We cannot go back to a previous point in history and see how events would have unfolded under a different set of conditions. The persuasiveness of such an argument rests on a feeling that the argument somehow "makes sense." Thus, there is wide agreement that the major European wars of the seventeenth century were instigated by opposing religious loyalties, that the Russo-Finnish War of 1939–40 and the occupation of Iceland by the United States in 1941 are best explained by military-strategic considerations, and that the wars over the possession of colonies were predominantly economic.

It seems to us that no explanation of the present East-West conflict can make sense without a heavy reliance on *ideological* issues and causes. If the conflict were entirely about strategic and political matters (Germany, Southeast Asia, and so forth), it could, in principle, be settled on that level. If the danger of war could be directly related to objective causes, for example, armament levels, then the admission by both sides that war would be disastrous would make for strong pressures to remove the danger. The facts of our time, however, are that explicit issues remain unsettled, and hopes for disarmament remain dim. We must conclude that more covert or more "irrational" factors are operating to inhibit the liquidation of the conflict. We shall try to derive these factors from the ideological commitments of the opponents, that is, from ways of thinking rooted in different world views.

This approach may seem to be in accord with conventional sentiments about the issues of the Cold War, invariably pictured in the propaganda torrents of both sides as an ideological struggle. While admitting the ideological underpinnings of the conflict, we shall also attack conventional ideological interpretations and try to separate the real ideological issues and causes from imagined ones.

In former days, failure to achieve a peaceful settlement of an international conflict did not necessarily imply that decision-makers were behaving irrationally. Before the advent of nuclear weapons, some wars could be rationalized on utilitarian grounds. Some countries, at least their ruling groups, actually profited from victorious wars. It could be argued that wars and risks of wars were undertaken on the basis of rational decisions. To make the argument convincing, at least four kinds of factors would have to be displayed:

(1) The net gains resulting from military victory;
(2) The probability of military victory (and the complementary probability of defeat);
(3) The losses resulting from military defeat;
(4) The gains or losses resulting from a proposed peaceful settlement (or status quo).

If numerical values could be assigned to all these factors, one could calculate the "expected gain" of war, i.e., the gains of victory weighted by the corresponding probability minus the losses of defeat correspondingly weighted. If this expected gain (positive or negative) were algebraically larger than the gain (positive or negative) from the proposed peaceful settlement, the decision to go to war would appear as a "rational decision."

In our own time, we find a crucial difference. There is now overwhelming agreement among policy-makers and their advisers (including some proponents of the toughest and riskiest military postures) that the "expected gains" of a nuclear war, *whoever* "wins," should be represented by a very large negative number. There are no arguments in favor of waging a nuclear war with a view of *gaining* something, as wars of conquest, commercial advantage, or national liberation were waged in the past. Risk of war is advocated openly only on two grounds: (1) to deter the opponent from making war, and/or (2) to avoid the losses incurred in an unfavorable settlement. We shall not be concerned with the first rationale (the deterrence problem) in this essay, but only with the second.

THE IMAGE OF THE ENEMY

War-risk advocates rely mostly on picturesque descriptions of what is likely to happen, often what will surely happen, if we falter in our posture of toughness. Sometimes these prognoses are spelled out in terms of an imagined sequence of events. For the most part, no explicit description is given. The disaster is summed up in a suggestive phrase: the Communists will "take over" like gangsters or "keep nibbling at the edges of the free world" like rats.

In the United States, grim visions are readily conjured up by these phrases because of our vivid, vicarious experience with analogous situations: the tyrannical rule of Wild West desperados over frontier towns, the domination of urban communities by racketeers and political bosses, and, somewhat more pertinently, Nazi blackmail and conquests and Soviet rule in Eastern Europe. A frightful image of the enemy emerges—the devil in his modern disguise as the bombastic dictator, the smooth chief of secret police with the foreign accent, the sadistic strawboss, or the psychopathic gangster.

On a somewhat less primitive level, the personalized image of the Enemy dissolves into the "System," or the "Ism." Here the personal Devil is replaced by the impersonal coercion machine and its corresponding newsreel images: marching boots, acres of children doing calisthenics, barbed-wire compounds, shrieking propaganda, debilitating conformity. These images also find echoes in our own experience. Certain aspects of American life have also become "regimented" through "The Organization," through mass production, through militarization.

In addition to the Devil and the "Ism," there is still a third image of the Enemy. This one has not yet pervaded the popular consciousness but is dominant in the minds of decision-makers and their advisers—the architects of "postures," military strategies, and diplomatic maneuvers. This third image is neither a villain nor a nightmare but a faceless Opponent, with whom we are playing a game of Winner Take All. The Opponent need not be motivated by hatred or by lust for power. Indeed he need not be human. He could well be a programed computer. He plays The Game according to rational strategic principles, he is always maximizing his advantage within the constraints imposed by *his* Opponent (us).

This image, like the others, makes sense to those in whom it evokes important and familiar experiences. It makes sense to the strategists because it invokes their professional experiences. Strategists work in the context of The Game. Their careers are invested in it. Their competence is judged by their grasp of its complexities. The Game has become their reality. In fact, The Game *is* a sizeable portion of American perceived reality. It is an idealized version of business competition, in which each entrepreneur is not only allowed but expected to maximize his profits under imposed constraints. The departure of actual economic life from the idealized version is not relevant as long as the idealized picture of the economic game is accepted as normal.

Of these three images, the first one, that of the personalized Devil, is not important. It can be, and frequently is, disavowed as primitive or naïve without changing the climate in which present policies are conceived. The individual leaders or the archetypes of the opposing camp need not be pictured as fiends. But they must be assumed to be entirely and irrevocably committed both to the System (which must be pictured as utterly evil) and to The Game. The essential image is reduced to this: The Game is being played exclusively according to strategy considerations, like chess, where it is certain, not merely probable, that whatever can be done to gain an advantage or to harm the opponent will be done by a rational player. The penalty for losing The Game is submission to the System.

Even the mention of the penalty is unnecessary if one is a strategist entirely committed to The Game. The penalty for losing The Game is simply losing the game, which is, by definition, the worst possible outcome. To play the game of chess well, the chess player need not be spurred either by the glory of victory or by the humiliation of defeat. He plays well, which means ruthlessly, because he is a chess player and derives gratification from playing well. In business life, men who care little about money, which they often squander, gamble away, or give away to worthy causes, nevertheless play the business game as red-blooded Americans are supposed to play it—to win.

But the game of global strategy is not played for chips or even for money. The "players" cannot avoid being reminded of the real events behind some of the "outcomes" of The Game. If these events were pictured realistically instead of symbolically, on the score board, there might be no escape from the conclusion that The Game is not worth playing. This is why the penalty for losing The Game—submission to the utterly evil System—must be kept constantly in mind. So must the image of the utterly ruthless Opponent. The image of the Opponent is necessary in order to assign certainty to the worst he can do; the image of the System is necessary in order to assign the largest negative utility to the "lost game."

THE CENTRAL CORE OF ETHOS

We have suggested that the image of the Enemy persists because it provides a rationalization for The Game in which the professional prestige of strategists is vested. This is not the only reason for its persistence. Like any other firmly held delusion, the conventional image of the world conflict, which guides the current policies of both sides, has a grain of truth in it. The idea of Communist conspiracy—as of capitalist encirclement—can be supported by properly selected and properly interpreted events and quotations. To point out that a grain of truth is not the whole truth, or that human lives should weigh more heavily in calculated risks, or that other extrapolations of experience are equally reasonable, is simply to plead for the abandonment of the established image. Such pleas are not likely to pierce the defenses of those who view the global conflict as a struggle between Good and Evil.

Why do so many cling to the Conspiracy or Encirclement idea so tenaciously? Explanations have been offered by drawing parallels with paranoid perceptions and reactions. But in view of the fact that a large majority of our population, who cannot all be paranoid, actually believe in the Conspiracy (as people in the U.S.S.R. believe in Encirclement), we must reject the "paranoid obsession" explanation as oversimplified.

We suspect that people cling to the conventional view of the conflict because this view is linked with fundamental *positive* values. An attack on the conventional view is instinctively interpreted as an attack on the *central core of one's ethos*. Such an attack cannot be tolerated. To be heard at all, a criticism of the conventional view must be so constructed that it does not threaten to destroy the ethos. The criticism must try to restructure the world view so that the central core of the ethos is preserved and even strengthened. But this is not always possible. It is not clear how one can proceed to restructure the world view of a White Supremacist or a Nazi or a dedicated member of the Birch Society without destroying its central core. However, in the case of a sincere exponent of "Americanism" or of "Communism," we believe this can be done.

Implementing a public policy directed toward re-examining our conception of global conflict presents a difficult problem in the United States, where direct governmental control over mass media of communication is lacking. Still a great deal could be done by an administration determined to modify the crude conventional view, whose most active proponents are the extreme right. To initiate a public reappraisal requires a decision to "write off" this political sector, to accept its permanent opposition or alienation. But it is a definite political sacrifice, an act of "bad politics" by professional standards, to assign zero weight to a political sector whose weight is not in fact zero.

AMERICANISM AND COMMUNISM

The problem is to re-examine *publicly* the nature of "Americanism" and of "Communism." I use the much-abused term "Americanism" instead of "capitalism" or "democracy" advisedly, because I believe an indigenous world view does exist in America, derived from specific cultural experience of Americans. Similarly, when I speak of Communism, I mean primarily Soviet Communism, for which unfortunately no special term exists.[a] There is a central core in both of these views which must be preserved if Americans and Russians are ever to participate in a world community freely and with full commitment.

The central core of Americanism comes from the roots of American history. The best features of American civilization, as well as the sources of nourishment of American genius, in turn derive from it. This idea may sound like an apology for a mystique, but there is really nothing mystical about it. On the contrary, the sources of Americanism are quite easy to trace and its modern manifestations are easy to identify.

The dominant sources of Americanism are two: the break with European society and the conquest of the frontier. The two are related, because the drive for the frontier, like emigration from Europe, also involved social and emotional breaks, a pulling up of stakes. The early American cry was "Leave me alone!" or "Don't tread on me!" This is the leitmotiv of the great American saga, *Huckleberry Finn,* the story of the boy who fled from riches, from Protestant respectability, from his father, from a senseless vendetta, from a pair of parasitic swindlers. The other hero of the saga is a fugitive slave. If the story of Huckleberry Finn is one half of the American epic, the other half is the romance of the Connecticut Yankee, the man "who could make anything."

The watchwords of Americanism, then, are liberty, self-reliance, and ingenuity, qualities which relate the individual to his milieu negatively if at all. Positive social virtues are not lacking in the American ethos, but they are "tacked on," as it were. *First,* the individual establishes himself as free, self-reliant, and ingenious. *Then,* he fulfills his obligations to other, perhaps less fortunate, individuals or to society at large. Philanthropy fits well into this picture. So does a career of public service; the individual is pictured as *giving himself* to the service of his society, never as being *made* by his society. Even in the context of social responsibility, the individual is seen as a free agent, whose fulfillment of social responsibility is a mark of generosity, possibly even a sacrifice, not an integral part of self-fulfillment.

[a] Bolshevism is not an accurate designation, being associated primarily with the early period of this philosophy, and Leninism is too intimately associated with a doctrinaire political creed rather than with an internalized world view.

The genuinely social, or communal, aspects of the fundamental American ethos are ordinarily confined to the local level. The barn-raising tradition (philanthropy in reverse, in which the community helps the unfortunate member or the newcomer), the town meeting, the school board, the church—these are felt to be the foundations of American democracy.

The emergence of the good society, then, is seen through American eyes as proceeding from the individual *out*. Free individuals make a good community. By some tacit extrapolation, it is assumed that good communities add up to a good society, an element of the scheme Americans have perceived only dimly. The good society is viewed as a matrix in which the individual has maximum opportunity to pursue his "happiness." This is the American Dream. Its philosophical expression is Rousseau's *Social Contract*; its manifesto is the Declaration of Independence; its nourishment came from an environment ideally suited to its realization—a vast, rich, empty continent. Its continual reiteration, ranging from the artless, through the pious, to the blatant and the arrogant, is found on every page of *Reader's Digest*.

The sources of the Communist ethos are more difficult to trace. Some see them in the primitive communism of early Christianity; others in the Roman ideal of the justice-dispensing state. St. Augustine's *Civitas Dei* appears to be an amalgamation of these two sources. The long history of protocommunist fantasies can be traced in the utopian literature, of which Plato's *Republic* and Thomas More's *Utopia* (sources acknowledged by Marx) are the best-known examples.

A fundamental difference between the respective geneses of American and Communist social ideals is immediately apparent. The American "pursuit of happiness" ideal is rooted in concrete experience. Its support was pragmatic. On the other hand the Communist (Utopian) ideal has never been realized, nor even faintly approached. Nevertheless the Utopian dream did not die. It received support from quite another source, namely a powerful social theory —the Marxist theory of history.

In the Marxist view, the history of human society is seen as a succession of stages, each stage being a reflection of a particular organization of the productive process. The form of organization of the productive process, in turn, gives rise to social classes, some dominant over others. These classes are quite easy to discern in European history: patricians and plebeians, landlords and serfs, entrepreneurs and propertyless workers. Social revolutions are seen as realignments of power among the classes. The gradual emergence of a new class, which derives its power from a new aspect of the productive process resulting from technological progress, paves the way for revolution. At some critical moment, the new class seizes political power and reorganizes society in accordance with its own interests.

Marxist theory, then, claims to have uncovered the "causes" of social change, especially of social conflicts. Again we have placed "causes" in quotation marks to indicate that a scientific interpretation of "cause" is

inappropriate. The Marxist theory of history cannot be corroborated or refuted because there is no opportunity to conduct controlled experiments or
to observe large numbers of cases. The theory is convincing to the degree to
which it "makes sense."

The theory made very good sense to those who saw in it a promise of their
own victory in the next social revolution—the propertyless workers of nineteenth-century Europe, for whom there was neither a frontier to flee to nor
avenues of social mobility to explore.

From a certain point of view, no theory can be considered as proved by
its successes and hardly any theory needs to be rejected because of its
failures. Every theory has a *range* of validity. The range of validity of
Marxist theory is probably to be found in aspects of European social and
economic history from 1350 to 1850. Unwarranted extensions of the range
of validity make for trouble, but long before the price of unwarranted generalization is exacted, extrapolation of a social theory provides valuable
leverage for political action. Such a theory in action *generates its own facts,*
which, properly interpreted, can serve to corroborate the theory. So it was
with Marxist theory. The proletarian revolution in Russia did not simply
"occur" as foretold like an eclipse. It was engineered by men who believed
the theory. Its accomplishment provided a powerful corroboration of the
theory. Accordingly, the world view proposed by the Marxists took hold and
with it the corresponding Communist ethos.

What is the Communist ethos? It is as explicit as the American and quite
as emphatic in terms of universal human values. (Note that we are not
speaking here of Communist social reality any more than we were speaking
of American social reality when we were describing the American creed.)
The starting point of the Communist ethos is different from that of the
American ethos. In the Communist version, the individual with his "natural"
inclinations and ideas of happiness is not taken as a given. Characteristically,
Marx, in criticizing the foundations of classical economics laid down by
Smith and Ricardo, dismissed as fictitious the hypothetical primary economic
units, the lone hunter and the lone farmer who come together to barter. He
argued that even before homo sapiens developed, he was already a member
of a community (family, herd, tribe, and so on). These social factors are the
givens. They shape the individual's consciousness and therefore his ambitions and his notions of happiness. A particular manifestation of the "pursuit
of happiness," such as the amassing of wealth, is not indicative of basic
human nature. It is a reflection of the social values of the society in which
the wealth-amassing individual finds himself. According to Marxist theory,
values are neither naturally given (a denial of the "natural rights" doctrine)
nor freely chosen (a denial of some Christian doctrines). They are imposed
on the individual by his social milieu, for example, by his class interests. As
long as there are social classes in conflict, values will clash and man will
know no peace. His energies will be expended in the social struggle and he

will not be really free. The way to peace and freedom lies through the organization of a classless society, which for Marx meant primarily the abolition of private ownership of the means of production.

So much for the Communist prerevolutionary ethos. Let us now look at the postrevolutionary Communist ethos, particularly its most clearly formulated variant, the Soviet. The social revolution has occurred. Has the classless society come into being? No. "Why not?" we might ask. "No one expected it to arrive," the Russian Communist would reply. "But now that we have taken our fate into our own hands, instead of being driven by the blind forces of history, we can build a classless society. In fact, by herculean effort, we *are* building it."

This answer contains the key to the present Soviet ethos. Just as we Americans assume that the individual is free to pursue his ambitions, provided only that his social milieu is sufficiently permissive, so the Russian assumes that a society (a portion of humanity, ideally all humanity) can embark on the true road to progress, provided only that it has freed itself from fratricidal class strife.

The Communist ethos naturally looks suspect to us. Does it mean that society is justified in imposing its collective goal on the individual? How is the collective goal determined in the first place? That is to say, we do not accept as "obviously good" even the goals of a classless society. We take it for granted that in *any* society individuals may have conflicting goals. Thus any society which pursues a single set of goals must, in our estimation, despoil the freedom of at least some individuals.

Similarly, the emphasis on the freedom of the individual seems suspect to the Communist. Does this freedom mean that the individual is licensed to act against the interests of society? The Communist, incidentally, specifically rejects the idea inherent in classical economics and tacitly assumed in American ideology that a collection of individuals, each pursuing his own economic interest, achieves through checks and balances, supply and demand, an equilibrium which is beneficial to all.

In Soviet society the problem of imposed goals is not nearly as serious as it looks to the individualistic outsider. Where peaceful goals are concerned, the main thrust of the national effort in the U.S.S.R. is perceived by the vast majority of Soviet citizens as directed toward goals which do coincide with theirs. This is because the major problems confronting Soviet society are still basic: how to grow more food, build more housing, insure more education for more people. The stated policy of the Soviet government and of the Communist party is demonstrably directed toward the pursuit of those goals.

At this point the Westerner is inevitably tempted to raise questions of cost and efficiency, whether, for example, the collectivization of land was indeed the best way to insure more food, whether the introduction of free enterprise would not have insured a more rapid accumulation of capital, and so on. We should keep in mind, however, that what is "best" is governed not only by efficiency indices but also by internalized values. In Soviet society, the highest value is attached to collective effort. Individual effort is valued only to the extent that it harmonizes with collective effort. Competition, with its concomitant ambition for personal gain, is ethically suspect in Russia and, in fact, has always been so. The most strongly held values are those that derive from personal and cultural experience, not those which are theoretically demonstrated to be superior. The Russian knew the man of property as the callous, idle landlord. He knew the entrepreneur as the usurer, the boss, or the shrewd operator who cheated the poor at every opportunity. The Russian never knew the capitalist as the innovator, the visionary, the inventor, the explorer, and the organizer of efficient production.

We, of course, have similar prejudices. With us "statism" is chronically suspect. In social and economy-regulating legislation, we have lagged behind every other civilized country. Arguments about the necessity of such measures often fall on deaf ears, for they violate the internalized ethos of liberty and self-reliance. The enterprising self-made man has remained our culture hero, a living proof of the class mobility which we identify with democracy. The politician and bureaucrat, on the other hand, have always remained suspect.

We see, then, that on the gross level, there is no conflict between internalized personal values and ambitions on the one hand, and existing social opportunities on the other, either in the United States or in the Soviet Union. Both societies are accordingly fundamentally stable with negligible "alienated" populations. The average citizen in both societies is truly convinced that he is "free" and that the structure of his society insures his "freedom." The American *tolerates* the power of the state as a guardian of his liberties. The Russian *identifies* with the power of the state, which he sees as promoting his interest. For the American a democratic government is government *by* the people (which is presumed to be for the people). For the Russian a democratic government is government *for* the people (which is presumed to be by the people).

EXPLANATION OF DISCREPANCIES BETWEEN
THE IDEAL AND REALITY

We have drawn two idyllic pictures of American and Soviet societies. We depicted these societies not as they are but as they are idealized, as they appear to the average American and to the average Soviet citizen, neither of whom is critical of the official or conventional view of the society in which he lives. Each thinks that his society would be as it is described, were it not for certain imperfections.

Now we must compare the prevailing American and Soviet ideas of what is responsible for the dissonant elements in their respective systems. There are two main views on these matters in the United States, the conservative and the liberal. The conservative view faces backward. It places the American Golden Age somewhere in the first decades of our century when the ideal of liberty, as the conservatives understand it, came closest to being realized. In the estimation of the conservative, American ideals have become corrupted by the infusion of alien elements, perhaps imported by immigrants, perhaps generated by a weakening of the moral fiber due to the "soft life," perhaps introduced by a hypertrophy of governmental institutions. The conservatives' cure for social ills is the re-establishment of unfettered individualism, which they believe can be accomplished by removing all governmental regulation of economic activities.

The liberals reject this view. They see the classical or primitive American ideals as inadequate to cope with the problems of the fully industrialized frontierless society. The liberals accept the necessity of modifying the private enterprise system by introducing social legislation and controls of economic activities. Typically they view such regulations as *ad hoc* measures. They are empirically oriented and shun the vision of a Golden Age either in the past or in the future.

In the Soviet Union the vision of the Golden Age is dominant. It is placed in the future. The shortcomings of the present are attributed simply to the fact that the Golden Age has not arrived. It is to be established, the people are told, and believe, when an adequate material base has been prepared—economic abundance—and when new generations have grown up under new conditions. The official view is that, although Soviet society is far from perfect, it is progressing toward perfection.

Because of the comparative meagerness of open criticism of public policy in the Soviet Union, we can only surmise that the role analogous to that of our conservatives is played in the U.S.S.R. by the Stalinists. To be sure the Stalinists have no Golden Age in the past to extoll, and it is doubtful whether there are many in the Soviet Union who are nostalgic about the austerities and the tyrannies of the Stalin era. But the Stalinists may well feel, as our conservatives feel about Americanism, that Communism has been corrupted by "liberal" tendencies, or by flirtation with the enemy camp.

CONFLICT OF DOGMAS

We have in Americanism and in Communism two views of society and of man's relation to it. Each view is adapted to the social system founded upon it in the sense of having been firmly internalized by the respective populations. Each view rests on reasonable generalizations from cultural experience.

Why is the mixture explosive? Why are the two societies poised for mortal combat? Why is talk of "coexistence" by either side always coupled with assurances that only one system will survive? Why is genuine coexistence for the foreseeable future not easily and sincerely accepted as, for example, religious differences have come to be accepted in the Western world?

One answer immediately suggests itself. Our own conservatives and presumably the Stalinists in the Soviet Union categorically reject the images we have sketched of the Soviet and the American systems respectively. Each will accept, with some modifications, our description of their own system but will dismiss our description of the other. To the extremists of both sides, the other system remains a brutal system of oppression sustained by terror, no matter what evidence is marshalled to the contrary.

But what about the liberal factions of both countries? Do they also cling to the infernal image of the other, which the extremists insist is the only true one? Perhaps some doubt the existence of hell. Can it be that they dare not admit it? To admit such doubts may seem equivalent to raising doubts about the perfection of heaven. There is no logical connection between the one doubt and the other. A man can go on believing in heaven even if he has lost his belief in hell.

The two systems are developing in two entirely different cultural contexts and may be equally "perfectable." But it is a common and successful demagogic trick to point to just one departure from accepted dogma and to denounce the heretic as an enemy of the faith. This is especially true in the Soviet Union, where it is still impossible to question publicly any statement made by Lenin. In the United States it is much easier to attack dogma directly. Indeed, it is being done by most of the authors in this volume and they have few misgivings about being ruined on that account. However, in the United States the politician is much more vulnerable than the professor. He feels, not without justification, that to credit Communism with a capacity to fulfill certain human needs and aspirations within certain cultural contexts is tantamount to insulting the American flag. Conservatives feed this fear. Charges of "treason" and "disloyalty" are political weapons. Here is one reason why the image of the utterly evil "Ism" is kept in focus even by those who do not believe it.

We have seen that the image of the "Ism," false as it may be, is not just an unfortunate delusion. The fearful image is an integral part of The Game, which could not be played without it. The Game, in turn, not only derives its rationale from the delusion, but endows the image with whatever measure of reality it has. While the popular conception of a Communist country as a vast concentration camp is sheer fantasy, communist expansion is a fact. While the official Soviet depiction of modern Western capitalism as a system of vicious exploitation and a source of ever-intensifying class struggle is silly, efforts of the United States to squelch popular uprisings against tyranny and corruption in underdeveloped countries are facts. We suggest that the aggressive tendencies of both Communism and of anti-Communism are by-products of The Game, hence depend strongly on the persistence of the distorted images of each other which the opponents nurture. As in the case of one of the "objective" causes of the Cold War, the armaments race, we have another closed cycle. The phony global issue "democracy versus Communism" or, if you will, "imperialism versus socialism," feeds the Cold War. The Cold War makes the issue seem real.

COMPLEMENTARY, NOT INCOMPATIBLE, IDEALS

The democracy versus Communism issue is revealed as spurious as soon as the two systems are seen as complementary instead of incompatible. Each system has evolved in response to certain deeply felt needs and could not be viable if it did not continue to fulfill these needs in many important ways. This is not to argue, *à la* Pangloss, that every existing social system is "right" by virtue of existing. Many exploitative and oppressive systems existed for long periods and still exist. But they were not and are not mass societies. We are speaking specifically of two highly successful mass societies, the United States and the Soviet Union. They are both successful in the sense that they command the genuine loyalty of the great bulk of their populations. This loyalty stems from faith—in the Soviet Union from the faith that the direction in which the society is going is the correct one; in the United States from the faith that the basic value, the "natural freedom" of the individual, is still cherished. On closer examination, it appears that the difference is one of emphasis and that both values are important to both peoples. Our gravest concern is the lack of positive "national goals," something in which the Soviet Union is so rich. An increasing number of honest Communists admit, if their own basic values are not threatened, that in certain respects individual freedom has been too severely circumscribed in their countries. Each system is a proud possessor of something the other lacks. In this sense, too, the systems are complementary.

In spite of all the anathemas in official pronouncements of both countries, each is cautiously incorporating certain values of the other. We are learning the values of collective effort and of the notion that, cracker-barrel adages and conservative consciences notwithstanding, society does owe each of its members a decent life. The Communists are learning that the best member of a collective society is a free and trusted man, that they cannot have educated men without having men capable of independent thought and initiative, and that independence of thought and initiative invariably lead to a questioning of established beliefs.

Freed from self-perpetuating, crippling fears of each other, Americanism and Communism could not only coexist but could each be enriched by incorporating the best of the other's features, properly adapted to its own needs and ideals. The world as a whole would benefit by the insight that there is more than one way to enhance the dignity of man.

Here is an opportunity for "ideological disarmament," that is, a liquidation of the ideological sector of the Cold War. It goes without saying that the ideological sector is tightly linked to the political and military ones. The ideological causes of the Cold War can be totally removed only when other more objective causes are also removed. But ideological disarmament seems a good place to begin. In contrast to the lack of progress in the military and political arenas, some timid steps toward ideological disarmament have already been made, for instance, in the cultural exchange program. An agreement on a joint condemnation of war propaganda was almost reached in Geneva. Thus a possibility exists for a toehold in this area. Unilateral measures in the direction of de-emphasizing the total evil of the "Ism" involve no risks of jeopardizing national security, except in the minds of the extreme right and of those strategists who insist that national security depends on keeping the nation at a high pitch of hatred and readiness to fight.

Steps toward ideological disarmament can be carried out only if both administrations proceed firmly and courageously against their respective "total victory" crowds. A major task facing both administrations is to spike the defeatist argument of the extremists, who maintain that the recognition of any virtue in the other "Ism" opens the floodgates for ideological conquest and subversion. This argument reveals that, for all their trumpeting, the extremists of both sides do not really have faith in their own systems. Patriotism which depends so wholly on vilification of the loyalties of others is a symptom of weakness, not of strength.

Ideological disarmament is not, as the term might suggest, a surrender of ideological defenses. It involves only the scrapping of offensive ideological weapons, offensive in the literal as well as the metaphorical sense. To refrain from attacking the faith of others does not weaken one's own faith. On the contrary, ideological disarmament, in recognizing the need for mutual respect and by emphasizing the positive aspects of both major secular faiths of our day, will contribute to the strengthening of both faiths through the removal of anxieties.

There is abundant evidence that the American ethos of individualism and the Communist ethos of collectivism are sources of great creative forces rooted in the noblest human aspirations. Once the hostility-generating anxieties are removed, these forces can be released for the benefit of humanity.

2

WILLIAM A. GAMSON

Evaluating Beliefs about International Conflict

Americans differ widely in their beliefs about the reasons for the Cold War and how we should cope with it. We have learned to tolerate our religious diversities, but we cannot afford the luxury of such tolerance about Cold War beliefs. Differences in assumptions about Soviet goals, for example, lead to radically divergent policies, some of which could produce tragic consequences.

Any comprehensive system of beliefs in this area is likely to be an amalgam of two sorts of propositions—empirical and normative. The empirical or factual propositions make statements about what *is;* the normative propositions are value judgments and prescriptions about what *ought to be.* In the belief systems described below, important disagreements may be found among both kinds of propositions.

This paper suggests an approach to the evaluation of the empirical propositions. In most general form, it raises the question of whether the various propositions put forward by Americans about the causes of the Cold War and the nature of Soviet intentions are true or false. It is wise to recognize at the outset that there is no possibility of finding absolute verification or rejection for any total belief system or even for any of their discrete parts. Instead, the quest is simply for evidence which provides relative confirmation or refutation for the belief systems being evaluated.

While intellectuals and others not directly involved in the formation of foreign policy have criticized the set of assumptions which underlie United States conduct of foreign affairs since World War II, there has until recently been no significant political challenge. Such challenges now seem to be emerging from two different directions, crystallizing quite separate sources of misgiving. Each involves a set of assumptions about the nature of the present international situation which either contradicts or changes the emphasis of current assumptions.

The first challenge is manifested by political candidates who criticize the "no-win" objectives of current policy; they would direct policy toward the expansion of American political influence and control and the isolation or removal of Communist control. The second challenge is manifested by "peace" candidates—some running as independents and some running as regular party candidates. Despite some differences in political goals, "peace" candidates share the desire for a reorientation of American policy toward a gradual accommodation with the Soviet Union which would lessen or eliminate the possibility of nuclear war.

Neither the administration nor any group of its critics has a uniform view. Administration policy is not the result of an orderly deduction from a series of consistent and explicit assumptions but is based on the pressure of competing views. There is diversity on important goals and assumptions about the causes of the Cold War within the ranks of those who urge changes toward "victory" or "peace."

I will describe three positions which are intended to represent the assumptions underlying present United States policy and the two political challenges mentioned above. More specifically, Position A characterizes those who desire a more aggressive policy toward the Soviet Union; Position B characterizes those who accept the general lines of current policy; and Position C characterizes those who desire a more aggressive policy toward the achievement of disarmament.

My own interpretation of these positions is only one among several possible variants. I am concerned *not* with how many people hold each position or the reasons why they accept one rather than another, but with an approach to evaluation. For this purpose, a high degree of explicitness and logical coherence is necessary. Inevitably the positions become "ideal types," somewhat removed from statements that their typical advocates might make in response to a public opinion survey.

THE BELIEF SYSTEMS: A GENERAL STATEMENT

POSITION A: The Soviet Union spearheads a well-co-ordinated offensive—political, economic, and ideological. The conflict is fundamentally a moral one between two incompatible social systems. To understand the Cold War one must comprehend the nature of Soviet intentions. The basic objective of Soviet policy is not the achievement of specific political goals but the destruction of the values and social system embodied by the United States and Western Europe.

Under these circumstances, United States policy cannot succeed in maintaining an uneasy truce which allows the Russians to pick points of confrontation at times and places of their choosing; such a policy will not lead to stability but to the ultimate defeat of the West. Similarly, given the nature of Soviet goals, any policy aimed at accommodation is doomed from the outset.

> The real issue is not economic but political—totalitarianism versus the open, liberal, democratic society, and the approaches adopted by each in its relations with other states. Different political systems can exist side by side, but not when one system is aggressive, geared to conflict and bent upon conquest.[1]

> We are engaged in a pervasive struggle with the forces of Communism— a conflict between two gigantic systems, each armed with massive military power, and both locked in a contest in which even a minor mistake may prove fatal. In this situation, we can find salvation neither in "gimmick" solutions nor in the leaven of compromise. The sources of conflict are not arms races, clashes of interest or the "unresolved issues" along the battle lines of the Cold War. The root causes of conflict are the closed monolithic society and revolutionary doctrine of an implacable adversary bent upon remaking the world in his own image.[2]

POSITION B: Two major power blocs are vying—one for the preservation, the other for the expansion—of political influence and control. The Soviet Union plans to extend its control through the achievement of specific political goals, many of which conflict with our own. They are willing to use weapons as an implicit or explicit threat but are not committed to the military destruction of the West. Ultimately, they wish to see the Western social system replaced by one more consonant with Communist values, but they are not willing to take excessive risks for such a goal. The basic objective of Western policy should be the containment of Communist expansion in the short run, combined with efforts at the gradual liberalization of Communist countries, including the Soviet Union itself.[3]

POSITION C: Two major power blocs—both led by countries with a strong stake in the maintenance of the status quo—are in conflict over artificial issues which frequently bear little relation to the real interests of either country. When real differences in interest are involved mutually advantageous compromises are available, but they are impossible to achieve because of the psychological atmosphere created by the Cold War. The key to Russian intentions is understanding that, in spite of its bluster, the Soviet Union has become very much a "status quo" power. It is more interested in maintaining and consolidating its gains than in making sacrifices or taking new risks in the interest of expansion. Western policy should be directed toward an accommodation which does not sacrifice freedom but which does eliminate the risk of a nuclear war.

. . . Mutual insecurity rather than struggle for power is the major source of international tensions.[4]

. . . One should not underplay the import of objective elements such as weapons capacities, their distribution among the contenders, economic capabilities, and geopolitical factors. . . . However, as the situation is developing at present the objective factors . . . enable settlement and require it. Hence, the removal of psychological blocks becomes crucial now.[5]

[The present-day Soviet Union] is not a revolutionary nor a socialist regime, but one of the most conservative, class-ridden regimes anywhere in the Western world.[6]

Means of Influence

The coherence of the belief systems can be made clearer if we focus, briefly, on the underlying means of influence which each system sees as basic to the conduct of international relations. *Constraint influence* involves the addition of new disadvantages to the situation or the threat to do so. This is the basic means for Position A, which sees threats and force as the most appropriate method of carrying on our relationship with the Communists. These are their methods as well, the argument runs; they understand and respond to them.

Inducement influence involves the addition or the conditional promise of new advantages to the situation. This is the basic means for Position B, which believes that the offering of inducements in exchange for counterconcessions by the other side is most appropriate. Essentially, we should use constraint only to create the conditions for genuine bargaining. We "arm to parlay."

Persuasion influence works on the motives of the other side rather than changing the situation. This is the basic means for Position C which believes that we should try to convince the Soviet Union that certain policies which we advocate are in their best interest as well as our own. Our aim should not be to destroy an enemy or to defeat an opponent but to achieve common goals.

These different emphases on means of influence underlie the policy implications described below.

Appropriate Defense Policy

POSITION A: THE CONSTRAINT SYSTEM   The continuation, and in some cases acceleration, of weapon development and production is required to make it clear to the Russians that we will respond fully to any aggression on their part. The United States enjoys a natural advantage in the arms race through its greater productive capacity. We have not used this advantage fully. Our goal should not be parity with the Russians but military superiority. We should be in a position to threaten the use of force with credibility if the Russians do not behave. Furthermore, such threats are a necessary backdrop to American initiatives in the Cold War.

The basic way to prevent war is to make certain, by maintaining strong quantitative superiority, that the would-be aggressor has no chance of winning. A one-to-one ration of equality cannot deter or prevent war, and could never prevail if put to the test of war.[7]

[Our strategies may] be pursued by many different means, but they must always be dependent upon our willingness and capability to use force whenever the nature of the Communist challenge leaves us no other choice.[8]

POSITION B: THE INDUCEMENT SYSTEM The threat of nuclear weapons should be used only to neutralize their possible use by our opponent. At the same time, we should be prepared to respond to other forms of military aggression at the appropriate level. Our military posture should be such that any use or threat of military force by the other side is effectively off-set. It is desirable, if possible, to achieve stability at an armaments level lower than the present one through arms control. With the threat system stabilized, we can negotiate and bargain with the Russians over the political issues which divide us and, hopefully, find acceptable compromises.

POSITION C: THE PERSUASION SYSTEM The major goal of our defense policy should be the dismantling of weapons of mass destruction and rapid delivery systems through multilateral disarmament. The continued existence of modern weapons, even when no explicit threat is made, contributes to an atmosphere of fear and distrust which makes the settlement of specific disputes and the establishment of effective international bonds extremely difficult if not impossible.

Preventing the Intensification of Conflict

POSITION A: The manipulation of conflict intensity has been used shrewdly by Communist strategists to weaken Western resolve and unity. As long as we respond to intensification by conciliation, we encourage such manipulation. We must be ready to accept fully the risks involved in the intensification of conflict to meet the Communist challenge adequately. Our unwillingness to take such risks except on rare occasions has been a major factor in the gradual attrition of the Western position.

Position B: Preventing intensification of conflict is generally a desirable goal. Unfortunately, intensification is frequently an inevitable by-product of necessary responses to specific Communist challenges. The willingness of the Communists to negotiate generally comes only after Western firmness in the face of threats. While we should never deliberately try to intensify conflict, temporary intensification is one of the unavoidable prices we pay for an ultimate resolution on satisfactory terms.

Position C: Preventing the intensification of conflict is a highly desirable goal, given the danger that intensification may trigger a nuclear war. It is not a necessary or inevitable adjunct to a policy aimed at dealing with our conflicts with the Communists. Far from making conflicts easier to resolve, intensification makes resolution more difficult by distorting each party's perception of its interests and heightening concern about national prestige.

Developing International Community

Position A: This is a desirable goal only if one refers to the free world community. Greater solidarity in the Western world will improve our capabilities in the struggle with Communism. However, it is an impossibility and a delusion to strive for a world community which includes incompatible values and social systems. We cannot establish integrative ties with a country bent on our destruction.

> The issue now before mankind is the political organization of the globe. The crucial question is who will provide a design for the future. . . . The issue before the West is the creation under its leadership of a world community in which free men make their own laws and live by them in peace.[9]

> The Communist system, as now constituted, will not accede to any just peace with that same Western civilization which it has vowed to destroy.[10]

Position B: The building of a world community is a desirable long-range goal. However, its achievement depends on the abandonment by the Communists of their expansionist goals. There is little which the United States can do until this prior condition is met, except to encourage the Soviet Union to meet it. In the short run, we must handle specific political challenges so that the Communists will find the pursuit of their expansionist goals unprofitable.

Position C: The strengthening and building of international integration is a major priority of the present. The necessary preconditions for many immediate steps in this direction already exist, including, for example, increased cultural exchange. The initiation of many other actions toward this goal can be undertaken by the United States.

THE BELIEF SYSTEMS APPLIED

There are many sharp differences in the positions outlined above. The differences in empirical propositions concern, for example, long-range Soviet goals, Soviet willingness to incur unprovoked risks, and general Soviet views of the West.

The task of evaluating them appears relatively straightforward. It is simply to confront the contradictory propositions with the same set of events. However, the complexity of both the belief systems themselves and the reality which they are confronting makes it possible for each position to find "facts" to support its own interpretation of the Cold War. Some perspective can be gained on the difficulties in establishing confirmability through an examination of the ease with which each position confronts two specific issues—Laos and Berlin.

Explanation of Events in the Laotian Issue

POSITION A: The agreement in Laos in the winter of 1961–62 to form a coalition government with pro-Western, neutralist, and pro-Communist elements will inevitably lead to the ultimate inclusion of Laos in the Communist orbit. The Communist victory is all the more impressive because it was achieved without military conquest, although the threat of armed force was ever present. When it became clear that a vigorous United States response to the Communist threat would not be forthcoming, the ultimate inclusion of Laos in the Communist bloc was an inevitable consequence. The Communists could afford to be generous about the terms of the American defeat. Such superficially co-operative behavior will encourage pseudo-compromises in the future. It is a wise strategy that gains the co-operation of the enemy in planning his own demise.

POSITION B: American firmness in South Vietnam and in the rapid dispatch of troops to Thailand, *combined* with our flexibility in finding a compromise solution in Laos, made possible Soviet willingness to reach an accord. Absence of the first element would have meant the takeover of Laos by the Pathet Lao; absence of the second element would have meant engagement in a lengthy military conflict on very unfavorable terms and at the risk of escalation of the conflict. American firmness set the stage for successful negotiation.

POSITION C: Soviet restraint in Laos is evidence of their desire for stability in international conflict. This restraint is all the more impressive in light of two facts: (1) the United States was originally instrumental in undermining the neutral status of Laos, and (2) a Communist military victory could have been obtained with relative ease and at very low risk of Western intervention. The resolution of this conflict, in spite of the weakness of the Western military position, is powerful evidence against the principle of always "negotiating from strength."

Explanation of Events in the Berlin Issue

POSITION A: American inaction in response to the construction of the Berlin wall and other Communist actions has allowed the gradual undermining of the Western position in Germany. Thus, a situation which has been and remains a point of great Communist vulnerability has been used to harass the West. Here, where we would expect the Communists to be on the defensive, we see an offensive aimed at weakening the freedom of West Berlin and the German commitment to NATO and the West. Continual timidity and efforts at conciliation as a response to Russian threats have encouraged the Russian offensive and undermined the confidence of the free world in the willingness of the United States to defend those who choose the Western way of life and values.

POSITION B: It is true that American policy in Germany has not yet led to a final solution at this writing, but it has proved an effective stopgap. This thorniest of all Cold War issues involves a basic conflict of interest between the Communists and the West. The West has made repeated efforts to negotiate a compromise which does not jeopardize our commitment to the West Germans. The Russians have remained unwilling to seek a genuine compromise solution. American firmness has forced the Russians on more than one occasion to retract an ultimatum and has prevented them from carrying out unilateral action threatening Western access to West Berlin. We can do no more than continue this firmness until the Russians recognize that we will not be cowed by threats. Only at that point can serious negotiation begin.

POSITION C: Russian initiatives in Germany have stemmed primarily from the insecure status of the East German government. The continued unpopularity of the German Democratic Republic is a great source of instability. Both sides share responsibility for having created a situation in which minor differences have become symbolic of the prestige of each. Many compromise solutions are available which could preserve Western access rights and the independence of West Berlin and also satisfy the Soviet desire for stabilizing the East German regime. Any such solution is impossible at present, given the atmosphere and relationship between the two sides.

DERIVING TESTABLE HYPOTHESES

The array of research tools which behavioral scientists customarily use is fully appropriate in the study of international conflict. The basic data for the particular research on evaluation of beliefs suggested here is a well-defined set of specific international events. Since the differences among the positions center on assumptions about long-range Soviet goals, strategies, and interpretations of Western behavior, the most appropriate events to test them are Soviet actions. More specifically, the investigator should examine Soviet actions which can be described as "conciliatory" or "refractory."

Calling an action "refractory" implies nothing concerning either its intended purpose or its justifiability. The focus is entirely on its immediate manifest content and effect. A manifest conciliatory action is any action by an agent of the Soviet Union, regardless of motive, which makes a disagreement less salient or which narrows the gap between the Soviet and American positions on an issue. A manifest refractory action is the opposite —any action by an agent of the Soviet Union, regardless of motive, which makes a disagreement more salient or which broadens the gap between the Soviet and American positions on an issue.

A somewhat more formal statement of the belief systems than the one given earlier is necessary to derive clear and testable propositions about Soviet behavior. They can be given a more systematic statement through a series of operating assumptions which each group makes about:

(1) Long-range Soviet goals;
(2) Soviet willingness to incur unprovoked risks;
(3) General Soviet view of the Western Alliance;
(4) Soviet monitoring of information;
(5) Bias in Soviet interpretations.

From these assumptions, the investigator can derive for each position a central hypothesis about Soviet conciliatory or refractory behavior as a response to Western behavior in the previous time period.

The operating assumptions are stated in language which is most congenial to the systems themselves. For this reason, the terms "resistant" and "aggressive" are used to describe Western and Soviet behavior. However, refractory behavior includes both of these terms. It is virtually impossible to make an empirically meaningful distinction between actions which are aggressive and actions which are resistant. Therefore, in the hypothesis of each belief system, the two separate terms "resistant" and "aggressive" are translated into the single term "refractory." In testing them, no use is made of the distinction between aggressiveness and resistance.

Position A: Operating assumptions

Long-range Soviet goals—The ultimate aim of the Soviet Union is complete world domination. They pay lip service to co-existence while they work to undermine the West.

Soviet willingness to incur unprovoked risks—The Soviet Union is willing to incur fairly high risks in order to achieve its goals, although it does fear a nuclear clash.

Soviet view of the West—In Soviet eyes, the Western powers are concerned only with retaining what they have, but they have lost the will to resist in any sustained fashion. Therefore, the Soviet Union believes that domination can be safely achieved by judicious but repeated application of pressure and a strategy which avoids confrontation at times when the West is passing through one of its sporadic fits of resistance.

Soviet monitoring of information—The Soviet Union scans Western behavior for information concerning momentary Western resistance. The more refractory Western behavior is, the more the West will be seen as temporarily resistant.

Bias in Soviet interpretations—Since the Soviet Union believes the West is not able to sustain resistance, it will tend to underrate the degree of resistance implied by any given refractory Western action.

POSITION A: CENTRAL HYPOTHESIS

Contingent Soviet behavior—If in a given period the West is generally conciliatory, in the subsequent period the U.S.S.R. will be highly refractory. Because of bias in monitoring, even if the West is mildly refractory, the Soviet Union will continue from mildly to highly refractory in the following period. However, if the West is highly refractory, the U.S.S.R. will be mildly conciliatory in the following period. (Figure 2-1 summarizes this prediction.)

FIGURE 2-1

Predictions of Soviet Behavior for Belief System A
Soviet Behavior at Time (T + 1)

Western Behavior at Time T	HIGHLY CONCILIATORY	MILDLY CONCILIATORY	MILDLY REFRACTORY	HIGHLY REFRACTORY
Highly Conciliatory				A
Mildly Conciliatory			A	A
Mildly Refractory			A	
Highly Refractory		A		

POSITION C:[a] OPERATING ASSUMPTIONS

Long-range Soviet goals—Despite its occasional bluster, the Soviet Union is fundamentally interested in maintaining the status quo and in co-existing with the West as long as the West shows a willingness to co-operate.

Soviet willingness to incur unprovoked risks—The Soviet Union does not wish to incur any risks unless it is forced to do so in self-defense.

Soviet view of the West—In Soviet eyes, the Western powers are basically aggressive countries which aim to undermine Soviet influence and control in

[a] Position B is presented last because it is the most complicated.

the world.[b] Only by being constantly on guard and constantly willing to resist or counteract such Western attempts, will the Soviet Union be able to persuade the West to accept co-existence.

Soviet monitoring of information—The Soviet Union wants to know when defensive measures must be taken. It scans Western behavior in order to ascertain temporary Western willingness to accept reasonable compromises on outstanding disagreements. The more refractory Western behavior is, the more the West will be seen as temporarily aggressive and unwilling to reach these compromises.

Bias in Soviet interpretations—Since the West is seen as intent on undermining Soviet influence, there will be a systematic tendency to overrate the degree of aggressiveness implied by any given Western refractory action.

Position C: Central hypothesis

Contingent Soviet behavior—If in a given period the West is highly refractory, in the subsequent period the U.S.S.R. will be highly refractory. Because of its bias, even if the West is only mildly refractory, the Soviet Union will be mildly to highly refractory. However, if the West is generally conciliatory, in the subsequent period the U.S.S.R. will be cautiously or mildly conciliatory. (These predictions of Position C are indicated in Figure 2-2 by the letter C.)

Figure 2-2

Predictions of Soviet Behavior for Each Belief System

Soviet Behavior at Time (T + 1)

Western Behavior at Time T	HIGHLY CONCILIATORY	MILDLY CONCILIATORY	MILDLY REFRACTORY	HIGHLY REFRACTORY
Highly Conciliatory		C	B	A
Mildly Conciliatory		C	A, B	A
Mildly Refractory		B	A, B, C	C
Highly Refractory		A		B, C

Position B: Operating assumptions

Long-range Soviet goals—The Soviet Union is interested in achieving a limited, cautious expansion of influence. It is willing to compromise when pressed and favors co-existence for the foreseeable future, but it persists in its attempts to gradually expand its sphere of influence.

Soviet willingness to incur unprovoked risks—The Soviet Union has a medium propensity to incur unprovoked risks. It will incur middling

---

[b] This is a statement of Soviet perceptions. Advocates of this Position C do not, of course, necessarily accept this view of the West themselves.

risks in order to expand, although it recognizes that even a conventional armed clash is in great danger of escalating into a major nuclear war.

Soviet view of the West—In Soviet eyes, the Western powers are sometimes intent on creating and exploiting Soviet weaknesses and are, at other times, either resistant or acquiescent in the face of Soviet expansion. Only by careful observation and experimentation can the U.S.S.R. ascertain the auspicious time for expansion, for abstention from such action, and for self-defense.

Soviet monitoring of information—The purpose of Soviet monitoring is to determine whether the United States is temporarily aggressive, resistant, or acquiescent. If in a given period Western behavior is conciliatory, the West will be seen as temporarily acquiescent and lacking in willingness to resist; if mildly refractory, then the West may be seen either as temporarily resistant or mildly aggressive; if highly refractory, then the West will be seen as highly aggressive.

Bias in Soviet interpretations—Since the West is seen neither as consistently devoted to undermining the Soviet Union, nor as consistently abstaining from such attempts, no systematic bias in interpreting Western actions exists.

Position B: Central hypothesis

Contingent Soviet behavior—If in a given period the West is generally conciliatory, in the subsequent period the U.S.S.R. will be mildly refractory. If the West is mildly refractory, then in the subsequent period Soviet behavior will be either mildly conciliatory or mildly refractory (depending on whether Western behavior was interpreted as resistant or aggressive). Finally, if the West is highly refractory, then in the subsequent period Soviet behavior will be highly refractory. (This prediction of Position B is also tabulated in Figure 2-2.)

The summary of the three sets of predictions in Figure 2-2 shows Soviet behavior at Time (T + 1) as a function of Western behavior at Time T. Although the belief systems start from radically different assumptions, it is interesting to note that they make three identical predictions:

(1) No position predicts that the U.S.S.R. will be highly conciliatory in the present situation.

(2) No position predicts that the U.S.S.R. will be mildly refractory following a period in which the West is highly refractory.

(3) All positions agree that the U.S.S.R. may be mildly refractory following a period in which the West is mildly refractory.

The reasons for each of these predictions, of course, differ in each system. Figure 2-2 also reveals that the point of maximum differentiation among the belief systems comes in their predictions as to what happens after the West has been conciliatory. This makes good sense; perhaps the most fundamental difference among the systems lies in their estimates of the extent to which the Soviet Union will take advantage of Western conciliatory behavior.

CONCLUSION

This paper has concerned itself with an approach to the problem of evaluating the empirical portions of belief systems about international relations where the systems differ radically in the policies they propose. I have tried to state positions in a form that makes such an evaluation possible. Proof of the utility of this approach lies in trying it out.[11] In this sense, the paper is no more than a suggestion for research.

One might ask what practical effect programs of evaluation could achieve. Certainly, a Barry Goldwater is not likely to be shaken in his beliefs by such evidence. Commitment to any of these belief systems is more than a rational and intellectual one; a convinced believer is not likely to be influenced despite substantial evidence that his predictions erred. Still, there are many whose commitments are more tentative. Belief systems are competitive; their advocates will be devoting increasing amounts of time in the years ahead to convincing others, and evidence of the sort suggested here is sorely lacking.

But there is a point to this evaluation over and above any specific contribution or clarification it might conceivably make to a discussion of foreign policy. Many social scientists, myself included, are advocates of some version of Position C. The role of the behavioral scientist does not require that he be neutral; the conditions of the world we live in demand advocacy and commitment. Yet social scientists have a special responsibility that other advocates do not—the responsibility to subject their own views to the same critical analysis and testing they give to the views of others.

N O T E S

1. Robert Strausz-Hupé, William R. Kintner, and Stefan T. Possony, *A Forward Strategy for America* (New York: Harper & Brothers, 1961), p. 8.
2. *Ibid.*, p. 252.
3. Some approximation of this position is held by many people formerly associated with the Kennedy administration who concern themselves with defense strategy. See, for example, Henry A. Kissinger, *The Necessity for Choice* (New York: Harper & Brothers, 1961).
4. Charles E. Osgood, "Reciprocal Initiative," in *The Liberal Papers*, James Roosevelt, ed. (Garden City, New York: Doubleday Anchor, 1962), p. 92.
5. Amitai Etzioni, *The Hard Way to Peace* (New York: Collier Books, 1962), p. 92.
6. Erich Fromm, "The Case for Unilateral Disarmament," *Daedalus*, LXXXIX (1960), No. 4, p. 1022. Fromm is somewhat more extreme in his assumptions than many others who are identified with this position.

7. Strausz-Hupé, *op. cit.*, p. 161.
8. *Ibid.*, p. 11.
9. *Ibid.*, p. 45.
10. *Ibid.*, p. 265.
11. I am making such an attempt. A progress report on this research describing some of the conceptual and methodological tools is contained in William A. Gamson and Andréa Modigliani, "Tensions and Concessions: The Empirical Confirmation of Beliefs about Soviet Behavior," *Social Problems,* XI (1963), No. 1, pp. 34–48.

3

KATHLEEN GOUGH

The Crisis of the Nation-State

The central argument of this paper will be that, in the modern world, the state is no longer an adequate form of human society.

THE DEVELOPMENT OF STATES

To understand the dilemmas faced by nation-states today, it is fruitful to consider the development of states in the evolution of human society as a whole and the distinctive properties of states. For such an overview, the following definition of the state has been found useful: "A state is a society having a sovereign power which possesses a monopoly of force and governs through the medium of territorial groups."

In the history of humanity, states are comparatively recent. The first states arose not more than 5,500 years ago, in Egypt and Iraq. Somewhat later— at various times between 3,000 B.C. and about 200 B.C.— states also appear to have developed independently in North China, North India, Peru, Mexico, and possibly on the Niger in West Africa.

Present knowledge suggests that all other states have been direct or indirect offshoots of one or another of these primary states. The state as a societal form has therefore existed for no more than one-hundredth part of man's history. Once this is realized, the possibility of the total disappearance of states in the future seems less strange than it otherwise might.

Before states arose, there were various kinds of prestate societies. It seems probable that most of them fell into three broad types: bands, tribes, and chiefdoms.[1] Instances of these types have persisted in many parts of the world until modern times, and their characteristics and range of variations are gradually becoming known to anthropologists. A brief consideration of them will highlight certain distinctive features of the state.

Bands, the earliest and simplest societies, have been groups of some twenty to a few hundred people who managed their affairs among themselves. Bands are usually too small and isolated to make organized war on one another. They are also small enough to maintain order in the absence of organized leadership. Offenders against the rules are dealt with by feuds between families, culminating in recourse to popular arbitrators, or by withdrawal of aid and services, institutionalized shaming or ridicule, ostracism, or, in cases of grave offense, expulsion or lynching by the group as a whole. Almost all band societies have been hunters and gatherers of wild produce. With few exceptions, the band has given way to the tribe with the domestication of animals and plants. Bands were thus probably universal until about ten thousand years ago, when cultivation and herding began in the Middle East.

Tribes, whose subsistence base is usually shifting cultivation, herding, or intensive fishing, are larger than bands. There are institutionalized links in the form of age grades, secret societies, clans, or other groups between several communities. As a result, disputes may be capable of settlement without recourse to all-out warfare within a society of several thousand people. Tribes, however, like bands, have no government, but only leaders whose advice is followed as long as they remain popular.

Chiefdoms, more complex than tribes, occur with more productive forms of horticulture, sometimes with elementary methods of irrigation or fertilization or with metal tools. Chiefdoms have elements of rank and formal authority. The chief's kin group is larger and controls more land and other property than do commoners. Chiefship is usually hereditary. The chief arbitrates disputes, leads war parties, organizes communal labor, and redistributes the surplus goods of the society at large. Though his authority is clearly institutionalized and is supported by supernatural beliefs, a chief, unlike the government of a state, does not monopolize force. He cannot compel men to go to war and cannot prevent feuds from breaking out between kin groups among his followers, although his own kin group and immediate following are strong enough to punish those who attack him. A chief usually exercises some customary rights of direction of agriculture and of specialized craft production. His right is, however, more co-ordinating than coercive and is backed mainly by popular support. His need to coerce producers is limited, because his role is one which emphasizes generosity rather than demand. A chief takes away only a small proportion of the surplus goods of producers for the benefit of his personal followers. The bulk of goods he merely collects and redistributes to the population at large, thus assuring them of a more varied livelihood than they could otherwise obtain.

States are, in general, societies of greater size, greater complexity of division of labor, and higher productivity than chiefdoms. They did not come into being until after several thousand years of improvements in the domestication of plants and animals. Most of the primary states probably did not arise until after the development of rather large irrigation works. States required a productive surplus sufficient to allow some men to be freed from producing goods, to spend their time instead in organizing and governing other men and in waging professional wars against other societies in competition for control of their natural resources and labor.

A state differs from a prestate society in possessing a ruling group or class which has authority—backed ultimately by physical force—over the rest of the population, to an extent which is only very imperfectly realized in chiefdoms and in a manner which is not found at all in tribes or bands. In a state, only the government—through its executive arms, such as the police force—has the legal right to use violence within the society; disputes must in theory be settled, and crimes punished, by law courts instituted by the government. It is true, of course, that in securely organized states most of the population acquiesces in the government's authority, which is supported not only by force but by supernatural beliefs, by the virtue of orderliness which resides in all established custom, and by the ethical system of the whole society. This does not, however, obscure the fact that in a state, as distinct from prestate societies, it is governmental monopoly of physical force which ultimately lies behind the maintenance of laws. The monopoly of force includes both the government's ability to maintain law inside the society and its ability to cause its citizens to engage in defensive or offensive war against other societies.

States differ further from prestate societies in that the government of a state has the ultimate authority, backed by force, to organize the production and distribution of goods and services. In the simplest agrarian states the government does this directly. Land and other resources are held with the permission of the ruler, who, through his agents, collects goods not required for the producers' own maintenance and redistributes most of them to those not directly engaged in production of goods or in specialized forms of production. The remainder is channeled into foreign trade, which is politically administered.[2] Such a system of allocation of goods and services in the simplest agrarian states in many ways resembles the redistributive system of a chiefdom. A crucial difference is, however, that, in an agrarian state, distribution of wealth is more unequal than in a chiefdom. Specific wealth privileges, defined by sumptuary laws, accrue to the ruling class and to those closely connected with it, and a larger proportion of the society's total product is normally absorbed by its armies.

Corresponding to this inequality of wealth distribution in a state, the government has at its disposal a greater degree of power than has a chief to enforce levels of production regarded as desirable by the rulers. Work, in the sense of labor for an authority who is responsible for fixing the conditions of labor and the amount of wealth which may be retained by the producer or remitted to him from other sources, thus appears unequivocally for the first time in states, although its appearance is foreshadowed in the co-ordinated forms of labor which occur in chiefdoms.

The state is also distinctive in its organization for competitive warfare. It is true that the men of tribes and chiefdoms often make war collectively on those of neighboring tribes and chiefdoms and sometimes displace them from their territories. Nevertheless, when a society has passed beyond a certain level of productivity, the state, with its centralized monopoly of force, is a much more efficient form of organization for competing with other societies for control of their natural resources and of the labor of their populations. Normally, the population of a state supports both the expansive and the defensive wars engaged in by its ruling class because the population, as well as the ruling class, hopes to benefit from such warfare.

This ability and readiness to engage in competitive warfare through the use of organized armies seems to me to be the most distinctive and central characteristic of the state. Although I am unable to prove this with presently available information, I would hypothesize that the state, with its centralized monopoly of force, arose in the first place among irrigation-based societies, out of the competitive struggles of chiefdoms for control of valuable and scarce resources in the form of irrigable land in arid regions. I further suggest that the ability of the government of a state to force its less privileged members to produce according to its regulations depends on the centralization of force, which in turn depends on or is justified by the benefits which the whole society derives from the government's ability to make organized war on other societies or to defend its territory against aggressors. Thus, if the competitive war system of existing industrial states were removed, through disarmament, I would expect governmental authority over production and distribution to become much relaxed or at least dependent on the government's ability and willingness to further the equal welfare of all sections of its citizens.

In more complex commercial and industrial states, government's authority over production and distribution has usually been exercised less directly than in predominantly agrarian states. In modern capitalist societies of the nineteenth and early twentieth centuries particularly, most of the direct authority over production passed to bodies of private property-owners, and most distribution was no longer politically administered but took place through markets. In these states, too, government nevertheless remained the ultimately responsible authority, in that the system of ownership and distribution was upheld by laws which government had framed and administered. It is interesting to note that the modern Communist states have reverted to a system of direct governmental authority over production and distribution which in some ways resembles the political economies of the less complex agrarian states. The main difference is that the Communist states, unlike the early agrarian ones, are deliberately expanding their technologies and increasing their production, with at least the avowed goal of ultimately devoting the product to the equal welfare of all the people.

THE MODERN STATES

Until shortly before the European industrial revolution of the late eighteenth and nineteenth centuries, a majority of people in most states had been engaged in producing food and in handcrafts. They were chiefly peasants and artisans; sometimes serfs tied hereditarily to the soil; or in limited areas, slaves who could be bought and sold. Trade did not involve great economic interdependence between states nor, with the partial exception of the Roman Empire, between states and their subject regions.

But, in the past three centuries, with the various technological changes that preceded or accompanied the industrial revolution, a much larger proportion of the population in the northwestern industrial states moved into industrial production, trade, transport, clerical work, or government service. States of the cool climates of the Northern Hemisphere—most of Europe, North America, and somewhat later, Japan—turned into predominantly machine producers. Among them they divided up the rest of the world—mainly, though not solely, the populations of tropical climates and, incidentally, of colored races—and turned these populations into subject states, either as outright colonies or as economic spheres of influence. Part of the energy of these subject regions was then devoted to the production of raw materials for the use of the dominant industrial states; the subject regions received in return manufactured goods and other products.

The extent to which colonialism was profitable to the conquering and the subject societies at various periods of Western expansion is highly debatable. Here we need merely note that colonialism profited certain powerful groups within the "mother" countries enough for them to prolong it as long as possible. In several cases, countries fought lengthy wars before abandoning colonialism in the mid-twentieth century. Correspondingly, large majorities in most of the former colonial regions probably feel that they were unduly exploited by colonialism, and their present attitudes to the Western nations are colored by this view.[3] In all cases, whether the subject regions were governed directly by the industrial states or were merely subjected to economic colonialism, power was exerted mainly from the industrial states to the nonindustrial regions, and the latter were obliged to change their productive structures and systems of social relationships to accord with policies emanating from the industrial states. The resultant general features of colonial societies have been described many times.[4] Significant among them are, first, that these regions changed from being relatively self-sufficient tribal societies, chiefdoms, or agrarian states to subject states producing raw materials destined for export, under Western capitalist, or associated native capitalist, enterprises, as well as subsistence goods for their own consumption. At various periods, production depended on slave labor; on one or another form of *corvée*; on indentured labor; or, in more recent times, on "free" wage laborers who were accorded living standards much lower than those of the industrial states and only very limited civil rights. During the colonial period, the gap in living standards between the peoples of the subject regions and those of the industrializing states appears to have increased greatly. On the credit side, the subject regions received modern political and economic institutions, some limited forms of industrialization and modern transport, and, in very varying degrees, a measure of Western education. They also received elementary forms of modern medicine, which in many cases enabled their populations to increase very rapidly while their productivity was not increased at a comparable rate.

It is, of course, from this subjection and dependence that the "underdeveloped" societies of Asia, Africa, and Latin America are struggling to free themselves today. In so doing, they gradually set up new, modern, independent states of their own and strive to mechanize their production.

During their periods of overseas colonial rule, the capitalist industrial states developed a particular form of representative democracy in government. It is an electoral system in which the people vote for candidates presented by political parties, which in turn tend to favor the interests of varying combinations of powerful pressure groups in the society at large. Such a system appears unquestionably (at least until the advent of mass communication) to have made governments more responsive to the genuine needs of their populations than in all previous periods of the history of the state. Especially during the twentieth century, legislation gradually tended to spread economic benefits more widely from the ruling groups to the less privileged. Imperfect though they are, the forms of government-sponsored redistribution, short-term national planning, and mass consumption that have developed in the "welfare states" of Western Europe and North America since World War II have further continued these trends toward more egalitarian wealth distribution. We may note in passing, however, that many of the democratic rights now enjoyed by citizens of the Western industrial nations (for example, votes for women and organization of labor unions) were won not only through the developing electoral system but also through civil disobedience of existing laws.

The Western nations' system of representative democracy appears to have been made possible in the first place by two conditions: (1) these nations' vastly increasing internal productivity, the result of industrialization, and (2) the existence of colonial or otherwise subject regions, which supplied indispensable raw materials for industrial production. These circumstances gradually made possible in the industrial states a level of living sufficiently valuable to all of its citizens so that eventually even the poorest of them could be trusted to vote. At the same time, the most oppressed portions of the imperial nations' work forces lived abroad in colonial regions where democratic voting rights were not extended.

In the modern world setting, the Western democratic electoral system does not seem practicable for most of the newly industrializing ex-colonial states. The reasons for this appear to me as follows. First, most of the new nations have the size of large modern nations without the technological structure to support them with any ease. If they are to increase their productivity to keep up with and surpass their population increases, the governments of these nations must carefully plan capital investment, work, and wealth distribution. This is difficult under a democratic electoral system because at the outset most property is still privately owned, after the fashion of Western capitalism. Many groups of property-owners are necessarily still engaged in more traditional "colonial" forms of raw-material production, of internal distribution, and of foreign trade with groups in the capitalist industrial states. The groups that profit most from these traditional economic institutions are reluctant to abandon them; yet, because of their wealth, they play a large role in the selection of candidates for government office and in manipulating the electoral process itself. In many cases the government itself, in a newly independent nation, is drawn largely from and is in sympathy with these older capitalist classes. In some cases, it has had to be removed by force and replaced by a more popular government before national planning for development could begin. Once such a nation acquires a government prepared to plan investment and consumption for the sake of rapid economic development, it is difficult for it to adopt or to revert to a party-electoral system. One reason for this is that continuity of planning becomes more difficult if there are frequent changes of government personnel. Another is that reversion to the electoral system may threaten to return to power older and more traditional vested interest groups. A third, and more tragic, reason is that many new states, having asserted their independence, are obliged to force their populations to work hard on extremely short rations in order to save for economic development. The Chinese state, with its huge population and inadequate technological resources, appears to be the most striking example of this last. There are signs that Indonesia, Ghana, Iraq, the Sudan, Burma, Cuba, and other new states may also find themselves obliged to apply some of the same internally coercive methods if they are to defend themselves from attack, to survive as united entities, and to develop economically.

The Record of the West

On the whole, in my view, the governments of the Western industrial nations, in spite of foreign aid and capital investment since World War II, have not fostered the best interests of many of the new nations. Even when they accord recognition and moderate approval to new governments bent on national planning, the Western nations have, in the past decade, often endangered their development by paying them low and unstable prices for the raw materials they are still obliged to offer on the world market in order to acquire foreign capital for new investment.[5] In some cases the ex-colonial powers have continued to patronize and protect their own nationals who have old-style private investments in the new nations.[6] Aid has been given, but it has been inadequate, and it has often been given with strings. In some instances, the imperial nations have bitterly opposed independence and have fought lengthy wars before withdrawing from their colonial regions, as in the case of France in Indochina and Algeria, and of Britain in Kenya. With American and European aid, the Portuguese are still fighting such a war in Angola. The United States has, since World War II, done much to hold up the political independence and planned economic development of many new nations. In its own traditional spheres of influence, notably in Latin America, it has supported governments that continued to favor its own private investors and that, on the whole, opposed planned development for the benefit of their own populations. In several areas of former European and Japanese control (for example, Iran, South Korea, Formosa, and South Vietnam), the United States' insistence on supporting anti-Communist and anti-leftist regimes has meant that it has again given massive aid to dictatorial regimes not primarily bent on raising productivity, improving living standards, or fulfilling modern ideals of social justice among their common people.

Meanwhile, the tide of opinion in the underdeveloped world is for immediate political independence, freedom from foreign economic controls, rapid economic development, and equal rights to the world's resources. Such values now permeate even the lowest class levels in the new nations. Indeed, it is these groups who are most determined to bring to power, if necessary by force, governments that will attain these objectives with maximum speed. Like that of factory workers in the older industrial states of a hundred years ago, the attitude of the new nations is "Damn your charity; we want justice." In spite of their present weaknesses in bargaining power, there seems no doubt that these nations will not cease to agitate until they achieve the levels of living and the international equality and justice for which their citizens yearn. And there seems no doubt that they will indeed attain them.[7] It seems to me that the more quickly the Western nations accept this fundamental postulate of international equality and seriously begin to implement it, the more happily they will be able to adjust to it when it is eventually realized.

Already, moreover, the revolutionary developments in the new nations are beginning to provoke readjustments in the production and distribution structures of the older Western industrial states. As far as they are able, the new nations have begun to produce under their own auspices, to sell their exports on their own terms, and to oversee the investment of foreign capital for their own benefit. Blocs of new nations in Asia, Africa, and Latin America are already arranging government conferences and attempting to unite in order to strengthen their bargaining power in relation to the older industrial states.

Perhaps partly in response to the new nations' growing independence and unity, partly in response to the attempts to form a unified economic system in Eastern Europe, and partly in response to modern technological changes which permit greater independence and over-all self-sufficiency for the Northwestern industrial states, these latter states are now also proceeding with attempts at economic integration. The European Common Market is striking evidence of this, as are the United States' recent overtures in the direction of an Atlantic economic alliance.

Increasing integration of the Western nations has positive features for the future of world society. It breaks down the insularity of the older nations, accustoms their populations to wider international co-operation, and appears to spread the benefits of the modern welfare state more evenly throughout the populations of these regions. The possible danger in such unity appears to lie in the older and richer nations' increasing ability to withdraw from trade and capital investment in the underdeveloped areas of the world. Partly because of the invention of synthetic products at home, the Western industrial states have less need than before for the raw materials of the tropics. If Western unity means that the richest Northwestern industrial states are to put up a united economic, as well as military, front against the new nations' demands for equal integration, this would seem extremely ominous for the future of both sides.

Meanwhile, the governments of some new nations already see the Soviet Union (although somewhat ambivalently) as a potentially more attractive economic partner than the Western industrial states.[8] There are at least three reasons for this. One is that, in spite of its incorporation or subjection of neighboring regions, the Soviet Union has never had overseas colonies in the tropical world and is therefore less suspected of "neo-imperialism." A second reason is that, at however great a human cost, the Soviet Union has proved that an underdeveloped nation may, through rigorous planning, become a highly productive industrial state within a generation. It can therefore in some respects serve as a model for the newer and even less developed states. A third reason is that the government of the Soviet Union, regardless of its specific actions in this or that region, envisions a future united, integrated world society where wealth, equality, justice, and order will prevail among all the world's peoples. The United States and the other Western nations have offered to the underdeveloped world no such hope of a united world future. The most that they have been able to offer has been a divided world, one half of which will be dominated by social institutions that they themselves developed in a bygone historical period.

The main conclusion to be drawn from the international scene appears to be that it is no longer profitable, and soon will not be possible, for the governments of rich nations to dominate poor nations in the sense of determining their policies and shaping their institutions. International domination is no longer economically profitable to the rich nations because, as we have noted, the products of the poor nations are in many cases less valuable than they were to the rich. Moreover, even when the rich nations desire the products of the poor, they have begun to realize that once the poor nations have passed beyond a certain stage of educational and organizational ability, they produce better if they produce freely in institutions of their own making. And international domination by the rich seems to be becoming less possible today, because the rich nations do not seem to have appropriate tools for continuing coercion. To use Kenneth Boulding's term, their "threat system" is breaking down. The Western powers have hitherto relied on conventional weapons to prevent social changes that they consider undesirable in the underdeveloped world. The experience of events in prerevolutionary China, French Indochina, Kenya, Algeria, Cuba, Laos, and currently in South Vietnam and Angola, however, appears to have demonstrated that conventional weapons are ineffective against a population determined on independence under a national leadership and institutions of its own choice. Conventional weapons cannot prevail indefinitely against civil disobedience, strikes, sabotage, and guerrilla warfare. Nor would nuclear weapons be a substitute for conventional warfare. They would annihilate rather than dominate a resistant population, and would invite the destruction of the aggressor by the Soviet Union.

It seems, therefore, that the only reasonable and humanitarian policy for the Western nations is to cease attempting to guide or determine the political and economic systems of the poorer nations, either by direct military intervention or by providing military aid to governments that favor the status quo. Such a policy might, it is true, involve short-term economic losses for Western business corporations if their property were expropriated by newly formed socialist governments. But with adequate national and international planning, the Western nations could afford to absorb and compensate such losses. Such policies could at the same time be accompanied by efforts to open Western markets more fully to the developing countries, while permitting them to retain tariff barriers to protect their own infant industries.[9] In the longer run, the Western nations would presumably find it to their advantage to provide such forms of aid and to help to build up the technology of poorer nations, regardless of their political systems. This is so for economic as well as humanitarian reasons. Trade with regions of high productivity is more advantageous than trade with nations of low productivity.

THE NORTHERN STATES

Today, for reasons other than the rise of new nations, the highly industrialized states of the Northern Hemisphere are reaching an impasse. Until recently, despite their despotism and inequalities, states have had a value for most of their citizens. The state has made sense in terms of the protection and preservation of human life. States organized and vastly expanded production, and they waged war in a relatively orderly fashion. At the least, the state prevented small private groups from wiping one another out by the indiscriminate use of ever more dangerous weapons. From the point of view of its own citizens, the state had value because it did, through its armies, protect women, the weak, children, and the old from indiscriminate external attack.

During the past decade, in the Northern industrial societies the state has been losing these bases for its continuing usefulness. The reasons for this are the exploitation of nuclear energy and the development of cybernation. These —a wholly new source of vast energy and a new set of tools for putting energy to work—constitute a technological revolution whose proportions have never before been imagined. If we are to survive, it seems clear that the corresponding changes that take place in social structure must be of a similarly immense scale.

Today the whole conception of industrial states' competing through war for control of the natural resources, wealth, and labor of other societies has become anachronistic.[10] First, the traditional motives of such competitive wars seem to be disappearing for the richer industrial states. Modern technology can exploit the natural resources of any given region more intensively and in many more ways than traditional methods could. Large industrial states can therefore, if they wish, achieve a high degree of self-sufficiency, and small ones can merge into larger, more self-sufficient units (as in the case of the European Common Market). With modern technology and high productivity, laborers have become more educated and more demanding of their rights; it would be very difficult—and no longer desirable—for one industrial state to conquer another and put its labor force to work. Further, even if nations should wish to conquer one another for purely ideological reasons, nuclear weapons are appropriate tools not of conquest but of genocide.

A less urgent and less spectacular dilemma of the Western, most highly industrial nations appears to be that these states are gradually losing the intrinsic need to coerce people with respect to work. This change is only now beginning; its implications are slowly becoming apparent primarily in the United States. There it is becoming clear that more and more, if governments and peoples will allow them, machines will do the work of men. In a pamphlet, *Cybernation*,[11] Donald N. Michael describes how automation and computers can already be used to do almost all tasks connected with making and rolling steel, coal mining, manufacturing engine blocks, and sorting and grading "everything from oranges to bank checks." It is true that there will always be some tasks for men. Machines must be organized, and people trained to operate and control them. But such work will presumably require a rather high degree of independent intelligence; it will not be carried out in the framework of coercive relationships that has characterized most wage work and even salary work in the industrial state. Further, as automation advances, increasing millions become wholly "out of work" in the traditional sense. It is to be expected that such numbers will expand greatly as modern technological advances come to permeate the culture of the industrial nations.[12]

The implications of this technological change are only dimly perceptible; I can make only a few tentative observations regarding them. It seems probable that the new technological advances are making anachronistic the relationships of production and distribution now obtaining in the Western nations and especially in the United States. In these societies it is still assumed that wages, salaries, and private profits should be the chief means by which most citizens acquire their shares in the nation's goods and services. This seems to mean that as socially necessary work decreases, the system can be kept going only by the development of large sectors of socially unnecessary or even positively harmful work, in order that citizens may do *something* to claim food and shelter from the owning and ruling groups who still control the means of production. Advertising and sales promotion activities; production of various unnecessary consumer goods; the planned obsolescence of some kinds of consumer goods; and direct or indirect employment of an increasingly awesome proportion of the labor force in armaments production or in the armed services seem to stand as evidence of this trend. In the United States even these occupations apparently cannot stem the growing tide of worklessness.[13] Meanwhile, the cultural goals of the society —even apart from nuclear war preparations—become meaningless under the system of enforced make-work. Meanwhile, large sections of the society, especially the less skilled working classes, are deprived of genuine physical and spiritual welfare in the form of incomes, adequate housing, medical care, schools, and facilities for recreation and travel. Policies of public spending developed in a period of lower productivity and lower expectations are inadequate to serve their needs.

In the United States Negroes are at present the main sufferers from the growing obsolescence of unskilled manual work and from the failure of development programs to take into account the needs of the whole population. In many respects Negro wage workers and unemployed persons are comparable to ex-colonial populations. In the past their ancestors in the Southern states played roles as raw materials producers comparable to those played by laborers in the colonies of the European industrial nations. Southern whites played, and to some extent still play, roles comparable to those of white settlers in such colonies and ex-colonies as Algeria, Kenya, or Central or South Africa. Today Negroes who are unemployed or who are shortly to become unemployed in some ways resemble the populations of ex-colonies whose work and raw materials are no longer valuable to the former imperial nations. Like the latter, they tend to be rejected from the mainstream of industrial development and to be given driblets of aid intended to appease them in the short run and enable them somehow to integrate into industrial society in the long run. Meanwhile, *pari passu* with developments in the new nations, a vociferous Negro demand has developed in America for justice without charity. And whatever form the demand takes, "justice," as in the new nations, means equality of economic as well as of social and political rights.

Readers may object to a view that sees the modern Negro struggle in the United States as a symptom of the decline of the nation state in the West. Unemployment, racial antagonisms and black nationalism were, after all, prevalent long before World War II. I would suggest, however, that these symptoms take on new significance because the cultural ecology of the United States is not what it was before World War II: The nation now operates in a different technological setting and in changed relationships with other societies. Unemployment is not merely the unemployment created by capitalist business cycles, but the beginning of the massive unemployment that automation can be expected to bring. Poverty and economic discontents take on a new meaning in a society where the problems of production have been solved and where poverty is technologically wholly unnecessary. The Negro struggle is no longer the struggle of a particular national minority attempting to improve its position with the help of benevolent white sponsors. It is part of a worldwide, irresistible movement for equality on the part of colored races, who confidently look forward to the end of their domination by the world's white minorities.

To sum up: The social systems of the Western nations have become anachronistic in view of modern technology. Nuclear war is a danger to human survival, impossible as a sane and practical policy. The traditional motives for conquest of other societies have become obsolete for the most highly industrial states. The underdeveloped nations are, moreover, reaching a stage where they can no longer be dominated by the Northern powers. Inside the nation-state in the West, automation has already made much work obsolescent, and this process is only just beginning. The continuation of private ownership and predominance of market mechanisms of distribution, unaccompanied by adequate national planning, have made the economy lopsided and ill-adapted to human needs. The arms race has become functional, in the sense that it temporarily fosters the maintenance of a traditional class structure, wealth distribution, and pattern of authority in Western society.[14] But it does so by forcing the society to concentrate on death, destruction, and domination as its most prominent cultural goals.

THE SOVIET UNION

My knowledge of the Soviet Union is inadequate for any but the most tentative statements. Nevertheless, I may suggest that although the Soviet Union presently looms as the West's archenemy in the Cold War, her position in the world as a whole is increasingly coming to resemble that of the Western nations.

It is of course true that the Soviet Union has reached its present dominant position through state-controlled institutions wholly outside the system of Western capitalism. The forced marches through which the Soviet government obliged its citizens to accumulate capital for rapid economic development offer some kind of example, albeit unhappy, for the most hard-pressed of the new nations today. The Soviet Union expounds a form of Marxist philosophy, however vulgarized and distorted, that appeals to millions in the new nations. The Soviet government and people no doubt look forward to a future in which a system they regard as socialist will unite the world. The Soviet Union is no doubt glad to foster avowedly Marxist governments as they may appear in the new nations if such support is not detrimental to her own national interest.

Yet the Soviets, like the West, have entered the period of the stalemate in nuclear weapons competition. More clearly than leaders in the West, Soviet leaders appear to see the futility of the nuclear arms race and the necessity to end it, although of course under terms that will not jeopardize their interests. Furthermore, the Soviet Union, like the West, is beginning to enter an era of high productivity in which it seems probable that the rigidly state-controlled economy of early Communism will become just as outmoded as will Western capitalist institutions. This anachronism is apparently not yet so visible in Russia as in the United States because industrialism and automation have advanced less in the total economy; it will presumably be some years before automated worklessness becomes an acute problem in the Soviet Union. Nevertheless, reports of a certain "decline of ideology" among Russian youth and of pressures for more consumer goods and a more flexible way of life suggest that the authoritarianism of Soviet government is, in the coming years, likely to be challenged more markedly than it has been since the death of Stalin.

Concomitantly, however, the Soviet Union now has an "empire" or sphere of influence of its own among the satellites of Eastern Europe. As in the case of Western dominance over less wealthy capitalist nations, the dominance of the Soviet government over its satellites appears to depend primarily on the maintenance of the Cold War and the arms race. In Russia as in the West, therefore, the arms race appears to have become to some extent functional for the maintenance of a particular kind of authoritarian internal class structure and a measure of dominance over other nations. But, as with Western nations in relation to their spheres of influence in the underdeveloped countries, there are signs that Soviet dominance over the satellite peoples cannot continue indefinitely. The uprisings and the modifications of Soviet control that have occurred in the satellite states over the past decade indicate that, for the

Soviet Union as for the West, the days of international dominance are numbered.

Like the Western nations the Soviet Union has thus become in some respects a conservative influence on the world scene.[15] Having entered into the nuclear age, the Soviet government finds it neither practical nor desirable to attempt further expansion through modern warfare; yet it attempts to maintain dominance within its sphere of the world through the threat of nuclear weapons. The Soviet Union does not, however, appear to be an instigator of popular leftist revolutionary movements in the underdeveloped countries, but seems merely to be attempting to accommodate to them and to take advantage of them after they have occurred. As a party to the nuclear stalemate, the Soviet Union is, like the West, evidently no longer a primary initiator of social change. Like the West, the Soviet government is threatened from within its own sphere by rising social forces demanding greater egalitarianism of wealth and power. As in the case of the Western governments, the only creative way forward for the Soviet Union would appear to lie in a relaxation of Cold War tensions, nuclear disarmament, withdrawal from positions of international dominance, and an attempt to come to terms with the rest of mankind in an integrated and fundamentally egalitarian world society.

THE FUTURE

I believe that in spite of the gravity and seeming hopelessness of the arms race and the present world situation, there are ways for the Western nations to escape from the dilemmas imposed by modern technology into a freer, more equal, more just, and more human world. But this would require the remolding of many social institutions and the surrender of much of the mythology by which the society presently lives. In short, it would require surrender of much of the autonomy of the nation-state as we have known it heretofore.

First, it seems necessary to recognize that nothing can be either won or saved through nuclear weapons and that it is essential to undertake complete, if gradual, nuclear disarmament. I shall not discuss here the technical problems of disarmament nor the period of time in which it would be feasible, given optimum political circumstances. I simply state my conviction that disarmament cannot be accomplished within the present nationalistic ideologies and within the existing climate of international mistrust and insistence on national sovereignty and on the dominance of weaker by stronger nations. Disarmament will rather require, I believe, an understanding that the age of national competition and international warfare has ended for the industrial nations and a willingness to voluntarily surrender a large measure of national sovereignty to supranational institutions. I would argue that, whatever the details of the settlement, the Western nations should make general and complete disarmament their serious goal and take steps, if necessary unilaterally, to initiate a withdrawal from their military positions.

Nuclear disarmament would of course also involve the removal of bases and the withdrawal of troops of both major parties to the Cold War from all other regions of the world. It would mean the surrender of any claims to international dominance on the part of major industrial powers. But it would open for the first time an era of increasingly equal co-operation and aid among the peoples of the earth.

The success of Western disarmament would of course require that the Soviet Union follow up our initiatives by carrying out its own nuclear disarmament. I would expect this to occur because of the Soviet Union's repeated suggestions in this direction in recent years and because of the Russian people's desire to avoid a third world war. Successful nuclear disarmament would also, however, require that other, now underdeveloped, nations not develop nuclear weapons with which to threaten their neighbors and the Western powers. The Western nations usually see China as the obvious danger in this respect, although probably some dozen other poorer nations could, if they wished, develop nuclear weapons within the next decade.

For this reason, as well as for economic and humanitarian reasons, it seems essential that disarmament be accompanied by the formation of a world administrative system above the several nation-states. So far as I can judge, the only motives that could prompt China or other poor nations to develop nuclear weapons would be, first, the fear of being attacked by others and, second, the possibility of forcibly appropriating the natural resources and wealth of other nations. Disarmament by the Western powers would remove the first threat. The second possibility would be removed by including all nations within a world community whose administration would plan the steady transmission of modern technology and scientific knowledge from the rich to the poor nations; would plan in broad outline the future production programs of the former nations; and would co-ordinate trade among them in a manner most beneficial to all. If such a state of affairs could be achieved, there seems no doubt that productivity would rise greatly in the rich as well as the poor nations, as the world's resources, technology, and brainpower became rationally directed toward peaceful programs for the betterment of mankind. The danger of reversion to competitive wars between the former nations would at the same time be averted. But such a future would of course require the surrender of much national sovereignty to a world administration and agreement to work out each country's development plans within a framework of world development.

The internal changes that would be necessary if the Western nations embarked on such a course can be only dimly foreseen at this time. First, disarmament itself would, in the earliest stages, require extensive national planning for transition to a peacetime economy. I am not competent to judge whether such a transition could be accomplished in the short run under the present system of private ownership, profits, and wages. It is certainly doubtful whether this would be possible in the longer run, if only because of the increasing obsolescence of manual work that rapid adoption of automation would bring. At the least, it would be necessary from the start to use public funds on a large scale to compensate those unemployed by disarmament and to educate them and others to take their place in a society in which manual work and much clerical work was disappearing. Public planning would also be required to coordinate, through a world administration, these nations' economic processes with those of the rest of the emergent world.

With the external threat of the Cold War and of the pressures of extreme nationalism removed, we might well expect that pressures for social and economic equality and for equality of civil rights would increase greatly on the part of the underprivileged within each nation. It would no longer be possible to stem these pressures by pleading that the nation-state must pull in its belt, sacrifice, and unite for common defense against enemies. The precise implications of the removal of the threat of war for the class structure within each Western nation can be only dimly envisaged, but they would no doubt be profound. At the least, I would expect that although structures of authority would probably remain within the post–nation-state society, positions of authority would cease to be linked with inherited social class positions or to be connected with marked inequalities of wealth, education, civil rights, or civil liberties.

It is difficult, perhaps futile, to imagine *in toto* the precise form that the over-all institutions of a united world society could or would assume. Its like would never have been seen before, and its institutions would develop step by step once the nations had agreed to disarm and to co-operate through a world administration. Here I can make only very tentative suggestions concerning the possible characteristics of a world society.

The Shape of a World Society

First, I would expect peace to be maintained through the actual growth of institutional forms of co-operation, of which the United Nations and its associated institutions may be the embryo. That is to say, peace would be eventually assured through the building of a sense of community and through the institutions of a world community rather than through the centralized monopoly of force on the part of a world government. For this reason I do not wish to speak of world society as a "world-state," for it would lack the essential ingredient of a state—a centralized monopoly of force for the sake of armed competition against states of like order. On theoretical grounds, it seems unlikely that a centralized monopoly of force could long endure in a world society, for such a monopoly in the states of the past seems to have been inextricably bound up with external competition. Further, the very existence of heavy weapons, especially nuclear weapons, in any hands poses the threat of genocide from which men are now fleeing; presumably it is primarily to escape this threat that men would be willing to enter into a world community in the first place. It seems probable of course that in a world community some form of police force, equipped with light weapons, would be required to restrain individuals and small groups from breaking the law. But I would expect peace between the former *nations* to rest on such factors as the absence of facilities for national rearmament, growing international interdependence, co-operative scientific endeavors, the growth of a body of world law, the free movement of peoples, and the growth of administrative institutions to plan the world's production and distribution and to arbitrate its disputes. Peace would not depend on a super police force armed with nuclear or conventional heavy weapons with which to threaten and coerce the former national units.

Some of the institutions of a united world society already exist in embryo in association with the United Nations. Among them are the Regional Economic Commissions, the Food and Agriculture Organizations, the International Monetary Fund, and the International Bank for Reconstruction and Development. While their operation in the past decade has been inadequate to solve the needs of the world's peoples, it is significant that they exist and could in the future form the basis of planned world development. It is noteworthy in this connection that, as Myrdal[16] points out, it has been chiefly the Western industrial nations that have resisted the degree of planning that full co-operation with these institutions would involve, while the newer and developing nations have been those most concerned to activate these institutions.

Second, I would expect that, connected with the disappearance of the centralized monopoly of force within each state as well as within the world as a whole, many institutions whose direction is now centralized in the government of the nation-state would become more decentralized. Concomitantly, I would expect personal freedom of action within such institutions to increase as their direct control passed into the hands of smaller groups. This means that greater centralization of broad planning of the world's basic pattern of law, of production, and of distribution would be expected to allow much greater decentralization of planning and of day-to-day controls in production units and in local communities. One reason for this is that, as Drucker[17] has argued, a highly centralized, bureaucratic control of economic processes is not feasible for the most modern forms of the world's economy. Technological and economic processes, in which designs and materials change rapidly, require constant experimentation, innovation, and risk-taking. A central body can therefore plan only in the broadest outline and must necessarily leave most decisions to local organizers and technicians. The highly centralized economy of the totalitarian state is feasible for a "backward" country only as long as it is trying to catch up with its neighbors and can set itself clearly defined, preordained goals.

A further reason why I would expect a high degree of decentralization in the control of production processes lies in the character of nuclear energy and of nuclear reactors, which can be expected to replace other forms of energy in large areas of the future world society. Pregel,[18] envisaging the nuclear-powered society of a few decades hence, foresees a breakup of the present pattern of congested city living in the industrial societies and the dispersion of most of the population into smaller, nuclear-reactor-centered communities, in each of which a small, highly skilled work force organizes and tends automated machinery. He foresees the bulk of the population engaged in a variety of service occupations carried on in a much-shortened work week, while a large proportion of the community's energy is devoted to education, research, entertainment, community and political organization, art, and travel. I may add that with the disappearance of nation-states as sovereign, mutually competitive units, I would expect educational institutions to become more free ideologically and in degree of self-government.

In general, in the world society of the future, I would expect a much higher degree of self-government by all sections of the population than has been possible in any state society of the past. In a society in which most manual and other routine work has disappeared, I would no longer expect to find the traditional divisions between mental and manual labor, between property owners or managers and workers, between rich and poor, nor, correspondingly, the same extent of separation between rulers and ruled. Instead, there might emerge a society with an almost uniformly high standard of universal education, with a high degree of homogeneity of wealth, and, correspondingly, with a leisured citizenry, all sections of which had some measure of direct control over the decisions affecting their day-to-day lives. With the obsolescence of the nation-state and the decentralization of many productive and distributive processes, representative government would be able to give place to new forms of direct democracy in which individuals expressed and made effective their approval or disapproval, not of candidates for election, but of specific policies affecting their daily lives. As Berkeley[19] has pointed out, the increasing use of computers would make possible the precise reporting and making operational of multitudes of individual decisions on specific issues of public interest in a manner that could not have been conceived in the preautomation era of representative democracy.

The characteristics that I have foreseen as possible for a united world society are based partly on the nature of atomic technology and cybernation. Without believing in technological determinism, I believe that each phase of energy exploitation and of technology opens a certain range of possible new social institutions and makes anachronistic other institutions that were appropriate to earlier technological phases. Thus, the flowering of the first industrial revolution in the West made possible economic institutions involving a high degree of free marketability of land, labor, and goods. In this situation slavery came to seem both morally outrageous and also economically undesirable.[20] I believe that, similarly, the full flowering of the second industrial revolution will eventually render anachronistic wage labor and many other related institutions. But what most distinguishes the second industrial revolution is that it will make possible such a high level of productivity throughout the world that men and institutions need no longer be dominated by techno-environmental and economic factors to the extent that they have been in all past ages. With the gradual obsolescence of manual work and of the need for some men, and some societies, to labor for others' leisure, it should prove possible to mold the society's technical apparatus and economic institutions to serve the aspirations of all men to an extent never before contemplated.

A second reason why I would hope for a high degree of decentralization and self-government in a future world society is that these already motivate the most dynamic movements for change in the world today. Our age has already seen the beginning of demands by oppressed peoples for greater freedom and international equality and justice. Already in many of the colonial and new nations, as well as in the older industrial nations, common people have shown their determination to struggle and sacrifice so that their descendants may live lives of dignity and freedom from tyranny. Similarly, the modern trends in the most advanced welfare states of the Western world appear, as Myrdal points out, to move in the direction of increasing decentralization of controls, leaving more freedom for municipalities, provinces, and local and occupational groups to decide how people shall live and work together.[21]

A final factor is that the extent of suppression of civil liberties in nation-states seems to have been closely related to the degree of ferocity of international competition. If this competition is removed, one would therefore expect that the need for suppression of personal liberties would also be relaxed.

IMMEDIATE GOALS

Many object to the idea of a united world society as so far removed from present possibilities as to be meaninglessly Utopian. The objection is also raised that if a world society is ever achieved, it will not be for one or several hundred years. In the meantime a large part of humanity is threatened with extinction, and more practical short-term remedies must be suggested.

First, I admit that it may indeed be several decades, although not, I think, centuries, before a united world society can be achieved. In the meanwhile, a variety of short-term programs can no doubt be drafted—including the continuation of the present nuclear stalemate that has already endured for a decade—under which the industrial powers *may* refrain from entering upon nuclear war. My point is, however, that I do not believe that the world will be safe from the danger of nuclear war until (a) the nation-states have divested themselves of all armaments that might be used for international warfare and (b) a world administration has emerged to encompass all of the former nations and to preside over a unitary body of laws and an integrated system of economic institutions. If the removal of the threat of nuclear war is our goal, I believe it incumbent on us to seek paths toward the creation of a world society.

With this in view, the most practical as well as the most ethical program seems to be an attempt to set up within each nation a national leadership that will be prepared, voluntarily and if necessary unilaterally, to disarm and to form part of or to surrender power to a world administration.

The chief objection to proposals for unilateral disarmament in the Western nations is of course that the Communists, chiefly the Russians, would overrun the world, including the industrial states in question. My reply to this argument is twofold. One is that plans for and the threat of nuclear war are infinitely more immoral and dangerous than the acceptance of any political and economic system, however unwelcome and alien. Even if unilateral disarmament meant the imposition of Russian-style institutions throughout the world, I would see this as immeasurably preferable to nuclear war. For the former condition would offer hope of survival and cultural betterment for our descendants, whereas the latter would not. Second, however, I have tried to argue that the permanent domination of one industrial nation by another is no longer feasible in the age of atomic power and automation. If the West disarmed, the cost of occupying it militarily would be uneconomic and probably physically impossible for the Russians or for any other Communist power. Even were they able to do so temporarily, the institutions of traditional Communism cannot be maintained in the coming era of high productivity and work obsolescence, any more than can the institutions of traditional American capitalism.

It seems probable that the real fear that lurks behind alleged fears of "Communist domination" in the West is in fact a different one. It is the fear, especially on the part of the wealthy and powerful, of loss of international and intranational forms of dominance and of having to modify or give up some of the institutions under which men in the Western world have hitherto enjoyed wealth, prestige, and authority. As in the case of white citizens in the Southern United States or in Africa, the real eventuality faced by the Western nations is not conquest or domination by others but the loss of one's own ability to dominate.

If this is true, I would simply say that the loss of such traditional forms of Western dominance is inevitable anyway, whether or not the West disarms. The tide of nationalism and the hunger for self-determination and for social and economic equality in the underdeveloped world cannot be stemmed indefinitely. It is surely better to acknowledge peoples' modern potentialities rather than to try to delay them and to threaten one's own and other populations with extinction through nuclear war.

An objection to unilateral disarmament, even by those who wish for disarmament and do not fear the loss of international dominance, is that such proposals are futile because they have no chance of acceptance by Western governments. Some persons also object that such proposals are so wholesale and apocalyptic that they cannot be broken down into piecemeal, practical suggestions, some of which might be acceptable to our governments.

My response to this is that if we believe disarmament—beginning with unilateral initiatives—and the creation of a world society to be the most reasonable and ethical program for the Western nations, we cannot pretend with integrity that we desire something less or something else. Holding this position does not, however, preclude us from requesting or approving small beginnings that would take the form of unilateral initiatives toward disarmament and the establishment of international trust. Such initiatives would include, for example, removal of military bases and withdrawal of troops from foreign nations near the periphery of the Communist zone, the voluntary and unconditional cessation of nuclear tests, an invitation to Communist China to join the United Nations, and diplomatic recognition and resumption of trade with the present government of Cuba. Such initiatives move in the direction of disarmament and the building of world community, yet are limited, practical, and relevant to the immediate problems of today. It is impossible to insure reduction of international tensions and the threat of nuclear war and at the same time to refuse to contemplate *any* unilateral initiatives toward disarmament or any of the risks involved in the surrender of national sovereignty.

APPROACHES TO A WORLD SOCIETY

It is clear that we are very far from achieving a world society. If, however, its creation is posed as the ultimate goal, this enables us to set up more limited objectives as intermediate steps. I have suggested that the primary objective should be to set up within each industrial nation a national leadership which will begin disarmament, if necessary unilaterally, with the ultimate aim of surrendering national sovereignty to a world administration.

In the Western industrial nations, and especially in the United States, the difficulty is of course that a majority in the population, as well as in the government, either do not feel or do not acknowledge the need to disarm and to effect fundamental changes in their social structures. This is perhaps not surprising, since these nations, the wealthiest in the world, still enjoy a measure of international dominance. Consequently, their populations tend to see disarmament in traditional terms, as a deliberate surrender of national security to would-be conquerors.

There are, however, growing signs of unease. In the past few years, peace movements have emerged that, although small, are increasingly vocal in their demands for an end to the danger of nuclear war. A portion of scientists and other scholars have begun to question the nihilism of the arms race. A growing number of women fear for their children's safety. In private and in public, racial minorities and the unemployed are questioning the whole structure and aims of Western society.

Among those in the United States at the present time who seek partial or full disarmament and some kind of alternative to the arms race are four apparent categories of citizens with fairly distinct methods and beliefs.

The first category favors attempts by specially qualified experts or already powerful persons to persuade the existing government to change its policies and prepare for a disarmed world.

The second, often closely allied to the first, seeks to influence and enlist a wide range of leaders in established social institutions—for example, industrialists, labor union leaders, educators, and church leaders, in addition to governmental and military officials—to support programs leading gradually to disarmament.

The third category attempts, through "peace groups" specially organized for "peace work," to enlist citizens regardless of their occupations and roles in power structures. These groups carry on the dual task of appeals and demands to the government for disarmament and education and propaganda directed toward the general public. By arousing large public support for their policies, such groups hope through legal and constitutional channels to bring about either a change of policy in the present government or a change of government through electoral procedures. Public demonstrations, petitions and letters to the government, advertisements, lobbying, public meetings, distribution of literature, and, more recently, election campaigns for "peace" candidates feature prominently in the activities of these groups. In England, and more recently in some other European and Commonwealth countries, the Campaign for Nuclear Disarmament has achieved political prominence. In the United States peace activities are at present carried on by a number of groups with varying shades of opinion. Among these are the newly united Women's International Strike for Peace, the Committee for a Sane Nuclear Policy, and a variety of student groups.

The fourth category of peace workers engages in direct opposition to the government through civil disobedience against laws that support the nation-state's exercise of military threats to the safety of its own and other populations. The actions of this category include refusal to pay taxes for the arms race, illegal sit-downs outside government buildings and military installations, and attempts at illegal entry of military zones. In the United States such actions, led by the Committee for Non-Violent Action, are chiefly confined to small numbers of religious pacifists, whose protests have the character of symbolic expressions of personal moral conviction. In Britain the larger-scale protests of supporters of the Committee of 100 begin to represent a somewhat more significant political force. Of all the peace groups, the Committee of 100 has also most explicitly indicted the nation-state for its threats to the safety of the world's populations.[22]

Given a goal of complete disarmament leading to a world administration, the first two policies seem to me the least likely to be effective, especially if they are unsupported by the third and perhaps eventually also by the fourth. The first and second approaches rely on direct appeals to those now in positions of power in Western society, on the assumption that such men control the attitudes and opinions of most of the rest of the society. In fact, however, it seems to me that those now in power have the strongest stake in maintaining *this* society—the society of competing nation-states—intact as long as possible. Nevertheless, we must acknowledge that the future is extremely unpredictable. Some grave, unplanned crisis might make the present leaders of the industrial states succumb to policies fostering world unity, which they would otherwise never have contemplated. Such a crisis might be, for example, an unplanned excess of fall-out from nuclear testing, which would cause large sections of the earth's population to die or to fall gravely ill. Another crisis might be a nuclear weapon's accidental explosion on a portion of the population of the nation that owned it.

The third approach—of attempts to awaken public opinion to exert pressure on government through the existing legal institutions—seems to me more promising than the first two and, especially in the United States, more desirable at the present time. I must admit, however, that I do not expect the peace movement to be very successful in converting the population until other kinds of events have further challenged the country's existing social structure. Among the conditions that might arise are: (1) increased unemployment resulting from automation; (2) failure of the United States to increase its productivity for peaceful uses at the same rate as some other industrial nations;[23] (3) increasingly forceful prosecution of the Negro struggle for equality, which will receive increasing support from the new nations and will itself call into question many features of the economic and power structures of United States society; and (4) the success of one or another type of "leftist" movement in increasing numbers of countries now dependent on the United States, notably in Latin America, and the setting-up of strongly state-controlled economies in such countries. Any or all of these events might create crises of policy-making in the United States in which groups favoring disarmament could eventually gain a popular hearing.

It seems uncertain whether all of the necessary changes can ultimately be brought about in Western society through the existing electoral system. In the United States, the electoral system does not yet represent the whole population. This is especially true with regard to underrepresentation of the

Southern Negroes and of the largest and poorest sections of the great cities —groups who might favor radical social changes under a leadership acceptable to them. Furthermore, the existing machinery of the two major parties is cumbersome and seems to be largely influenced by the same groups that most support nationalistic and militaristic policies. Even if a majority in the population became convinced of the need for disarmament, it is questionable whether the electoral system could be made responsive to their demands. The danger might indeed arise of a military dictatorship assuming control of the nation and suspending the traditional democratic procedures.

The fourth approach—of civil disobedience against existing military policies of the national governments—seems to me amply justified on moral grounds in the present world situation. The laws of representative democracy were framed in an historical period when national governments lacked the technological ability to plan the instantaneous murder of hundreds of millions of people. Since the governments have acquired this power and, at the same time, have lost the power to protect their populations from destruction, it becomes the individual's moral right, and perhaps also his highest duty, to disobey the laws that uphold governmental powers of genocide.[24]

In the present climate of nationalist opinion, however, civil disobedience against military policies has little chance of political efficacy within the United States. It is possible, however, that if a large popular movement for disarmament does arise in the future, it may be obliged to exercise mass civil disobedience in pursuing its ends. This would depend on whether the national government was open to popular pressure through democratic procedures or whether these were further curtailed or even suspended through the actions of political factions having the support of military and industrial groups.

In the United States at the present time the peace movements have a very narrow popular appeal. In my view this is not only because the population is exposed to continuous nationalist and militarist propaganda. It is perhaps also because the peace groups have not been able to make clear the kind of society that they wish to build in the process of effecting disarmament. In particular the peace groups are hamstrung by two basic issues: their approach to Communism and to the Communist nations and their approach to social change within American society.

Peace groups vary in their evaluation of Communism as a force likely to affect the Western way of life. At one extreme are peace workers who, in the main, accept the official American stereotype of a Communist conspiracy to dominate the world from Moscow or Peking and to subject it to the type of totalitarian dictatorship found in Russia under Stalin. Such groups tend to attribute most of the blame for the arms race to the Soviet Union. While they see the necessity for reduction of international tensions and gradual disarmament, they are much afraid of making contact with organizations in the Communist countries independently of their own governments, or of being tagged as Communist sympathizers at home. The same groups also tend to shun discussion of radical social changes in their own society, perhaps because social change is in the United States so often equated with Socialism, and Socialism, with Communism.

At another extreme are those who, like myself, see a variety of socio-political forms in the Communist bloc but note that repressive, totalitarian and police-state features, undesirable in our own society, certainly appear to be present in all of them. We do not, however, see Communism as threatening the highly industrial Western nations. It seems to us that, given modern forms of technology, levels of productivity, and aspirations for personal freedom, neither traditional communism nor traditional capitalism can be the "wave of the future" for the already industrialized zones. It does however seem obvious that deep social changes will be required in the Western nations *pari passu* with disarmament, and that, because of the necessary extension of public planning and of the public sector of the economy, they will involve some measures traditionally associated with the goals of democratic socialism. In an age of nuclear power and cybernation, we expect all citizens to be able to attain to a degree of equality and of personal liberty greater than that foreseen by democratic socialists in the past. While agreeing that the Soviet Union also contributes a share to the tensions of the arms race, we tend to focus on and to criticize those power groups that hold up disarmament in our own, Western, societies.

Between these extremes are to be found peace workers with a great variety of political theories, as well as many who are interested only in disarmament and hold no political views at all.

A Compelling Need of the Peace Movement

As mentioned before, organized peace groups have not, on the whole, stated clearly the kinds of changes which they would like to see accomplished inside Western society. Some have attempted to plan for reconversion to a peacetime economy. But they have tended to treat the problem as purely economic, without questioning how disarmament could or should be linked with spontaneous struggles for social justice on the part of groups now excluded from the mainstream of American culture. Most peace workers come from the wealthier and better-educated segments of American society. Except for some students, few apparently feel the need to make contact with, understand, and amalgamate their cause with those of other disaffected groups, such as Southern rural Negroes, Black Muslims, the unemployed, or workers in factories. Although the peace groups vary in this respect, most give an impression of concern to "save this society" as it is. Social issues not directly connected with nuclear war are pushed aside as irrelevant to disarmament and as distracting from the main issue, since consideration of them would break the present precarious unity of the peace movement by introducing political, class, or ethnic divisions. In some quarters there is even a view that all other social changes should be postponed until disarmament has first been accomplished.

My own view, by contrast, is that if it is to succeed, a disarmament movement in the Western world must attempt to ally itself with all of the social forces in the world that seek an end not only to the threat of nuclear war, but also to the domination of one people by another or of one group by another, whether internationally or intranationally, in light of the most modern, emergent ideals of social justice and equality.

This means that those who wish disarmament must first seek to form an international movement with a co-ordinated program. The first filaments of such a movement are beginning to stretch out through cross-national peace marches, international conferences of scientists, international peace conferences such as those recently held in Moscow, Accra, and Tokyo, informal meetings of women from East and West, and the gradual internationalization of such groups as the Campaign for Nuclear Disarmament and the Women's International Strike for Peace. They must, I think, be strengthened and co-ordinated into a single movement that demands the surrender of national sovereignty to a world leadership responsive to the needs of the world's citizens. In the process of internationalization, all help is required from those governments and people's organizations in the new nations which favor world unity and an end to international domination both by the U.S.S.R and by the Western industrial nations.

Second, disarmament movements must, I believe, begin to embrace and to be influenced by those segments of industrial societies that are in some way oppressed by present nation-state systems for other reasons than the threat of nuclear war. In the United States, these include in particular Negroes, underprivileged immigrant minorities, migrant and nonunionized laborers, and city workers whose employment is threatened by automation. The inclusion of such segments of the population is essential if only because no large popular movement can be built without their support. But it is also essential on humanistic grounds, for their deprivations have no justification in the world of modern technology.

Embracing other than "intellectual" and "middle-class" segments of the population means that "peace" must be given clear social content and that all elements drawn into the movement must be allowed to present their own goals for discussion and ratification as part of the total program. In order to "contact" these submerged social segments, it is not enough to meet their members only through the traditional organizations that purport to represent them—for example, the labor unions. The official leaders of such organizations may lag behind their fellows in the urgency of their demands, since they themselves usually have some stake in preserving the social structure in its present form. Rather, efforts should be made to reach the people themselves and their local and less formal leaderships and to form co-ordinated programs with them.

In the process of forming an international movement for disarmament and for world society, it seems to me that professional "intellectuals" have special roles to play. First, they should not cease to make plain to their governments and peoples their dissatisfaction with present foreign policies and their plans for disarmament and social change. But this is not enough; it is all too easy for intellectuals to talk only to one another and to do their protesting in a void. They should also, I believe, attempt to unite in an international group that has its roots in and is responsible to the already emerging peace movement of women, students, and other nonprofessional citizens. Finally, in the process of consolidating themselves with a growing popular movement, intellectuals should make it clear that their first loyalty is to this movement and to the broader interests of world society, rather than to the narrower, short-term interests of their separate nation-states. Using their professional leverage, but working jointly with nonprofessional disarmament workers, they should ready themselves not only to advise but, when necessary, to take stands against their national governments and to refuse their co-operation with those national policies that run counter to their emerging, supranational conscience.

NOTES

1. Cf. Elman R. Service, *Primitive Social Organization* (New York: Random House, 1962).
2. For an extended discussion of politically administered trade in archaic states, see Karl Polanyi and others, *Trade and Market in the Early Empires* (Glencoe, Ill.: The Free Press, 1957).
3. See, for example, Kwame Nkrumah, *Address to the Opening Assembly of the Accra Conference on a World without the Bomb* (Accra, Ghana: Government Printing Department, 1962), pp. 3–4.
4. See, for example, Barbara Ward, *The Rich Nations and the Poor Nations* (New York: W. W. Norton & Co., 1962), pp. 1–90; Gunnar Myrdal, *Beyond the Welfare State* (New Haven: Yale University Press, 1960), pp. 102–103; and also Myrdal, *An International Economy* (New York: Harper & Brothers, 1956), pp. 149–222.
5. See, for example, U. W. Kitzinger, *The Challenge of the Common Market* (Oxford: Blackwell & Mott, 1961), p. 12.
6. Myrdal, *Beyond the Welfare State*, p. 212.
7. See Barbara Ward, *op. cit.*, p. 111, on the ideals of international equality and justice as the driving force for development in the new nations. See also Boris Pregel in Johnson E. Fairchild and David Landman, eds., *America Faces the Nuclear Age* (New York: Sheridan House, Inc., 1961), p. 30: "Within two generations . . . every have-not nation can become a land of plenty. Where literacy and other circumstances permit, the change can come even more swiftly."
8. Kitzinger, *op. cit.*, pp. 38–39.
9. *Ibid.*, p. 84.
10. Nkrumah, *op. cit.*, p. 4.
11. Donald N. Michael, *Cybernation* (Washington, D.C.: Center for the Study of Democratic Institutions, 1962).

12. Pregel, *op. cit.*, p. 38: "The inevitable growth of automation, more than anything else, will make the great city obsolete. In the New York metropolitan area alone, hundreds of thousands of white collar workers, skilled and semi-skilled workers will lose their jobs. In other urban areas like Detroit, where the emphasis is even greater on hard goods, the number of the technologically unemployed will be greater."

13. See, for example, H. Brandt, "Disarmament and the Prospects of American Capitalism," *Dissent,* IX (Summer 1962), p. 239.

14. *Ibid.,* p. 238.

15. See, for example, Erich Fromm, *May Man Prevail?* (Garden City, N.Y.: Doubleday & Co., Inc., 1961), pp. 67–118.

16. Myrdal, *Beyond the Welfare State,* p. 212.

17. Peter F. Drucker, *Landmarks of Tomorrow* (New York: Harper & Brothers, 1953), p. 53.

18. Pregel, *op. cit.*, pp. 37–41.

19. Edmund C. Berkeley, *The Computer Revolution* (Garden City, N.Y.: Doubleday & Co., Inc., 1962), p. 164.

20. See Nkrumah, *op. cit.*, pp. 3–4.

21. Myrdal, *Beyond the Welfare State,* p. 127.

22. See *On Trial, A Report, with Comments, Disallowed Evidence and Profiles, of the Old Bailey Official Secrets Act Trial* (London: *Peace News,* 1962).

23. See, for example, Brandt, *op. cit.*, pp. 236–251. Brandt argues that defense spending has become a major prop to the American economy and that it is popular with the owning classes because it preserves high profits, equity values, and interest rates and prices, and has in general helped to maintain the economy in operation without the necessity for major changes in the economic and social structures. He further argues, however, that the arms race will in the long run prove unprofitable to the financial and industrial interest groups themselves because it leads to stagnation in other sectors of the United States' economy and thus to the loss of a competitive position in the world market.

24. This view has been most fully and clearly stated by the five members of the British Committee of 100 who were defendants in a trial in February 1962, involving the charge of endangering the safety and security of the British state through civil disobedience against nuclear weapons. See *On Trial,* a Special Supplement to *Peace News,* April 1962.

4

KENNETH E. BOULDING

Toward a Theory of Peace

Without theory, the search for peace is like a game of hide-and-seek in which we do not quite know what it is we are looking for and in which nobody is able to tell us whether we are getting "warmer" or "colder." In the mythology of ordinary life there is an unfortunate identification of the theoretical with the impractical. In the case of the physical and medical sciences we have at least got beyond this point: we almost universally recognize that without theory we would not have been able to make the extraordinary accomplishments of the modern age. People are less willing to acknowledge the value of theory in social systems, perhaps because in this field each man believes himself an expert. Nevertheless, if we are to manage the complex social systems in which we find ourselves, we must have theoretical structures that can enable us to think about them, to identify the problems, and to create an information system upon which to base wise decisions.

First we must identify the system in which the problem lies. This, fortunately, is easy. Peace, whatever it is, is a property of a social system, not of a physical or a biological system. Furthermore, it is a property of some social systems and not of others. The theory of peace, therefore, must be a theory of certain aspects and properties of social systems.

A social system may be defined as the relevant history of two or more persons in contact. Persons are in contact if behavior by one affects the behavior of the other. The contact may be either conscious or unconscious. If one person has an image of the other that affects his behavior, the interaction is conscious. If he has no image of the other, the behavior of the other may still affect his environment and so may affect the system that binds them together. The study of social systems must include both unconscious and conscious elements, or what Merton calls the latent as well as the manifest. There are great forces in society—such as population trends, inflation and deflation, technological development, and so on—which are not consciously planned and of which no individual may have a conscious image but which profoundly affect the history of the social system. On the other hand, there are conscious images that also affect the behavior of those who entertain them. In examining the international system we must observe both the great latent forces and the manifest operating assumptions that lie constantly in the minds of the decision-makers. These are not unrelated. If the decision-maker's operating assumptions are strongly out of line with the latent forces of history, decisions may be made, but they will not produce the intended results.

One of the major problems that must be faced in the study of social systems is that the dynamic properties of these systems include strong random elements. Social systems are not like the solar system, in which the random elements are so small that we can predict the movements of the heavenly bodies with almost 100 per cent certainty—or could, before the advent of artificial satellites. This means that we cannot, by reason of the nature of the system itself, ever arrive at a state of knowledge in which we can make exact predictions of social systems. It does not mean, however, that there is no system in society or that history is chaos. We can make probabilistic predictions and, furthermore, can apply controls, at least within limits.

A good illustration of a dynamic system with random elements of great importance in both the biological and the social sciences is a growth system. If we take a fertilized egg, we have a pretty fair chance of predicting the kind of organism it will become. We would be very much surprised, for instance, if a chicken egg grew into a horse. On the other hand, we cannot predict exactly the properties of the individual that any given egg will grow into, simply because there are essentially unpredictable elements in the process. We have a similar phenomenon in social systems. If we understood the growth processes better than we do, we might have been able to predict, for instance, that the egg that was laid at Plymouth Rock would grow up into something like the United States. In social systems, however, it is hard to detect which eggs are fertile, and it is much harder to predict the consequences of these growth systems. We are, however, always on the lookout for these patterns, and the images that people have of the growth or decline of various social systems is an extremely important element in their behavior.

PEACE AS A PART OF CONFLICT

If we now look for that element of the social system in which the concept of peace is important, we shall find it in the notion of the conflict system. Peace is not a particularly important problem in such social systems as buying a shirt, listening to music, or reading a book. It is important when we observe the quarrels of children or the conflicts of races, economic groups, and national states. It may sound a little odd to say that peace is a property of conflict systems, as we frequently regard peace as the absence of conflict. It is, however, the very negative definition of peace that makes it so troublesome as a concept, and even perhaps rather unattractive as a symbol. A theory of peace must be part of a more general theory of conflict. Without understanding conflict, we cannot understand that particular aspect of conflict that we call peace.

Once we identify peace as a property of conflict systems, it becomes apparent that it has two rather different meanings. In the first place, we think of peace as referring to some characteristic or property of the system as a whole. We say that one family, for instance, is more peaceable and less quarrelsome than another. Or we might say that the relations between the United States and the British Empire in the past hundred years have been more peaceful than the relations between France and Germany. Here we are looking for some index or scale that measures the general level of hostility, or consciousness of conflict, within a system of relationships—of persons, of groups, or of organizations. It is not easy to construct indices of this kind, and there is probably no perfect theoretical solution for the problem. But we do in fact make such estimates in common speech, and it should be possible to construct a rough scalar measure of this magnitude. Professor Robert North of Stanford University is currently experimenting with such measures.

The second, and perhaps the more important, concept of peace is that of a system boundary that divides the possible states of a conflict system into two kinds, one of which is defined as peace and the other as not peace. Conflict systems frequently exhibit sudden changes in the intensity of conflict. Two children, for instance, may play fairly quietly and happily for a while, and then hostility may arise between them, resulting in a fist fight. In international relations, the distinction between peace and war is fairly sharply drawn. The world social system, for instance, was very much different in 1942 from what it had been in 1938. In international relations the transition from peace to war and from war to peace is formalized in many ways by declarations and treaties, even though, as in any other distinction, there are marginal cases that are difficult to categorize. Between any two countries at any particular time, however, it is usually possible to say whether a state of peace or war exists.

The concept of peace that is important here is that of a system break, representing a sharp transition from a milder to a more acute form of conflict. Thus in the case of a marriage increasing conflict may eventually lead to separation and to divorce; in an industrial relationship increasing conflict may lead to a strike or a walk-out; and in an international relationship increasing conflict may lead to the rupture of international relations or eventually to war. In any such system there are a number of different boundaries and phases of this kind. We should not think of the system as simply having a single boundary, but there is likely to be one boundary that represents the most fundamental system break such as divorce, strike, or war.

The two concepts of peace are not unrelated. If we think of peace as an index of the general state of peaceableness of a system, it is clear that the magnitude of this index is of great importance in telling us whether we are going to cross the boundary from one phase to another. The exact position of the boundary on the scale of peaceableness depends on the nature of the system itself. Some families, for instance, can stand a high level of conflict and hostility without producing divorce. Similarly, there may be some international relationships that also can stand a high degree of hostility and "Cold War" without going over the edge into war itself. If anything breaks, even a stick or a piece of chalk, it is because the strain on it was too great for its strength. A strong system can stand a lot of strain before it breaks; a weak system can stand little. The first concept of peace measures the strain on the system; we may be concerned about decreasing that strain. The second concept of peace refers to the strength of the system relative to the strain. If our main concern is the prevention of system breaks and the passage from peace into war in the second sense of the term, then we may legitimately be as much concerned with strengthening the system as with diminishing the strain on it.

We must not assume, incidentally, that all strain is undesirable. For any system we can postulate an optimum degree of strain or of peaceableness in the first sense of the word. A system may be peaceable to the point of dullness. For instance, a family without conflict is likely also to lack many of the qualities that we regard as desirable in family life, such as creativity. The problem, then, is first to identify an optimum degree or range of strain, and then to make certain that the system is strong enough to withstand it without recourse to war.

THE NEED FOR CONTROLS

These simple concepts throw a good deal of light on what we are looking for in the search for peace. In the first place we are looking for a machinery to control the general state of the system in terms of peaceableness or strain. If the system is too peaceful, we can stir it up; if it is too warlike, we can tone it down. This implies that we are capable of identifying, within a reasonable measure, what is the optimum degree of peaceableness for a system. This is not an easy task, because some people and some cultures seem to enjoy quarreling, and others do not.

It may be, paradoxically enough, that the better the means of controlling the peaceableness or quarrelsomeness of a system, the higher the level of quarrelsomeness the system is able to enjoy. We can enjoy conflict only if we are quite sure that we are able to control it and that it will not lead to disaster. The development of sport is a very interesting example of a social system in which conflict is so well controlled that its optimum level is high. In intercollegiate football, for instance, conflict artificially generated is perfectly legitimate, for there is little fear that it will get out of hand. But in the case of international relations, unfortunately, we have no such confidence in our ability to control the level of conflict.

If then we define peace as "ideal conflict," it is clear that it must involve a social system capable of controlling the general level of hostility and capable also of pushing the boundary of system break well beyond any level of hostility that the system is likely to attain. In more technical language, the system must have a cybernetic mechanism capable of bringing the general level of conflict toward an ideal, either from above or from below, and also a mechanism sufficient to insure that the general level of conflict is well on the "peace" side of the line of system break. A system of this kind must have the following requisites: (1) an apparatus of social perception that can inform a sufficient number of persons in the system when the system is diverging from the ideal or when it is beginning to approach the boundary of system break and (2) an apparatus of dynamic control to permit the persons who perceive that the dynamics of the system are moving in an unfavorable direction to alter their behavior in such a way as to reverse the movement of the system.

It is important to recognize that systems of this kind can have varying degrees of centralized control. It is perfectly possible to create a completely noncentralized cybernetic social mechanism simply through unilateral behavior. A great deal of conflict control is, in fact, of this kind. Indeed, one of the great lessons a child growing up has to learn is to control conflict situations by his own behavior. A young child is incapable of this, and so gets into all kinds of fights. As he comes to be an adult, he learns to modify his own reactions to evidences of the hostility of others in such a way that the hostility is diminished rather than increased. In any social group, we find some tendency toward specialization of this process. In the family or the work group, for instance, certain individuals act as peacemakers, who absorb tensions without giving them out and tend to diminish the general level of quarrelsomeness. Any given social system, in fact, is likely to contain some equilibrium level of tension that depends very largely on the number and quality of the peacemakers within it. One of the questions on which we need to do much more research is that of the role of the peacemaker in social groups and especially the learning process by which the peacemaker is produced. If peacemakers are absent from the society, then it is almost impossible to set up a social organization strong enough to prevent system breaks. Yet we have put astonishingly little effort into identifying this particular social variable and even less effort into trying to develop it.

We cannot always rely, however, on the ability of individual peacemakers in a social system to perform the necessary control function; therefore we must introduce a centralized cybernetic machinery or government. Our object may be in part to diminish the general level of quarrelsomeness by absorbing some of the hostility into the central government itself. But we are also concerned with providing machinery by which quarrelsomeness may be sustained without system break. The law is, of course, an important element in this machinery. Arbitration and conciliation services are important too. Where conflict has legitimate channels, it can afford to be more intense.

ILLUSTRATING THE DYNAMICS OF CONFLICT

Up to this point we have treated the problem in extremely general terms; now we must try to focus the discussion on more particular systems, for general theory is useful only as it leads to particular applications. We may begin by illustrating the possible dynamics of interaction of two parties which may, of course, be either persons or organizations.

In Figure 4-1 we measure the welfare of Party X along OX and of Party Y along OY. Any point on the field then represents a combination of the welfares of the two parties. If we think of the directions of movement in this field in terms of the conventional points of the compass, then a move north benefits Y without hurting X. A move east benefits X without hurting Y. A move northeast benefits both Y and X. Being an economist, I have defined such a move elsewhere as a "trading" move. Those who dislike the dubious virtues of exchange may prefer to call such a move "benign." A move southwest similarly might be called "malign" as it makes both parties worse off.

A move to the southeast makes X better off and Y worse off, whereas a move to the northwest is beneficial to Y and detrimental to X. Moves in this direction are conflict moves. They serve to define the concept of conflict very accurately as any change in the position of the social universe that makes one party better off and another party worse off.

What will be the dynamics of a system of this kind? Let us start at point A and adopt the convention that X moves and then Y and then X, and so on. We can define X's area of freedom as bounded by the solid line surrounding point A in the diagram. This means that A can change the social universe in a number of different ways, all of which, however, fall into distributions of welfare of X and Y within the boundary as drawn. If X is actuated only by short-run considerations of his own welfare, he will move to point B, where his own welfare is maximum. In the figure as drawn, this happens to diminish Y's welfare. Although this does not have to be the case, there is nothing to prevent its being a property of the system. Suppose that Y's area of freedom is bounded by the dotted line, and he responds by moving to position C. X now responds by moving to D, Y to E, and so on. We have here what

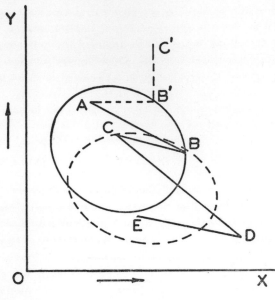

FIGURE 4-1.

might be called a perverse dynamic process, in which the reaction of each party produces a movement of the whole system in a malign direction. It is perfectly possible, however, for the movement of a system of this kind to be benign, as in Figure 4-2, where the succession of moves leads to positions that improve the welfare of both parties.

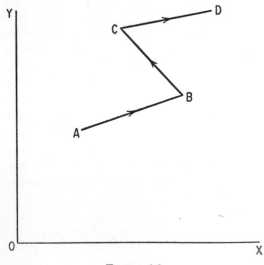

FIGURE 4-2.

An important element of a system of this kind is the shortsightedness or longsightedness of the parties. In the example above, we assumed absolute shortsightedness in the sense that each party considered only the consequences of his immediate move. If the parties take into consideration the long-run consequences of their moves, including the reaction of the other party, the dynamics of the system may turn out to be quite different, and actually more benign.

With the aid of this apparatus, we can distinguish more clearly between the role of internal limitation of behavior on the one hand and of external limitations on the other. In Figure 4-1, for instance, we might suppose a third party, which may represent a government or a central stabilizer, intervening to say to each of the parties, "You must not move to any position that will make the other party worse off." In these circumstances X will move from A to B′, where he is as well off as he can be under the limitation that Y must not be made any worse off. Then we may suppose that Y had to move to some point such as C′, where he is better off but X is no worse off. In these circumstances we clearly have a benign process—in this case, indeed, spectacularly benign. This suggests that we can almost certainly get away with a less restrictive rule and still assure benign processes of interaction. We do not have to go to the extreme of saying that the other party must never be injured; even if we impose a slight limitation on the degree to which he can be made worse off, the interaction may remain benign. The exact nature of this limitation presents some difficult mathematical problems still to be worked out.

The internal limitation on behavior that can guarantee benign processes of interaction may depend not only on longsightedness but also on community or altruism. If A conceives Y's welfare as in part his own, then he will limit the shape of his area of freedom by his own choice, so as virtually to guarantee that he will not make a conflict move. He will voluntarily move to positions such as B′, where at least Y is no worse off. The process of mutual benefit or detriment, incidentally, will not necessarily go on forever. There will come a time at which neither X nor Y can improve his position by any move. We may think of this as the long-run equilibrium.

In such a position, alas, only conflict moves are possible, as we see in Figure 4-3. If XY represents a welfare boundary imposed by scarcity, then when this is reached at, say, P, we can only move either toward Y or toward X. Two solutions are possible in this situation. One is to devote resources to pushing out the welfare boundary, say to X′Y′, which allows further benign moves, say to P′. This is the "research and development" solution. The other solution is to limit the field of behavior by either internal or external boundaries so that it falls within the rectangle OKPL. Then, from any point in this rectangle, benign moves can carry the system to P. But at P no further moves, either conflictual or benign, are possible.

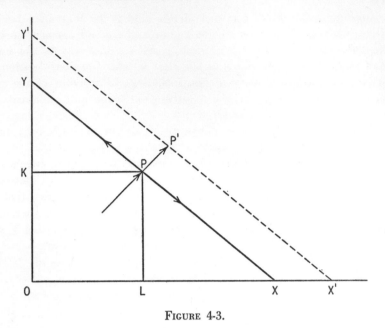

FIGURE 4-3.

THREE MAJOR SUBSYSTEMS

To each position in the field of Figure 4-1 we have supposed that there is a corresponding position of the social system in general. A social system, however, consists of a very large number of variables, which we will wish to break down into subsystems. I have elsewhere distinguished three major subsystems of the social system, which I have called the exchange system, the threat system, and the integrative system. In the exchange system, the relationships between individuals are organized primarily by promises: "If you will do something nice for me, I will do something nice for you." In the threat system, attempts are made to organize behavior by creating expectations of unfavorable circumstances: "You do something nice to me, or I will do something nasty to you." In the integrative system, persons acquire empathy with each other, so that one says to another, "If you want something, I will be happy if you have it."

Conflict may be present in all three of these systems. In exchange, as has frequently been pointed out, there is a community of interest in the very fact of exchange. Exchange is a positive-sum game in which both parties are better off, and we have a benign movement in the field of Figure 4-1. But there is frequently a conflict about the terms of the exchange or the relative price structure. The seller, for example, prefers a high price and the buyer a low price. Within a certain range of prices there may be mutual gain, but there is conflict about the distribution of this gain. Even in integrative systems, there may also be conflict—conflict, for instance, in unselfishness, or conflict for the affection of another. And even integrative systems may lead to malign moves in the field of Figure 4-1—when trust is misplaced, love is deceived, or empathy is felt and there is emulation of people of ill will.

These relationships are illustrated in Figure 4-4. Here we suppose the rectangle ABCD represents the whole social system. This we divide into three subsystems: threat systems, exchange systems, and integrative systems, represented by rectangles AEFD, EGHF, and GBCH. Cutting across is a further subdivision into systems involving violent conflict, area AKCD; peaceful conflict, area KLMC; and no conflict, LBM. At the extreme left, where we find pure threat systems with hardly any admixture of exchange or integration, we see the Hobbesean system of the war of all against all. At the other extreme, in such highly integrative systems as the happy family, the coterie of congenial friends or the perfect team, war disappears altogether, even peaceful conflict is small, and the bulk of the system is nonconflictual.

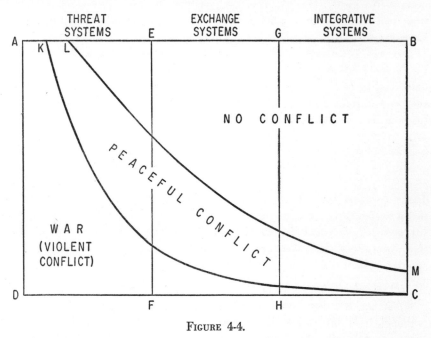

FIGURE 4-4.

It is in the threat system, then, that the element of conflict is most conspicuous, and it is here, for the most part, that we must look for the analysis of a theory of peace. I would argue that all social systems are in fact mixtures of these three elements and that social institutions and organizations tend to embody all three. Nevertheless, there are institutions and organizations in which one of the three elements predominates over the others. Thus a business firm is predominantly concerned with the exchange system, even though there must be integrative elements, for instance in the morale of its work force, and there may also be elements of threat in the discipline of the organization. The family and the church are primarily integrative organizations, but here also there are elements of exchange and of threat. An armed force, on the other hand, is primarily concerned with the threat system. The Department of Defense, for instance, is a very different kind of social organization from either General Motors or the Methodist Church. Similarly, if we look at the place of weapons in the social system, which we must do if we are to develop a successful theory of disarmament, we must look primarily at the place they occupy in the threat system, even though weapons are an element of exchange in that they are bought and sold, and they also may have a place in the integrative system. We may want to have them, for instance, in order to acquire the respect and admiration of another, and they may be a symbol of or a substitute for manliness. There is no implication here, incidentally, that threat systems are, in themselves, "bad" and that the other systems are necessarily "good." Nevertheless, the fact that the word "threat" has a somewhat bad meaning in English is not wholly surprising. The threat system has a greater potentiality for getting out of hand than the other two systems. Threats also constitute a cost in a way that the other system elements do not, for threats are hardly ever regarded as good things in themselves. They can only be justified by their effects, and an organization embodying threats, such as an armed force, is likewise seldom regarded, in these days, as a good thing in itself; it is desired only for its supposed good effects.

ANALYSIS OF THREAT SYSTEMS

Threat systems may be classified as unilateral and bilateral. A unilateral threat system takes the simple form noted above—"You do something nice for me or I'll do something nasty to you." The response to a unilateral threat then determines the subsequent dynamics of the system. Four types of responses (which may be mixed) are noted:

(1) *Submission.* If the threatened party obeys the demand of the threatener, the threat will not be carried out. This transaction tends to be, though it is not necessarily, a conflict move in the field of Figure 4-1, in the sense that the threatener is then better off and the threatened worse off.

(2) *Defiance.* If the threatened party refuses to comply with the request of the threatener, the next move is up to the latter. He may not carry out the threat, in which case the system returns to its pre-threat position with one exception—the credibility of the threatener is likely to be changed for any future threats. Although it seems probable that this credibility will be impaired, there may be circumstances in which the failure to carry out

the threat one time may create a greater presumption that the threat will be carried out the next time. The threatener can stand not carrying out one threat, but his reputation may suffer severely if he fails to carry out two! The credibility of the threatener is of course an important part of the system, as on it depends the reaction of the threatened. If the threat is not believed, defiance is a much more likely reaction than submission.

(3) *Counterthreat or deterrence.* The threatened party may threaten in turn, "If you do something nasty to me, I will do something nasty to you." This possibility is the bilateral threat, or deterrence system. If both the threats are credible, the situation, apart from the threats themselves, may return to what it was before the first threat. The difficulty with a system of this kind, however, is that the credibility of threats tends to depreciate with time unless the threats are carried out. Such a system, therefore, has an element of time depreciation, which almost inevitably insures that, if particular threats are never carried out, their credibility will decline to a point where they no longer command a change in behavior. The system then relapses either into defiance or into carrying out the threat. A possible reaction to such a decline in credibility is an increase in the magnitude of the threat. This contingency introduces instability into the situation, however, because the threat easily becomes inappropriate and cannot be carried out without disrupting the system. If you say to a child, "I will kill you if you steal the cookies," and he then steals the cookies, what do you do? Another element of instability in deterrence systems is that deterrence is inherently an anxiety-producing situation which is likely to become increasingly uncomfortable for both parties as time goes on. The sheer increase in anxiety may create a predisposition to carry out the threat pre-emptively, simply to relieve the anxiety.

(4) *Integration.* The threatened party neither submits nor defies but tries to bring the threatener into a richer, more integrative relationship or attempts to create an organization that includes both the threatener and the threatened. The integrative relationship operates directly on the value systems of the parties concerned; its main object is the convergence of these value systems and the creation of a mutual empathy.

Establishing Credibility

A major weakness of the threat system as an organizer of human behavior arises out of the cost of establishing credibility. The threat is only valuable to the threatener if it is believed and therefore influences the behavior of the threatened in directions that the threatener likes. Credibility may be built up, of course, by breaking down the threat into small parts that do not cost much individually to carry out, but that build up an expectation of escalation. In these circumstances, carrying out a small threat may restore the credibility of a large one. On the other hand, carrying out a large threat is almost always costly to the threatener. Where this is so, the threat may engender defiance.

The effectiveness of a threat is therefore a complicated function of the potential cost of carrying out the threat, both to the threatener and to the threatened. The ratio of the potential cost to the threatened divided by the potential cost to the threatener might well be a rough measure of the effectiveness of the threat. The greater the cost to the threatened and the less the cost to the threatener, the more effective we may expect the threat to be. We must emphasize that the significance of threat lies in the image it evokes in the mind of the threatened. It does not therefore have to be a verbal threat; it can well be a symbolic act that creates fear in the mind of the threatened.

Combining Threat and Integrative Systems

The success of the threat system in organizing society and in changing human behavior depends to a large extent on the extent to which it is combined with an integrative system accepted as legitimate. The threat that is accepted as legitimate, like the threat of legal sanctions, is much more likely to evoke the response of submission than the response of counterthreat. Most of us submit, for instance, to the threats involved in the tax system; we do not issue counterthreats of blowing up the tax office. We submit because the threat here is allied with an integrative system involving patriotism, respect for law, and so on. If this integrative system disintegrates, the threat system will disintegrate along with it. On the other hand, the threat system may also be important in maintaining the integrative system. If the tax system, for instance, contains no threats, and if as a result a lot of people get away without paying taxes, the legitimacy of the whole system is threatened. Threats, furthermore, will not be perceived as legitimate if they seem to be inappropriate. Here there is a complex web of reinforcing relationships that deserves careful study.

Threat Systems and Armaments

An analysis of threat systems should throw light on the significance of weapons and armaments in the social system, for the principal purpose of a weapon is to augment a threat. A particularly important aspect of a weapons system is its impact on the geography of the threat. Ordinarily, the ability of the threatener to carry out a threat depends on his distance from the threatened. Distance usually diminishes threats. A major function of weapons is to increase the distance at which a given threat can be effective, as well as to augment the threat itself.

We can make an analytical distinction between a weapon's offensiveness, which is measured by the amount that it increases the threat of the threatener, and its defensiveness, which is the extent to which it diminishes the threat faced by the threatened. Offensive weapons diminish the cost of transport of threats, whereas defensive weapons increase this cost of transport. History reveals a constant tendency for weapons to become more offensive, in the sense that people can make greater threats over larger distances than they formerly could do. This trend has occurred in spite of the fact that defensive weapons increase the stability of the system as a whole, with some important exceptions where a change in defensive weapons—as in civil defense—may be a signal for pre-emptive war. A possible explanation for this phenomenon is that the immediate payoffs to the innovator are greater with offensive than with defensive weapons, in the interim before the innovation is imitated. Hence the system can run into arms races, "perverse dynamics" or "prisoners' dilemmas," to the detriment of all parties.

A party's viability to threat depends on its ability to withstand it without submission to the point of system damage. This in turn depends very much on the geography of the threat system. Generally speaking, an "improvement" of weapons diminishes the number of unconditionally viable organizations. When unconditional viability disappears, however, it may be replaced by conditional viability if the integrative system permits it. The impact on personal armaments of weapon improvement, beginning with the cross-bow and going on to the firearms, is an extremely interesting case of a system of this kind. As long as the principal armament was the sword, the individual had some chance of being unconditionally viable; hence a system of fairly stable war, or armed threats among individuals, was possible. With the improvement of weaponry, personal armament became so expensive that weapons tended to disappear from the personal threat system. The replacement of threat systems by exchange or integrative systems warrants careful historical study; we do not seem to have either theoretical models or empirical descriptions of this transformation.

INDUCING CHANGE IN ORGANIZATIONS

War and peace in the international sense is a function not of the relations of individuals as such but of organizations of individuals, especially those organizations known as national states. Systems of interaction among organizations may have many of the properties of systems of interaction among individuals, but they also possess many peculiar properties of their own. In particular, the fact that organizations are not homogeneous, that they are themselves composed of many individuals who may have personal relationships with individuals in other organizations increases the complexity of the problem.

An organization can be considered essentially a structure of roles. The fact, however, that a role must be occupied by a person means that a change of person in any particular role (and especially in the top roles of an organization) may perceptibly change the behavior of the organization. The replacement of Eisenhower by Kennedy or of Stalin by Khrushchev produces a perceptible change in the behavior of the organizations known as the United States and the Soviet Union, even though the role itself largely determines the behavior of the person in it, and though there is a great deal of continuity in organizations despite the change of occupants in the roles.

The perception problem in the case of organization likewise depends on the nature of the organizational structure. In reaction processes, it is not the "realities" that are significant, but the *perception* of reality on the part of those who are reacting. In the case of organizations these perceptions are channeled through an informational hierarchy and consequently may be more subject to corruption than they are in the case of an individual. That an organization permits a greater division of labor, however, operates on the other side and at least makes it conceivable that an organization could be so organized that its decision-makers enjoy perceptive powers superior to any that an individual could enjoy by himself.

The problem of the nature of integrative systems among organizations is of great interest and importance, but also of great difficulty. An organization is itself an integrative system among the individuals it comprises. For this very reason an organization finds it difficult to maintain integrative relationships with other organizations on any but rather low levels. Organizations exchange with one another and threaten one another, but they seldom love one another. This fact is particularly important to the international system, where it is difficult for nation-states to maintain an integrative organization that unites them externally without losing their individuality and internal morale. This problem is particularly difficult for the armed forces. Their task is intrinsically disagreeable, and if they are to maintain their internal integrative system, they must almost inevitably develop a myth of an enemy or one of unquestioning obedience. A saint of almost any kind would be an immediate threat to the integrative system of an armed force.

The role of ideology in the integrative structure within organizations and between them must not be neglected. If individuals were arranged in some kind of social space according to their susceptibility to various ideologies, then over this space the geographical structure of the power of ideologies would look very much like a threat system. This area of the social system is extremely difficult to reduce to any simple quantitative forms, yet we must not neglect it on that account, especially as it is peculiarly relevant to the present world situation. Our great need seems to be for ideological changes, even within the structure of existing ideological images, that reduce the intensity of the threat system and that increase tolerance of ideological differences. The movement of Marxist ideology toward the doctrine of peaceful co-existence is a case in point. Sometimes a change of this kind is too threatening to the formal pretensions of the ideology and has to be made tacitly.

Something like this seems to have happened with the ideology of the Roman Catholic Church. In principle, it is universal, but in practice, at least in predominantly non-Catholic societies, it is prepared to recognize tolerance.

One way in which the threat system can be modified to strengthen the integrative system, as Dr. Lieberman suggests in this volume, lies in rephrasing threats in terms of assurances. A threat in itself implies hostility and a denial of any integrative bond between the threatener and the threatened. The more it can be formalized, ritualized, and made to resemble an objective law—"If you do this, something unpleasant will happen to you, which I shall be powerless to prevent"—and the more threats can be placed in somewhat negative terms—"I will not do anything nasty to you if you do not do anything nasty to me"—the more the form of the threat system can be changed to build up integrative bonds rather than to tear them down.

The Role of Learning

The most important single key to understanding social dynamic processes is learning, that is, the process by which the information the individual acquires affects his image of the world around him. The behavior of individuals, and indeed the behavior of organizations, is a function of their image of the world and of their value systems. These images change under the impact of disappointment or of reinforcement of expectations. Images, like everything else, move toward the payoffs or toward higher utility. The payoffs themselves, however, are part of the image, and we know little about how they change. The process of development, whether economic development toward greater productivity or political development toward more refined methods of conflict resolution, must be conceived essentially as a learning process. Unfortunately, learning theory is almost purely individual; we have no good models of the learning process in the society as a whole. The problem is complicated enormously by the symbolic nature of the human image, an aspect which is extremely difficult to reduce to simple, scalar terms. Our image of relationships in the present and possibilities of the future is determined very largely by our image of the past. But our image of the past, especially when it is the result of formal education rather than of family tradition, is mediated through an elaborate set of national, religious, and social symbols.

The crisis of our times is primarily a crisis of the threat system. Its equilibrium has always been precarious and it is now itself threatened with destruction by new weapons. The problem of achieving stable peace, which has become a necessity, can be seen as essentially a problem in rapid learning on the part of large numbers of people, as well as on the part of their leaders and rulers. The difficulty is that we cannot learn from the actual payoff system, for mistakes can be fatal. The payoffs from which we have to

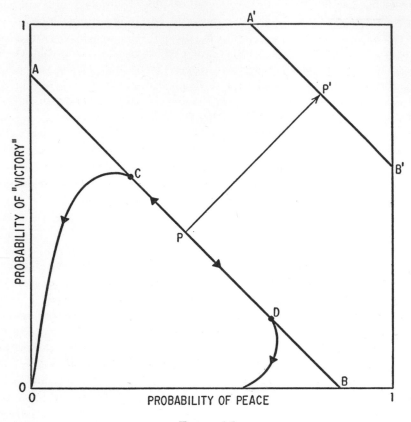

FIGURE 4-5

learn can exist only in the imagination; hence the problem may very well be one of quickening the imagination so that the evolutionary process may go on within the image, rather than outside it. In this process the development of a convincing body of theory is of the first importance. The body can learn only from experience; the mind can learn from the imagination. We learn by imagining theoretical models and projecting consequences from them. An experience that is fatal offers no opportunity for learning. We do not learn not to fall over cliffs by falling over them. We learn by having an image of the cliff and projecting the consequences of falling over it. When systems are stable, we can learn from precedent; when systems are unstable, learning from precedent produces crisis; unfortunately, crisis generally impairs the learning facility, although it creates an incentive for learning. If we are to learn properly from crisis, we must be prepared. Those who are prepared and who have learned in advance what the crisis can teach can then, in a crisis, act as teachers to those who are unprepared.

The Task of Peace Research

The dilemma of our time and the nature of its major intellectual task can be summarized in a diagram, Figure 4-5. Here we plot the probability of peace horizontally and the probability of "victory"—meaning the establishment of values dear to the party concerned—vertically. Unfortunately, this system seems to have a boundary, line AB. When we increase the probability of peace, we seem to diminish the probability of victory. When we increase the probability of victory, we decrease the probability of peace. All moves in this field, so long as we are on line AB, seem therefore to be conflict moves. Those who wish to move toward A are accused of warmongering, those who wish to move toward B are accused of surrender. The situation is further complicated by the fact that the boundary is certainly not linear. When we arrive, for instance, at point C, the boundary is likely to bend over toward the origin O. Beyond a certain point, as we diminish the probability of peace, we also diminish the probability of getting anything else we value. If the probability of peace were at zero, it is quite likely that the probability of getting other values would be at zero too. And it may be that, as we move in the other direction beyond a certain point, D, the boundary also bends back, and that pursuing peace without regard to other values may actually diminish the probability of peace itself.

The great intellectual task, however, and the major task of peace research, is to move line AB outward, say to A'B', so that benign moves, such as PP' which increase both the probability of peace and the probability of victory, are possible. If by "victory" we mean the preservation and extension of values dear to us, it may even be possible for both sides to be victorious. Perhaps this conclusion is unduly optimistic, but we do not have to have everything in order to have something. And in this area, a move in the right direction is always preferable to one in the wrong direction, even though it may not take us all the way to where we want to go.

PART II

Handling Conflicts

5

ROGER FISHER

Fractionating Conflict

The problem of avoiding war is usually seen as one of establishing an alternative means of settling the important questions over which countries fight. Cures are designed not to alter the character of the dispute but to provide a substitute for armed conflict. Governments are urged to adjudicate or arbitrate those issues over which they would otherwise go to war.

Looked at in this way, the possibility of international adjudication or arbitration seems remote. The issues for which the United States, for example, would go to war are large and important; they include national survival, freedom, democracy, and our way of life. It seems unlikely that the United States will ever be prepared to refer such an issue to the International Court of Justice or let it be decided by any group of neutrals. Wherever a country believed that so much was at stake in a controversy that nuclear war was preferable to losing, it would almost certainly believe that too much was at stake to be entrusted to a court. Little issues can be adjudicated, but big issues appear to be different.

DANGERS INHERENT IN OVER-ALL CONFRONTATION

If we look at the relations between two hostile countries, we find that each international incident tends to be perceived as part of a large total confrontation, nation-to-nation. Rather than being considered as a small isolated event, each issue is seen as, and thus tends to become, an integral part of an over-all contest between freedom and Communism, or between colonialism and independence, or between NATO and the Warsaw Pact powers. In particular, the relations between the United States and the Soviet Union are perceived and described as a Cold War—a major all-out contest which is like a war except that there is no shooting.

When all incidents are considered part of a big dispute, the relationship is precarious. All eggs are in one basket. Similar situations occur between individuals when relations become on an *ad hominem* basis. Not what is said but who said it becomes important. The merits of particular issues are lost in one big over-all controversy. Statements, proposals, offers, and concessions are judged not by their content but by their source. Little controversies are pictured, understood, and dealt with as—and hence become—integral parts of a big controversy.

If we look at the relations between countries where there is the least possibility of war, we find that issues are more often dealt with separately. As problems come up they are formulated as small matters, each to be considered and negotiated in terms of what is most immediately relevant.

The danger inherent in big disputes and the difficulty of settling them suggests that, rather than spend our time looking for peaceful ways of resolving big issues, we might better explore the possibility of turning big issues—even issues like Hitler and Communism—into little ones. Each side plays a part in determining the scope of a controversy. It is well recognized that moves made in the bargaining and negotiating process often increase the stakes, raising the controversy from a small one to a big one. It is also well recognized that on occasion part of a dispute can be settled, leaving the balance unresolved. But a change in the size of a conflict is usually the unintended by-product of action taken for some other reason. This paper focuses attention on the sizing of disputes. It considers the conscious formulation of issues in conflict, and the advantages and disadvantages of breaking up big issues into little ones. Viewed from this perspective, adjudication appears not as a process for settling big conflicts, but rather as one that is valuable because it tends to fragment conflict situations by cutting off and serving up for decision one small issue at a time.

To suggest that what is now seen as a major conflict should often be dealt with as a number of small ones is not to assert that the smaller issues have a greater objective reality than the large one. A detached observer from Mars might conclude that a useful way to understand current Soviet-United States relations is to consider "Communism" and "democracy" locked in political combat; each move is part of a single large conflict. It could also be true that many moves on the part of the Soviet Union are taken by Communist leadership as part of a master plan for a Communist world. Fractionating such a conflict will not make existing differences disappear. It will affect not the diagnosis but the prescription for dealing with issues on a day-to-day basis.

Issues between people and between governments do not have objective edges established by external events. These problems of life lie in a seamless web of interrelated facts and circumstances. People and governments can choose which congeries of events shall be considered as a unit for the purpose of working out relations with others. Related events may be joined together for some purposes and treated separately for other purposes. Ideological, national, racial, and religious differences may be "fundamental," but may nonetheless be treated either as relevant or as irrelevant to economic questions that come up daily for decision.

A few examples show that the United States does have a choice in defining issues. In August, 1961, a civil aviation agreement between the United States and the Soviet Union was negotiated. The United States might have signed the agreement, treating it as a separate matter. We chose, however, to decline to sign it, and considered the matter related to Berlin. Sometimes, as has been the case with cultural exchange agreements, we agree to treat a particular problem between us and the Soviet Union as a matter that can be settled independently of other outstanding issues.

Another way in which an issue can be fractionated was illustrated after Brazil expropriated an American-owned telephone company in 1962. There were suggestions in Congress that if Latin America treated the United States in this way, we should give no further aid to the Alliance for Progress. The president, however, at a press conference defined the dispute as one between the governor of a province and a single American company over the form and amount of compensation due. A potentially big issue was turned into a small one. The way in which a government defines a dispute obviously does make a difference.

In short, this paper is not concerned with debating whether major conflicts of interest exist between countries; it is concerned with dealing with them. It does not suggest that any one country has complete control over the formulation of international conflict issues, but that it has a measure of control. It does not suggest that it is always wise to fractionate conflict into little issues, but that it is often wise to do so. Actions affecting the size of an issue should be undertaken consciously, with the advantages and disadvantages in mind. The formulation of issues in dispute between our country and another should not be undertaken accidentally or emotionally. Defining an issue in big terms—for example, defining issues in South Vietnam or Berlin in terms of freedom versus Communism—may satisfy the human desire for clear, simple black-and-white choices. But it may be as ineffective as arguing military policy in terms of whether one is for peace or for war.

Within the last few years, it has been recognized that bigger military weapons do not necessarily mean better ones. Study of the complex questions involved in determining the military restraint which a country should exercise has developed the field of arms control. It is obvious that with international disputes, as with weapons, the bigger does not necessarily mean the better. Yet little study has been devoted to the criteria and methods by which a country should formulate and expand or contract issues in controversy.

Arms are used only over issues. Perhaps more important than the field of arms control is the field of "issue control."

CRITERIA OF SUCCESS

The way in which a country wishes to carry on a dispute must be judged in light of the nation's objectives. The foreign policy objectives of the United States can be roughly divided into two categories. The first covers our substantive social goals: we want to preserve the freedom, equality, and prosperity that we have and to extend such values to other people throughout the world. We are concerned with both defending and advancing the American position when it is in conflict with the social objectives of other governments. These goals are implicit in such phrases as "defending America from Communism" and "winning the Cold War."

The second major category of foreign policy objectives lies in the field of international procedure, the process by which conflicts between nations are resolved. Here again, our objectives are both defensive and offensive. We want to protect America from the dangers involved in the present method of adjusting international differences and to develop better methods of dealing with situations in which one country's goals collide with those of another. The second category of foreign policy objectives is implicit in such phrases as "avoiding war," "ending the arms race," and "developing a world rule of law."

In short, the United States' basic objectives are: first, to win each dispute with another country and, second, to avoid war and develop a fair way of settling such disputes—objectives which are somewhat inconsistent. While the United States would like to win *each* dispute, it is not seeking a world in which any one country wins *every* dispute. Internationally, as well as domestically, our government is simultaneously interested in winning each case and in promoting the rule of law—a regime in which the government does not always win. It is interested in winning disputes and in settling them peacefully. No absolute priority can be established between these two objectives; both need be kept in mind in each dispute. It is against these objectives that the process of formulating and fractionating conflict issues must be judged.

There are, perhaps, an infinite number of ways in which international issues might be sliced. For a first approximation, it may be useful to consider five dimensions which measure the size of a conflict issue:

(1) The parties on each side of the issue;
(2) The immediate physical issue involved;
(3) The immediate issue of principle;
(4) The substantive precedent which settlement will establish;
(5) The procedural precedent which settlement will establish.

With respect to each of these, there is a certain amount of choice as to how big or small the issue is made. Although these variables are not wholly independent, they will serve as a basis for exploring different ways in which conflict issues may be increased or decreased in size.

PARTIES ON EACH SIDE OF THE ISSUE

Objectively, there is no single correct definition of the parties on each side of a dispute. Each party is often free to define one or both sides in the way that best suits its interests. For example, if a Polish fishing vessel has damaged a trans-Atlantic cable, the party on the "left-hand" side of the dispute might be taken as the helmsman of the ship, the captain of the ship, the department of the Polish government concerned with regulating fishing, the Polish government, the Soviet government, Khrushchev, or "the Communists." The party on the "right-hand" side might be considered to be the private company owning the cable, the United States, or the West.

In traditional international law, the nation is considered as the proper unit to represent the interests of a citizen who is injured. In some circumstances, the nation is held responsible for wrongs committed by its citizens. Thus history as well as nationalism support the present tendency to attribute to the Soviet Union and the United States positions taken by individuals or groups within each nation. If an editorial writer in *Pravda* criticizes the New York Stock Exchange, it is likely to be reported in American newspapers under the headline SOVIET UNION ATTACKS WEST. Similarly, if a retired United States Air Force general makes provocative remarks, Soviet spokesmen are likely to treat them as official statements of the United States government.

Disputes between people ruled by different governments need not be treated as intergovernmental disputes. Disputes between groups in different states within the United States are rarely treated as interstate disputes. Among nations, even actions by government officials are often deliberately treated as though the government itself were not involved. When the first secretary of the United States embassy in Moscow is accused of spying, the charge is directed against him as an individual. He is declared *persona non grata*, and when he leaves the country the dispute is usually treated as closed.

There are advantages in downgrading a dispute and in treating it as one between individuals, or at least as one in which the other government is not involved. As long as disputes are considered in this way, there is little chance of war. Part of the strong emotional outburst by the Soviet Union over the U2 incident in 1960 was apparently due to President Eisenhower's insistence that the flights were official governmental action, not unauthorized conduct on the part of the Central Intelligence Agency.

Treating disputes as cases between individuals or groups rather than nations has the further virtue of establishing crosscutting conflicts. In such conflicts, the opponents in one controversy are not identical with the opponents in another. If a number of different disputes divide the same two nations or the same two groups of nations along a common boundary, the conflict situation becomes aggravated. But if the lines of one conflict cross those of other conflicts, divisions become less sharp, people begin to recognize some common interests. On the international scene today, Yugoslavia and Poland have helped this country understand that our disputes with the Soviet Union and our disputes with Communism are not always the same thing. By identifying more accurately our opponent in certain Far East situations as "China" rather than as "Communism," we may find that we have reduced the size of our opponent and also that on occasion we have an ally in the Soviet Union. We may be able to identify our opponent still more narrowly on some occasions as a particular guerrilla leader and further increase our chances of establishing crosscutting conflicts.

On our own side, we can insist that some matters are nongovernmental. The New York World's Fair Committee asked the White House whether the Peking government should be invited to exhibit at the 1964 fair. A White House decision that the Peking government should *not* be invited turned a possible nongovernmental matter into a governmental one. The issue would have been downgraded if either the committee or the White House had decided that it was a matter for decision by the committee.

There are often, however, conveniences in treating a single government as the responsible opponent in what would otherwise be a mass of unrelated problems. A simple over-all solution may be possible only by considering matters on a government-to-government basis. Using one dispute as leverage on another, as discussed below, often requires a preliminary step—that of treating as governmental two disputes which otherwise would be considered to involve different groups or individuals.

Defining the parties to a dispute is thus a basic way of making disputes bigger or smaller.

IMMEDIATE PHYSICAL ISSUE INVOLVED

Any particular conflict can be thought of as having a certain minimum size in factual or physical terms. This is measured by the inconsistency between the physical events desired by the two adversaries. If two men want to sit at the same time on a particular chair that will only hold one, a conflict is defined which can hardly be further reduced.

If the Soviet Union wants to keep a certain number of soldiers in Cuba and if we want them to have a smaller number, these facts set a certain minimal physical size to the conflict issue. It is possible to take action which makes the issue larger, and it is possible to take steps which will reduce the issue back to its physical dimensions, but often there is a minimum size below which it cannot be reduced. The apparent minimum size of a conflict can often be broken up by spreading it over a time scale. For example, assume that one country wants to increase the number of authorized border-crossing places by twenty, and the neighboring country is opposed. The issue might be broken down to consider whether one new crossing place should be opened this month, leaving open the question of the rest.

There are two ways of expanding the physical size of an issue: first, by defining more broadly the subject matter in dispute; second, by bringing in different subjects which are related only because the parties are the same.

By rational extension, almost anything can be related to anything else. The question for each party is whether it would prefer to deal with issues separately or together. Should it seek agreement on a portion of a problem and be willing to postpone consideration of other aspects, or should it insist that nothing will be agreed upon until all of a defined subject matter is settled? For example, countries can agree on co-operative development of weather satellites as a separate issue or insist that the subject is intimately connected with military satellites and that a single agreement must cover both aspects of the problem. The question of releasing prisoners from the April 1961 landing on Cuba could be treated as a special issue (in fact, each prisoner could be considered separately), or it could be treated as part of a single over-all political dispute between the United States and Cuba.

It seems clear that if a subject is too narrowly defined, there will be little possibility of a bargain. The narrower the point, the more likely it is that a change will benefit one party only. It would seem desirable to expand the subject until it is large enough for a bargain which benefits each, if not to the same extent, at least to some degree. As a general rule, enlargement of the issue beyond that point is unwise. If either party tries to get a still greater benefit, it runs the risk of cutting off its nose to spite its face. It is impossible to settle all matters simultaneously. The argument for settling disputes in small units so long as a bargain is possible is comparable to the argument for free trade versus state trading. It is possible that by state trading a nation, using its full economic leverage to make large bargains, will do better on a particular occasion. As a general rule, however, it will probably do better under a system in which individual trades are made wherever a bargain can be reached.

The Technique of Coupling Issues

The immediate issue under discussion between two sides may be expanded by coupling one dispute with another. Here the connection is made not by broadening the definition of the subject matter but by recognizing that two matters involve the same parties. The considerations involved in coupling one dispute with another deserve more study. If the joining of problems is made as an offer, the process seems constructive, facilitating agreement: "I will let you have what you want in the X dispute if you will let me have what I want in the Y dispute." Without such bargaining, it may be difficult to settle either dispute. If the proposed solution of the X dispute will benefit the other side by, say, sixty "utility units" but cost us twenty, we will suffer a net loss and hence have no incentive to accept the solution unless some other matter is thrown in—a matter in which we benefit by twenty units or more. Coupling disputes in this way may increase the chances of agreement.

Even here, however, shifting the nature of the dispute—from a narrow subject matter to one in which the only common denominator is the parties involved—tends to bring up all possible issues in the relationship and may do more harm than good. It encourages the unfortunate "over-all confrontation" described earlier. The joining of issues as leverage or bargaining currency, even when constructively looking toward a negotiated agreement, tends to shift the focus away from the merits of a problem and to put relative bargaining power in issue.

One way to improve the relationship between two adversaries may be to treat different subjects as separate issues. At roughly every other stage in the escalating process, each party has that option and should be aware of it.

In international negotiation, it may be difficult to couple apparently unrelated disputes. A large part of international negotiation is conducted in public view; governments are under some compulsion to justify their conduct. As national positions are increasingly expressed in terms of principle, it becomes increasingly unacceptable to engage in unprincipled bargaining. Coupling the Cuban problem with the Berlin dispute might make it objectively easier to draft an agreement benefiting both the Soviet Union and the United States. But both countries operate under political inhibitions that tend to make such a trade unacceptable, particularly when the interests of third states are involved.

Pressure in a Dispute

It seems important to distinguish talking about an additional issue by way of a counteroffer, as discussed above, from taking action on an otherwise unrelated matter by way of pressure. When pressure produces counterpressure, the escalating process is much like that by which limited hostilities grow into all-out war. As is the case with limited war, the more unrelated the action of one country is to the action taken by the other, the more difficult it is to find a boundary to the conflict.

In such a process, it is also difficult to keep a limited objective in view. Although no shot may be fired, the situation becomes warlike, particularly in that the aims become unclear. The pressure is no longer being applied for a specific and limited purpose. Relations between the United States and China have broadened out in this way. The United States is applying pressure on a country that is now widely regarded as its enemy. But we are not sure what we want that pressure to accomplish or what China would have to do in order to yield to it. In effect, our pressure is for unconditional surrender, an objective so broad that it becomes impossible to attain by negotiation or otherwise.

When pressure, though substantively unrelated, is applied for a narrow, specific objective, the dispute in one sense remains quite small. This was the case in Laos when the United States suspended economic aid and brought substantial pressure on the government. The pressure was directed at causing the government to accept the specific terms of a particular agreement on the neutralization of Laos.

An unrelated matter may also be brought in by way of reprisal or punishment: "I am doing this to you since you did that to me." Such action may provide grist for future disputes but does not seem to be part of the process of formulating an international issue. Punishment, which functions as a lesson for the future, should apparently be distinguished from actions which broaden a dispute. The latter are taken or threatened in order to induce a change in an adversary's immediate position.

THE IMMEDIATE ISSUE OF PRINCIPLE

The size of a dispute is determined not only by the parties and physical issues involved but by the issue of principle which each side considers to be at stake. To some extent the immediate issue of principle can be considered apart from the problem of the precedent which a settlement may establish. The position which a country takes in a particular controversy is usually not an *ad hoc* position applicable only to those circumstances; it generally reflects broad political and moral principles of wide applicability. A major difficulty in settling a dispute lies in the fact that it is often seen in terms of principle, and on matters of principle countries are usually unwilling to yield.

To be strong and effective, a country apparently needs principles and needs to adhere to them. Principles can be flexible, however, and the extent to which they are involved in a particular controversy can be limited in two ways. The first is by recognizing that we can be loyal to our principles without insisting that our opponents be disloyal to theirs. To arouse the maximum support of our own people, we often identify a dispute as a conflict of principle, in which one principle or the other must yield. We do this also as a form of commital strategy in which we strengthen our negotiating position by tying our own hands and making it harder to back down. If we wish to win a controversy, it would seem wiser to say that the solution we seek is not only consistent with our principles but is also consistent with those of our adversary—at least if properly construed and applied. By insisting that our adversary can come along without abandoning his principles, we make it easier for him to do so. In this way a country can remove an issue of principle from a controversy without in any sense abandoning its principles. If another country is prepared to accept a physical solution which we regard as consistent with our principles, no principle of ours requires that it first accept some generalized statement of what it is doing.

In many instances, an issue is defined differently for several different audiences. Each government may tell its own people that a particular issue is an important step in furthering its national goals and is an application of strongly-held national principles. At the same time, it may be explaining to its adversary that the particular matter can be settled pragmatically without regard to differences of principle. While explaining to the American people that the Antarctic Treaty was furthering the principle of complete inspection for any disarmament agreement, the United States government could point out to the Soviet Union that it could accept this practical solution without abandoning any matter of principle.

The Application of Principle

The second way of limiting the extent to which principle is involved in a controversy is to recognize the difference between principle and the application of principle. In almost every dispute, there are conflicting principles involved. In a lawsuit, each side urges that a different principle should be the controlling one. A resolution of the dispute does not necessarily mean that either principle need be abandoned; it often means that, at this point, a particular accommodation between them has to be worked out, leaving both principles intact. The United States government rarely argues a case in the Supreme Court except to further some principle in which it believes. To lose a case, as the government often does, is rarely to abandon its principles or to be disloyal to them. Litigation may simply determine that, in this case, the principle does not properly apply. The same determination can be reached through negotiation; to do so is not to be disloyal to principle.

Recognizing where possible that a dispute involves a question of the *application* of principle rather than the central principle itself should make it possible to decrease the stakes. Nonetheless, in every controversy, a certain minimum amount of principle is involved; it cannot be further reduced. This is probably best identified in terms of the precedent which will necessarily be established by resolution of the controversy. The size of a controversy may be measured in terms of both the substantive and procedural precedents which its resolution will set.

SUBSTANTIVE PRECEDENT WHICH SETTLEMENT WOULD ESTABLISH

In almost every conflict each side is thinking not only of how much it would lose immediately if it yielded a point, but of how much it would lose by way of precedent. Similarly, a country may press a position, not for the immediate consequences, but with the hope of establishing a precedent for the future.

A nation's concern in international affairs over the problem of precedent is substantial. Even those who contend that the precedents embodied in international law are wholly ineffective are often the first to contradict themselves by saying that the United States must not yield on a point because it would set a dangerous precedent which would be difficult or impossible to overcome. Those who contend that the Soviet Union respects no rules are often those who also insist that the United States must press certain propositions as precedents for the future. A precedent is a piece of a rule. There can be no doubt that it has some effect. The impact of a precedent depends upon its *strength* and its *scope*. To the extent that these can be controlled, the size of the matter in conflict can be changed.

A precedent no doubt has some strength. Even without an implied promise to be consistent, governments, like people, find it much easier to do what they have done before. A precedent is a fact which cannot be undone by accompanying the action with a statement that it is not a precedent. The fact demonstrates to oneself as well as to others what actions one is prepared to take under particular circumstances. Also, basic fairness tends to require that different people be treated in the same way under the same circumstances. A highly bureaucratic government like that of the Soviet Union is particularly bound by precedent on small matters—those which top authority is too busy to decide and which lower bureaucrats have no authority to decide.

The scope of a precedent is always somewhat ambiguous. In political affairs as in the legal system, ambiguity permits a nice accommodation between consistency and flexibility as new circumstances arise. The minimum scope of a precedent is determined by that which cannot reasonably be distinguished from it. Additional scope may be established by what is said before and during the resolution of an issue. The language used by one or both sides may turn a simple case into a test case. Significant possibilities exist for limiting the size of a conflict by limiting the precedent. Apparently either party to a controversy can, by itself, limit the substantive scope of the precedent that will be established. It takes two to make an agreement, but either one can create a dispute. If the parties agree that a controversy is a test case which will decide a broad category of issues, the scope of the precedent is thereby enlarged. But if the parties disagree as to the scope of the precedent, it is thereby reduced. For if the yielding party truly considers a particular settlement unique, it will ignore it when other questions come up. It will not have been effectively bound by the precedent, whatever the other party contends.

For several days in the fall of 1962, Russian guards for the war memorial were allowed to enter West Berlin in armored cars instead of buses. Later the United States told the Russian guards to revert to transportation by bus, which they did. The United States was not effectively tied up by the armored car precedent because it distinguished the circumstances. The armored cars were allowed during a period of rioting. Once the rioting had stopped, the cases were different.

PROCEDURAL PRECEDENT WHICH SETTLEMENT
WOULD ESTABLISH

Since international substantive issues can usually be distinguished from each other, greater concern is generally expressed over the broad procedural aspects of a precedent. The United States is constantly being warned against establishing the precedent of giving up something for nothing or of yielding to threats of force. We are told that particular issues are not so important in themselves but because a line must be drawn somewhere. We hear that appeasement does not work; that once concessions are made, further concessions are almost inevitable.

A close relationship exists between the substantive issue involved and the procedural precedent established by reaching an agreement. To the extent that a settlement is substantively sound, it can be justified "on its merits"; the fact that concessions were made will have limited effect. If both parties have made some concessions, the effects are likely to be in balance. If one party has made all the concessions, the Munich situation obtains. The effects of such a concession need to be examined in terms of their influence on each party and on third states. The lessons learned from Munich deserve more study than they have received.

The first lesson—that a country may not succeed in pacifying another by yielding to its purportedly last demands—has been thoroughly absorbed. In fact, appeasement has become such a bad word that there is little attempt to identify situations in which it might be politically effective. The fact that a particular concession may not accomplish its purpose has, however, little to do with the precedent established.

The second lesson of Munich is that the party to whom the concession has been given may think that a procedural precedent has been established and may seek further concessions in the same way. Having discovered that the British would not fight over one issue, Hitler apparently assumed that they would not fight over a comparable issue. Third states may have reached the same conclusion.

The third lesson of Munich, however, is that Hitler was wrong. Governments, like individuals, are tolerant to a degree. They will co-operate with others on a give-and-take basis, but unless concessions are reciprocal, it is less likely, rather than more, that additional concessions will be made. Each concession a country makes diminishes the number of its citizens who perceive the other country's demands as legitimate. Finally it becomes clear that further concessions will accomplish nothing. Instead of weakening British will, the yielding at Munich tended to stiffen the subsequent British determination to resist. Of course, if a country gives up territory or arms of substantive importance, it may become weaker through concessions. The Munich example, however, suggests that the effect of a procedural precedent on a country that yields has been widely exaggerated. It suggests that the famous "slippery slope" goes uphill, not down.

FRACTIONATION AND THE PEACEFUL SETTLEMENT OF DISPUTES

When considering only the "procedural" objective of the United States—to avoid war and to improve the method of settling international differences—it appears that the practice of fractionating conflict issues is definitely to our interest. Separating issues into their smallest components and dealing with them one at a time reduces the risk of war significantly. No country is likely to fight over what it perceives as a small issue. It is only when a country fears that it might lose a great deal, or hopes to gain a great deal, that it will go to war.

When issues are considered separately and in terms of their smallest size, the process of settling disputes should be peaceable. But some disputes may not be settled. Unlike judicial settlement, negotiation requires scope for bargaining. Ideally, one country should yield on a dispute about which its adversary cares more than it does, confident that on some subsequent occasion the process would be reversed. But realistically, the chance of settling an issue when one party's gain means another party's loss seems to be increased either by enlarging the substantive issue until it includes enough ground so that a settlement will benefit each or by coupling it with another issue in which the position of the parties is reversed.

Fractionating conflict should avoid the stalemate that comes from a nation-to-nation confrontation in which neither country feels that it can make any concession without losing part of an over-all war. To the extent that issues are decided separately there is an increased chance that they are decided on their merits, that is, in light of their particular facts and circumstances. In this sense, agreements reached might be objectively better. Piecemeal settlement also recognizes that everything cannot be done at once and permits progress in certain areas while other matters are being worked out.

Thus, one technique of lessening the risk of war and improving the process of international settlement is to separate and reduce the size of issues. Apparently this technique ought to be pursued unless significantly better results can be obtained by the contrary technique of enlarging and coupling issues. Fractionating conflict can help in coping with disputes peaceably, but how does it stand up in terms of our companion objective—winning disputes?

FRACTIONATION AND THE WINNING OF DISPUTES

No general statement, of course, can be made that either fractionating a conflict issue or enlarging it will always be better for a country from the point of view of winning the matter in dispute. Sometimes a country will gain a point by coupling one issue with another, or by enlarging it in terms of a broader subject matter or in terms of principle. On other occasions, it will do better to treat the issue in its narrowest possible context. Some tentative guides as to when one strategy or the other will help to obtain a substantive payoff can perhaps be formulated.

Coupling one issue with another may be useful as a form of pressure. If one country has sufficient power for effective arm-twisting, the desired substantive result may be accomplished. Such substantive gain must be weighed against the procedural loss which deciding disputes on the basis of superior power involves. There are other limitations on the pressure technique. Usually, a country must possess superior power and be willing and able to use it to make the method effective. When dealing with an opponent who has the opportunity to escalate a conflict issue by throwing in counterleverage and counterthreats, the tactic can backfire. It is not at all clear that the consequence of raising the ante will result in winning the original dispute.

Even when one country of superior power is applying pressure in large quantities, the effectiveness of that pressure is likely to depend upon keeping the issue on which it is focused small. The effectiveness of pressure is a function of the difference between how much the pressure currently hurts and how much it would hurt to yield on the issue involved. Economic sanctions against Cuba or Mississippi or South Africa, for example, would be more effective if it were made clear that they would stop upon the attainment of an identified, limited objective, than if pressure were directed against "Communism" or against "discrimination." The effectiveness of pressure is increased by keeping the objective narrow and making it easy for the adversary to back down.

The coupling technique may also be a useful way of winning one dispute at the expense of another. If an issue that is likely to be lost anyway is on the table, a country may be able to retrieve something by coupling that dispute with one on which the adversary might yield. If an issue that a country strongly desires to win is on the table, perhaps it can be bought by coupling it with a "loser."

Similarly, expanding the subject matter under dispute may make it possible to work out an agreement in which we win something. Negotiating the allocation of a single radio frequency between several countries would be difficult. There would be more likelihood of success if the subject were broadened to include enough frequencies so that each country would get at least one. Finally, if it is already clear that one side is going to win in a particular conflict situation, the larger the terms in which the issue can be defined, the more that side will win.

These instances indicate that fractionating a conflict situation—insisting that the issues be dealt with separately and in their narrowest possible scope —may not always be the wisest strategy. However, they do not cover the most frequent occasions on which countries tend to insist that big issues are involved.

ESCALATION AS A DEFENSIVE TECHNIQUE

Perhaps the most important proposition developed in this preliminary consideration of the field of issue control is that a country which defines an issue in large terms has adopted a negative strategy. An issue is often defined broadly as a deliberate defensive maneuver. Rather than treat the transit of men and materials from West Germany to West Berlin as a group of narrow, pragmatic questions, the United States has defined the problem in terms of freedom versus Communism. The West has insisted that any interference with its access to Berlin would be serious enough to justify a war—including, perhaps, a nuclear war.

This tactic of issue escalation was deliberately adopted as a form of committal strategy. It makes the West less willing to yield. By turning an issue into a test case, by insisting that what is involved is not a small and unique event but a major principle, a country makes backing down more difficult. In addition, citizens, allies, and friends can more easily be rallied to fight for a big, clear-cut principle than for a particular case. In seeking to preserve the status quo, a country insists that any change would be catastrophic. The technique is common in domestic as well as international politics. In an effort to stop a threatened change, groups will argue that the proposed measure is the first step toward socialism or totalitarianism, or that it threatens the entire American way of life. Internationally, the United States has sometimes taken the position that recognition of a government is not simply a question of deciding what authority is in fact in charge, but involves the larger question of approval of the regime. Those opposed to the admission of Red China to the United Nations insist that the issue is a large one of principle, not a small one of credentials.

Insisting that a small change from the status quo would bring disastrous consequences is a defensive move, a kind of rear-guard action, slowing down the pace of change. It retards the loss of a substantive point, but is unlikely to be wholly successful in preserving the status quo. The United States can insist that any interference with our right of access to Berlin will be viewed as grounds for war. This may slow down the slice-by-slice "salami tactics" of the Soviet Union, but it can hardly stop them. To insist that a small change would be a justification for war does not by itself make it so. An additional five- or ten-minutes delay on a convoy of trucks to Berlin, or the addition of one more inspector to the routine, does not mean the end of freedom or democracy, whatever we may say. If the slices are thin enough and are taken slowly enough, the prophesied doom does not in fact materialize. The country which defines small issues and presses forward on them is likely to make headway which its adversary, by insisting that large principles are at stake, may delay but is unable to stop.

ESCALATION AS AN OFFENSIVE STRATEGY

If increasing the size of an issue has little long-run promise as a defensive strategy, it has even less promise as an offensive technique. If a party desires to alter the status quo, defining an issue as one involving a large subject matter or big principles tends to make success less likely. Almost inevitably, change from the status quo must be brought about incrementally. Even those who have the power to bring about major changes and would like to do so must face the question of where to begin. A group which defines its action program as "for peace" is likely to be as ineffective as if it were for virtue and against sin. If one is to be effective in domestic politics, he must combine the public support which broad issues and principles can arouse with the pursuit of narrowly defined goals.

It would seem equally important for a government which wishes to alter the behavior of another government to define its immediate goal in narrow and specific terms, to break up the big issues into smaller ones, and to press for these separately. At this writing, the United States is carrying on a dispute with Cuba over major issues. The Cuban government is pursuing policies which we would like to change; the United States has been applying increasing pressure on Cuba to that end. While broadening the pressure, we have, consciously or unconsciously, broadened our demands at the same time. We have stated our goals in such terms as "a free and democratic Cuba"— a goal which, like "peace" and "ending the arms race" is admirable, but too broad as a focus for effective action. We are interested in particular issues— for example, the removal of Soviet weapons from this hemisphere, no armed subversion in other countries, respect for international law, free elections. By asking for more than we need and more than we really want, and by lumping all our demands into one big issue, we make our case an extremely hard one to win. Furthermore we rally and unify the opposition. In seeking "to topple the Castro regime," we are defining the issue in the largest possible terms, as we did in seeking unconditional surrender during World War II. The British experience in seeking "to topple Nasser" is instructive. By defining an issue in all-or-nothing terms, we tend to make sure that we get nothing unless we are prepared to exert the force required to get all. Having declared that the choice is between Communism and freedom, little victories look like compromises with Communism. In this context it is difficult for us to apply the "salami tactics" of moving forward slice by slice.

Escalating a matter into a large issue of principle appears to be somewhat effective as a defensive strategy; at least it can gain time. It would seem generally unwise as a strategy to pursue in areas in which we would like to change the status quo.

Fractionating issues, on the other hand, seems almost invariably the best tactic for a country seeking to bring about change. And in a world in which change is inevitable, the best defense is probably a good offense. The situation anywhere could always be better. The best way to preserve and advance our values would seem to be to press constantly for *small* improvements in all areas. Ironically, those who take a "tough" position in international affairs are usually against breaking up the issues; they unwittingly inhibit action which could bring about changes they desire. Routine insistence upon the big issue would seem a prescription for an unsuccessful defense of the status quo.

THE SOUTHERN EXAMPLE

Within an organized society the legal system facilitates the fractionating process; domestic experience may nonetheless be useful in illustrating its virtues. In the South today, a fundamental and major conflict exists between differing views that are strongly held. Leaders of the Negro community and proponents of the conservative Southern point of view see the conflict in terms of broad principles—and they are correct. Each side also has a problem of strategy. Without in any way abandoning their over-all objective or their principle of full and equal rights, Negro leaders, by and large, have proceeded by fractionating the conflict issues and moving step by step. Small issues have been raised: including Negroes on a particular jury list, allowing Negroes to register to vote in a particular county, admitting Negro students to a particular school, and serving Negroes at bus terminals and restaurants.

On most occasions, the White Citizens Councils and others opposed to integration have adopted the strategy of escalating the issue into broad political terms. They insist that what is involved in this case is a choice between the Southern way of life and mongrelization of the races. This strategy may have caused some delay, but it has not served the White Citizens Councils well. The freedom riders and others have experienced substantial success by pursuing the salami tactics of one slice at a time. At almost no point has the loss of a particular slice been painful enough to cause a united uprising of the opposition.

If one were advising the conservative Southerner on the strategy he ought to take, one might well suggest that he fractionate the issues and proceed with his own salami tactics. For example, starting with the established base that a purely social club may exclude from membership whomever it pleases, one might proceeed through a series of incremental cases; the country club that owns land; the country club where members live on the club property; the "residential" club where only members may use the swimming pool and take lessons at the private school; the two or three blocks which form a residential club, and so on. How successful such a series of cases might be in limiting the consequences of the racial covenant and school integration decisions is an open question. But the strategy appears to have far greater promise of success than the "big issue" strategy currently being pursued.

CONCLUSION

Internationally, it is more difficult to force a decision on the little issues. The lack of compulsory jurisdiction for the International Court of Justice means that we have no institutionalized method of bringing up and disposing of one case at a time. The virtues of adopting and pressing for a small specific objective, however, go far beyond the legal machinery. In international politics as in domestic politics, the strategy of separating out small and immediate issues and dealing with them one at a time would seem likely to advance our social and substantive goals.

Instead of identifying every issue as a part of a Cold War to be dealt with as a single major conflict, it would seem wiser to insist that each issue, whether or not it reflects basic and fundamental differences, be dealt with independently on its merits. By separating out the Antarctic problem, and dealing with it outside the context of the Cold War, the United States accomplished in the Antarctic Treaty a significant victory for its own objectives. By urging the United Nations to deal with the Middle East and Congo problems in terms of what the particular circumstances required we advanced our objectives of strengthening the United Nations and world order more than we would have had we cast these problems as part of an East-West conflict.

If the United States continues to press, in the United Nations and elsewhere, on many small and separate issues—issues in which our position makes more practical sense than the position of our opponents—we have a fair chance of prevailing. If the issues are small, no one defeat will be serious enough to cause any country to pick up its chips and go home. By dealing with issues in their narrow and immediate factual context, there is a greater chance that the position of other countries will be determined by the merits of the problem rather than by broad ideological points of view. To the extent that our position has merit, and to the extent that countries normally opposed to us are persuaded to pay less attention to ideological differences, we may find that the opposition has been lessened and divided. In Berlin, Cuba, the United Nations, Latin America, and elsewhere, we would seem well advised, in applying whatever political, economic, or military pressure we deem appropriate to the situation, to define immediate objectives which are limited and precise. The salami can be sliced either way.

Fractionating conflict would thus seem to be a promising strategy not only for reducing the risk of war but also for promoting victory for our values. This does not mean that such a strategy is opposed to the real interests of any other country. As we need to be reminded so often, the world is not a zero-sum game where victory for some automatically means defeat for others. If we examine all the detailed social objectives of any two countries, including the United States and the Soviet Union, we find an enormous area of overlap. Each believes that the people should have better schools, better health, better highways, better homes, a chance to benefit from the experience of others, and so forth. However basic and significant other disagreements may be, in perhaps 90 per cent of the detailed factual issues our interests are not in conflict. In this area, measures can be taken which benefit us both. As long, however, as most issues are dealt with in terms of a nation-to-nation conflict, common interests will be lost in the major conflict which precludes agreement. It would seem that only by dividing up the issues and considering them separately in small units will we be able to find and to work together in those areas where we have common goals and common interests and thus obtain the optimum accommodation possible.

6

E. JAMES LIEBERMAN

Threat and Assurance in the Conduct of Conflict

The most powerful military weapons cannot eliminate conflict from international life. The existence of ultimate weapons confronts policy-makers with a tremendous new dilemma, for which deterrence strategy is at present the only solution. Our task is to develop the capacity to engage in vital international conflict, responsibly aware of possible holocaust, yet free from overwhelming fear.

Change is a constant challenge to individuals and groups, and in our culture generally a welcome one. The very word "challenge" suggests a desirable stimulus. "Threat," on the other hand, suggests an undesirable one. Yet the two stimuli may be quite similar. A fearless yet responsible approach to conflict would maximize challenges and minimize threats, with a view toward enhancing the adaptability of the parties involved. Individual and institutional stability and progress depend on the ability to change and be changed, to challenge and be challenged.

All nations are faced with the problem of coexistence in a world community which has and will have highly antagonistic members. Failure to develop stable forms of vigorous, integrative conflict can only lead to nuclear disaster. "Integrative conflict" implies a nonmilitary strengthening of the nations involved and the parallel development of a strong international community.

DETERRENCE

An assumption underlying present nuclear policy states: We can best *prevent* certain behavior in an adversary by means of our ability to inflict injury upon him.

This is deterrence; and, even if it works admirably, it leaves open the question of *persuading* the adversary to act in ways that would be favorable to us. Deterrence is intended to prevent bad behavior, not to evoke good. But a theory of conflict must also be concerned with evoking good behavior and face the problem of reconciling deterrence with positive persuasion. Ideally the strategist evokes good behavior and prevents bad behavior simultaneously; he cannot do so, however, if self-contradictory acts are involved in the pursuit of these two aims.

Physical force plays two roles in deterrence: it punishes transgression and it exercises restraint, or control. Obviously, punishment is designed to prevent a future recurrence of undesirable behavior. External control is applicable in only a limited way; we cannot keep all potentially dangerous people in strait jackets or behind bars.

While the army that successfully defends a boundary line is primarily an instrument of control and only secondarily punitive in its use of force, large nuclear weapons are useless for control, since they punish by total destruction. The very presence of these weapons on both sides precludes military defense as it was once known; we cannot expect true protective defense ever again to match offensive capability. The threat of retaliatory destruction—deterrence—is substituted for the missing defenses. If fear of punishment adequately deters, then the threat of nuclear retaliation should suffice; it is capital punishment for nations. However, nations cannot afford a single major failure, namely a nuclear strike. Prevention is all-important, and the punishment is all but meaningless if it has to be used.

As a result of the technological revolution in weaponry (hardware), the use of maximum physical force has tremendous punishment value, but little control value. Although the actual use of such force is hypothetical, the threat of its use is part of everyday policy. Strategists acknowledge that if it becomes necessary to carry out the threat of nuclear retaliation then deterrence will have failed. *The defense strategist's problem is to establish a deterrence policy which is as effective an instrument of control as the weapons are an instrument of destruction.* In past eras, and even in conventional wars of the present, using the military deterrent was feasible; the risks were not absolute and implementation of the threat served both to protect nations and to enhance the credibility of similar threats in the future. With megaton weapons, however, the exercise of power implements nothing; *only the threat has policy value.* Actual blows only signal the failure of deterrence with an onslaught of revenge, an act which provides no more than momentary emotional satisfaction.

Absolute power to destroy probably does not provide an absolute deterrent. Lester Van Atta recognized this in pointing out a weakness of early approaches to arms control: "Even the deterrent effect of hardware was measured entirely by its military capability."[1] Conversely, effective deterrence may well be achieved by positive incentives rather than by threats alone. A consideration of this broad range of possibilities, certainly warranted by present knowledge in the behavioral sciences, may usefully enlarge the repertoire of national policy responses in conflict situations.

AN EXAMINATION OF THREATS

A threat is a communication intended to coerce or deter another person or group. It is, in effect, a negative promise, bearing the same relationship to punishment as promise does to reward. Indeed promise and threat share many characteristics, for example, credibility.

When examining a threat, we should consider whom it involves, how it is communicated, and what is its message. Further useful characteristics to observe are specificity, credibility, legitimacy, and appropriateness. A key concept in deterrence—credibility—depends not only on physical power, but also on the reputation and circumstances of the threatener. The secretary who shouts at her boss, "I'll shoot you if you start dictating letters at five o'clock," may deter by the strength of her anger, but probably not by the content of the threat; a threat to quit might be more credible since it is more appropriate. A person in street clothes would not be effective in directing traffic or ordering soldiers; perceived legitimacy is part of credibility. Past performance is another factor but an equivocal one: no one has dropped H-bombs on cities before, but this fact may either add to or detract from a threat to do so. Russia's failure to carry out one threat to sign a separate peace treaty with East Germany might reduce credibility of a subsequent threat or might enhance it, since, because of the failure, self-respect or political reputation might be more significantly at stake the next time. A further complication arises when we consider the evaluation of threat credibility by all parties concerned. Is A convinced that B perceives A's threat as credible? Can we be confident that Khrushchev believes that Johnson will engage in nuclear war over West Berlin? De Gaulle, a third party, assesses the credibility of this American threat from still a different viewpoint.

Threats differ greatly according to the nature of the demand. "Change your status quo!" is extremely aggressive, in contrast with the usual deterrent "Don't attack—or else." Defensive rather than aggressive threats are the rule in nuclear deterrence, because the latter are far more likely to escalate into a nuclear showdown. The rare aggressive threat—a threat requiring affirmative action—produces great alarm: witness the Cuban crisis of October 1962. Even then, Kennedy justified the blockade in terms of defense, and he was careful to facilitate Khrushchev's compliance.

In the following sections, we will examine some of the human aspects of threats in a deterrence system, observing the threatener, the threatened, and the conflict process between them. Though we are mainly concerned with threats of nuclear attack, threats to embarrass, to frustrate, and so on, occur as often in international relations as they do in everyday life. Furthermore, while our discussion is largely a critique of threats, we must consider the constructive functions which threats, like promises, have in human relationships.

We issue threats only if we care about an issue, and thus we convey important information about our state of mind and heart: values, expectations, imagination, and feelings. It is far more constructive politically—and more healthy, psychologically—to give warning via threat than to maintain silence and to strike suddenly out of the blue when one's threshold of tolerance is finally crossed. In addition, threats may have utility as a form of ritualized fighting, like the nonlethal combat among many social animals which decides issues and keeps the animals in fighting trim while avoiding wear and tear on the species.[2] Man has several important systems of ritualized fighting. The legal system, economic competition, the United Nations—all involve threats, though they are crucially modified. However, as indicated by Boulding in this volume, and corroborated by the analysis to follow, a pure threat system is unstable and dangerous.

Effects of Threats on the Threatener

Freedom of choice of subsequent action is limited by commitments embodied in threats. Designed to control or influence the recipient, threats also constrain the threatener to the extent that he obligates himself to respond in certain ways to given eventualities. If reputation for credibility is at stake, then the threatener must carry out the threat when its demands have not been met. There are occasions when the threatener may escape the constraint of credibility without losing integrity, for example, by forgiving rather than by punishing the offender. George Washington's father withheld punishment in the fabled cherry tree incident because the boy told the truth. Rewarding a virtue outweighed punishing a sin. But in military deterrence, such human transcendence of the threat runs counter to the heavy emphasis on credibility. *The threatener is not really free to respond to the merits of the situation; he is much more constrained to punish sin than to reward virtue.*

A subtler, if more dangerous, aspect of a threatener's lack of freedom is that *his credibility increases as his array of alternatives decreases.* By backing himself into a corner—"I have no choice"—the threatener maximizes credibility at the cost of flexibility.

Deterrent threats must be made in a defensive context. The threatener is liable to precipitate a power showdown with an aggressive threat: "Do as I say, or else!" A power showdown occurs when the threatened cannot comply, and the threatener cannot transcend his self-imposed constraint. Nuclear technology makes a power showdown completely untenable. The consequent need to avoid threat interactions which may cause such a showdown accounts for the predominance of defensive threats, often general and vague. The crises over Berlin and Cuba are striking exceptions, characterized by aggressive threats and widespread alarm over the possibility of escalation into all-out war.

A versatile foreign policy requires flexibility, aggressiveness, and initiative. It could well be that, paradoxically, the power of modern weapons inhibits the creative, experimental exercise of policy-making skills—in other words, that the limitations of military deterrence interfere with optimal political decision-making. The threatener's commitment to deterrence is likely to detract seriously from constructive approaches. There are limits upon what finite economic, political, and scientific resources can be made to do. A garrison state is hardly compatible with a vigorous democracy. Dissenting opinion about defense within a nation may be perceived as weakness by military leaders, with oppressive conformity the result. Recent military strategy in the United States is an example of the ways in which military requirements can increasingly dominate the political and socio-economic life of a nation.

Deterring unlikely events gives the threatener a false image of reality. When a threatener has used defensive threats, his opponent may have had no intention of performing the forbidden acts. An offensive threat, demanding action, is particularly vulnerable to misinterpretation if the opponent would have taken the action in any event. Seeing apparent success, the threatener places confidence in an untested, perhaps imaginary, deterrent. Just as talismen become invested with fancied magical powers, so may our nuclear weapons have acquired much of their presumed power to deter. The danger here is that fantasies of power, blossoming in the absence of reality testing, may lead to increasingly provocative behavior and subsequent escalation. *An explicit deterrent posture may have only circumstantial relationship to the prevention of undesired behavior; the assumption of a causal relationship may thus lead to unrealistic behavior on the part of the threatener.*

One who uses threats cannot be immune to them; he tacitly reveals his own susceptibility to intimidation. Sensitivity to this may in turn lead him to deny that he can be intimidated by force, even though he expects his opponent to be. The denial is self-contradictory, thinly veiled by such statements as, "The only language *they* understand is force." Meanwhile he must demonstrate—or pretend—that he does not respond to force, that he would die for his ideals, as in the line, "Better dead than Red." The opponent may feel—or pretend to feel—the same way, and escalation may follow. Since it is rational for both sides to fear annihilation and to hide the fear, there is no ready exit from the vicious circle of denial, belligerence, and escalation.

Threats allow little room for doubt. Extreme emphasis on single-minded determination does not allow the threatener flexibility in handling his own uncertainty and mixed feelings. Global decision-makers are not exempt from doubt and ambivalence, undesirable as these may be for split-second decision-making. Requirements for credibility may demand more or less than human responses from the threatener. He may want to build a "doomsday machine" to blow up the world automatically in case of nuclear attack, or he may let the weight of responsibility for decisions fall upon other humans or upon computers. Although computers feel neither responsibility nor ambivalence, the programed abandon with which they work is hardly suitable as a model for sane human beings!

Recent developments of game theory and strategic simulation exercises produce such conclusions as, "It always pays to threaten cities; it never pays to hit," and, "The longer the decision time for retaliatory strike, the less likely it is that it will be made." Tenable as these logical paradoxes may be to practicing strategists, the propositions reveal a profound emotional dissociation between strategic decisions and their human consequences. Rather than accept and deal with ambivalence and doubt, the "perfect" threatener, it would appear, must try to live with inhuman intellectualizations.

Another problem involving ambivalence—uncertainty, ambiguity, inconsistency—occurs with respect to conciliatory behavior by the opponent. The threatener needs to deny friendly feelings toward the opponent lest he weaken his position by revealing lack of will. This attitude reflects the extreme all-black or all-white stereotypes in international relations. The belief that the opponent is capable of acting amicably only in order to plot diabolically against the unwary leads the threatener to increase his threat even after the opponent becomes genuinely conciliatory. Thus the threatener's perception of conciliatory behavior in the opponent is impaired, as well as his perception of his own coercive power. An ambivalent threatener wavers between the feeling that he can coerce conciliation (and wants to) and that he cannot (and does not want to). The threat system, by virtue of its premium on single-mindedness, does not readily allow for ambivalence which, in the context of a threat system, may cause the threatener to deny and distort vital reality factors.

Ambivalence, moreover, may lead the threatener to exaggerate the severity of the threat in order to compensate for his own indecisiveness or lack of will. As long as a real test does not occur he can continue to overcompensate unchecked, reiterating a threat which may be objectively quite inappropriate. A variation on this theme is the tendency to exaggerate a threat regarding a unique, unprecedented event. Since there is no prior experience on which to base credibility, the threatener may attempt to strengthen his hand by exaggerating the severity or likelihood of his threat. Nuclear retaliation is in this category of uniqueness. (See Rapoport's discussion of the probability of unique events in his "Critique of Strategic Thinking" in this volume.)

In questions of national policy, it is usually an oversimplification to refer to "the threatener" as a single person; it is done here for grammatical convenience. In a group of decision-makers enjoying some freedom of expression, ambivalent feelings may come to light readily and be handled with due regard, or they may be summarily squelched. That the latter approach is strongly favored in some quarters was revealed in the controversy over Adlai Stevenson in the aftermath of the October 1962 Cuban crisis. What was the reason for such an uproar over (alleged) differences of opinion in secret, high-level policy discussions? As a psychiatrist, I cannot resist the speculation that Stevenson became the scapegoat for those who were scared during the crisis but managed to resist the hidden urge to make tension-relieving concessions toward Russia.

Another problem of the threatener which may well be related to ambivalence is the inconsistency, or self-contradiction, of means and ends in deterrence strategy. We hear repeatedly that both the United States and Russia love peace, and are ready to go down fighting for it. Thus we are brought to the brink of war. Both nations are using means contradictory in combined effect to the end sought; benign ends are made to justify increasingly malignant means. Non-Western observers gravely point to the peace-disturbing behavior of the self-appointed defenders of peace. Each side tries to make the world safe for itself by making it conditionally dangerous for the other. The result is a world unsafe for everybody. The rationalization for this dilemma is deterrence, which, however, is not assured by ultimate destructive weaponry. A macabre circle of reasoning justifies overkill for the sake of deterrence, which remains—in contrast to all the hardware—an unknown and immeasurable abstraction. In effect, the main reason we possess all our dreaded weapons is so that such weapons will not be used. How men live with billion-dollar conundrums such as this is a study in itself; to do so would appear to require both wishful thinking and denial of painful reality. We must concern ourselves with integrity as well as credibility if we would make our nation worth defending with our lives.

Effects on the Threatened

The well-intended deterrent threat may provoke rather than deter or coerce. Most of us will accept the highway patrol as an appropriate deterrent—if not for ourselves, then for our neighbors. A few hell-bent souls might take the deterrent as a dare, but not in sufficient numbers to make us scrap the system. Quite a different deterrent relationship exists between the United States and Russia. We are told (as the Russians are by us) that we are held by the bomb as a nation of hostages, in order to deter our aggressive expansionistic ambitions. Not only do we feel uncomfortable standing on a target, but we resent the accusation, deny it, and throw it back, along with a duplicate deterrent threat. The last thing either side will admit is that it is deterred from anything evil by the opponent's might. Both sides will be quick to assert, however, that their heavy involvement in arms building is in response to the opponent's arsenal, which is, from this point of view, a provocation rather than a deterrent.

Of course, we do not ordinarily take such denials and assertions at face value. And the foregoing model ignores the eternal questions of who started it, and which side is right. These questions, historically so crucial, would be irrelevant after a major nuclear exchange.

Nations do not like to be pushed around. We see this in the fantastic value nationals place on independence and self-determination. When we act to deter someone with arms, we place a strong constraint upon him, at least in our imagination. While we may be "deterring" something that he had no intention of doing anyway, the other party may be provoked to demonstrate blusteringly that his autonomy has in no way been limited. After all, a weak-looking premier is hardly more comfortable or secure than a "soft" president. The threatened party may feel, "If I can't go where I don't want to go, then my freedom is reduced." Autonomy, independence, and freedom are sensitive matters; one may go to great lengths—even defiance—in order to assert them. This, of course, may lead to a final power showdown. No matter how defensive a deterrent threat seems to its author, its impact on the adversary may be provocative. Flying extra planes through the challenged Berlin corridor illustrates this mechanism.

Deterrence may backfire, though in a subtler way, through inducing resistance in the opponent to desirable change. Rather than appear to comply with the adversary's wish, the threatened party avoids a beneficial change. Opponents of a test ban agreement pointed worriedly at Khrushchev's kind words about Kennedy's proposal. "If *they* think it's good, it must be bad for us." The issue is not seen on its own merits or in a context of mutual benefit, but only as a move in a zero-sum game: A's gain is B's loss. Similarly, this mechanism gives external support to regressive internal policies. Russia justifies much of its paranoid secrecy, as we justify extra-legal CIA activities, by blaming a provocateur: A's defense is B's excuse.

Threatening messages may impair the receiver's ability to perceive and/or to respond rationally and appropriately. Grinspoon, in this volume, elaborates on this phenomenon, which is often ignored in game-theoretical approaches to deterrence. Fear and hatred, which threatened persons and groups are likely to experience, may reduce internal dissension and facilitate solidarity against the threatener—an untoward result from his point of view. Severe stress probably reduces the variety of responses while intensifying the irrational component. Fear of domination by the developing counterforce of an opponent might precipitate a surprise attack. A nation might resort to a similar policy of desperation or vengeance if it could no longer compete in the arms race, for example, with a massive shelter program.

Military deterrence, by definition, slights the role of internal psychological and political factors in the good behavior of an opponent. Internal factors should produce controls as effective as the specter of a long-range missile. But strategists continue to rely on missile threats as though they were analogous to a pre-atomic national guard. They are not. Actually, deterrence by threat ultimately depends on internal controls. The missile threat is not a physical restraint, like a pair of handcuffs, but a harsh tocsin: "Control *yourself*, or else." It is, ironically, a symbolic admission that true external military control no longer exists. In fact, the missile threat *undermines* those stabilizing internal processes which, in the view of neutral observers, are the major inhibitors of aggression. *The conciliatory faction within a country is weakened by the external threat, and the militant-hostile faction is strengthened.* "It is reasonable to suppose that moral and political restraints on all-out surprise attack are least effective when one party feels seriously threatened."[3]

The deterrent casts the opponent into the role of an incorrigible, who understands only the language of force—an epithet common enough on both sides of the Cold War. The degree of mistrust expressed in the nuclear deterrent stance may itself help confirm the expectation. The Powers U2 episode, though highly embarrassing to the United States, produced the unprecedented "justification" that we take such risks for necessary espionage, in which practice we are no different from others. Once we had accepted the delinquent role, caustic Russian criticism was easier to take—and flout. The real danger is that when we lose our ethical integrity we also lose the self-restraint involved in preserving that integrity. "Might as well hang for a sheep as a lamb" seems to apply to the subsequent sale of U2 planes to Taiwan, to support of the invasion of Cuba, and to the condoning of torture in Southeast Asia. Russia, meanwhile, went back on its own statements of a year previous by resuming nuclear testing. The argument here is not against strong criticism where justified, but rather against a stereotyped, automatic assumption that the opponent can only understand ruthlessness and violence.

Having looked at several aspects of threats separately, we are faced with the much more difficult problem of assessing them as a whole. Both Cold War camps rely on nuclear deterrence, believe in it, and, of course, at the same time deny intimidation by the other's weaponry. But both are increasingly open regarding the need to avoid nuclear war and to curtail the spread of nuclear weapons. As the 1963 test ban treaty showed, the deterrence race is being modified. (To some extent modification had taken place earlier: when the United States substituted the invulnerable Polaris submarines for "soft," first-strike-only missile bases in Italy and Turkey, it removed a significant first-strike threat.)

Nuclear deterrence may have prevented a Russian takeover of Berlin, and an American takeover of Cuba. While nuclear deterrence fits popular notions of behavior and is a natural derivative of pre-atomic military strategy, its psychological and political aspects are as radically different from the old defense process as are the weapons on which it is based. Technology has far outdistanced political and psycho-social skills in many areas, of which deterrence is a most important example.

We are unable to evaluate the effectiveness of deterrence by threat or even estimate its credibility to friend and foe.[4] Perhaps this is why the strategy persists. We are so heavily committed to the theory—historically, economically, and politically—that we avoid questioning its assumptions. The result is that each side in the Cold War sees its own behavior as self-controlled, the other's as deterred, while reality is bypassed somewhere in the middle. A corollary of this lack of reality-testing is that each side is under pressure not to examine its own real weaknesses. Deterrence is not the best way to foster internal freedom and enlightenment in either party. It enables each side to blame its own faults on the need for national security; thus hostile giants provide mutual reinforcement for crass internal politicking. In the deterrence system, minimizing one's choice—making it automatic or predetermined—maximizes one's credibility. This factor leads to the notion of the doomsday machine, in which human ingenuity is used in the service of perfect destruction.

Stable deterrence should make attack unthinkable, not simply unprofitable. Nations do not act on economic and military considerations alone, important though they are. Threats will certainly have their place in deterrence but not without accompanying factors. Deterrence at present is a mixture of effectiveness, illusion, and provocation which has yet to be stabilized. And, if we are to survive the nuclear age, active conflict strategies must exist which permit delving into political issues without touching off a holocaust.

THE ROLE OF ASSURANCE

A positive factor must be inherent in successful deterrence and in the constructive conduct of conflict as a whole. The word "assurance" best describes this phenomenon, which can be observed in nonviolent strategy. A sit-in, Salt March, strike, or boycott is announced, along with specific demands, and then is carried out if the demands are not met. The element of threat is relatively mild, and the strategy is notable for the implicit or explicit assurance that violence and destruction will be avoided. Persuasion rather than intimidation is the intention of this approach. "Assurance" has two connotations in Webster's Dictionary: safety and certainty. One is safe in believing that the proposed action will be nonviolent, and one can be certain that it will take place—unless persuasion takes place first. In Gandhian nonviolence, there is the global assurance that mutual benefit, not unilateral victory, is the goal.

The tactics noted above—sit-in, strike, and so on—deliberately combine threat and assurance. Sometimes the purest nonviolence may be a vigorous attack on the status quo and those institutions which maintain it. But while challenging their ideas and behavior the attack is designed to preserve and dignify people, not to destroy them.

Challenge is the tactic of aggressive nonviolence, as threat is the tactic of defensive deterrence. Challenge, by our definition, means a combination of threat and assurance, intended to activate constructive conflict. The opponent is placed under stress, but not intimidated, by the challenger, whose aim is to facilitate change. Deterrence is relegated to an incidental role. If adversaries are engaged in constructive combat which is challenging but not too threatening, then this very engagement has a value of its own for the participants. The hostility of the challenged is modified and his fear allayed by the investment of his challenger in a relatively benign form of conflict. The legal system is an example of a widely acceptable means of waging conflict which, as Fisher points out in this volume, has such high continuing value for contestants that they will abide by unfavorable decisions rather than scrap the system. Economic competition, with scruples or regulation, is another system of constructive conflict which can carry the weight of its own decisions, because the participants will adhere to the rules voluntarily for their own long-term self-interest.

It should be clear now that challenge and assurance are not limited to the sphere of deliberate nonviolence but apply to other systems of conflict—in fact, to some of the oldest and most deeply established ones. These systems rest solidly on the fact that self-interest in human society requires adherence to common interest. The deterrence system rests, in contrast, on the assumption that self-interests are mutually exclusive. In its extreme form, it holds that they are mutually contradictory: What is good for A must therefore be bad for B.

Forthright legal, economic, and political conflict is not lacking in aggressiveness or hostility but provides for their expression in constructive channels. We can view legal, political, and economic conflict, along with sports, as forms of ritualized fighting which, unlike war, contribute to the survival of the species as a whole. Forensic and economic conflict are highly evolved, vital forms of ritualized fighting for human beings. They are nonviolent social institutions through which men pursue conflict in what Albert Szent-Gyorgyi (echoing Gandhi) has called the scientific manner. Our adversary becomes our helper in the search for truth, as long as the verdict goes with skill and strength of argument rather than with strength of arms. Add to this form of conflict the dimension of personal appeal, empathy, and popular participation, and we have a useful model of nonviolent *political* conflict—the most powerful weapon in the civilized struggle for human rights and social progress.

THE USES OF ASSURANCE

No rational party will initiate political conflict unless he respects the strength of his own position. But human beings are more than rational. The Montgomery, Alabama bus boycott was touched off unwittingly, but effectively. Political conflict of this kind can be launched unilaterally. The power showdown of challenging ideas is creative. The challenge should produce a dialogue, and if well done will motivate adherence to the discipline of argument. Departure from that discipline should cost the deviating party more than can be gained by the lapse. A critical element of deterrence emerges from the affirmative structure of the contest, with its credible assurances. The mechanism of this deterrence is that departure from the discipline of creative politics signals defeat in that particular conflict area, and a general lack of integrity.

Obviously, a kind of political diagnostic skill is needed to prevent the opponent from becoming dangerously frustrated or, on the other hand, overconfident. Keeping the adversary engaged in constructive competition is more important than winning points, if peace and progress are indeed the goals of the challenger. The responsibility for failure, including the eruption of violence, rests with both parties in the relationship, though not necessarily equally. The more skilled one party is in persuasive strategy, the more possibilities there are for lasting and fruitful interactions with others. This focus on activity and engagement runs counter to the old adage of deterrence, "Wait for them to learn how to behave." The passive wait is likely to be infinite; it prophesies an incorrigible enemy—an assumption which, as Deutsch points out in this volume, is deadening.

In order to challenge rather than to attack, one must make clear that he wishes to test the opponent's constructive potential for mutual benefit, not to undermine him. If the opponent is vulnerable, he should be moved by the stratagem to strengthen his capability in the challenged area or be persuaded that the challenger's way is better. This mechanism holds for the conduct of conflict itself. The evolution of more and more effective nonviolent institutions will only occur through persuasion and example. This does not mean that we cease to be normal, emotional human beings. "Nonviolent" does not mean "passive," and the practice of nonviolence requires the ability to threaten (but not to terrorize or intimidate), to be firm, even harsh, and to be spontaneous as well as careful and deliberate.

Actually, the strategy of assurance is more difficult when the opponent is weak, embittered, divided within, or paranoid. Then any challenge is likely to be perceived as an attack. But the effort to find a nonviolent solution should not cease. It did at Goa, which was a minor operation to all but the Portuguese. Unless, however, a more constructive way of freeing Angola can be found, Portugal may go down with a terrible death grip on that country. The desired effect of assurance from outside, instead of threat, is to strengthen the political moderates within the adversary country. As the moderates in one nation are strengthened, they will respond reciprocally to their counterparts in others. The mechanism is the reverse of the arms race.[5]

To sum up the characteristics of the challenge, let us recall the patterns of pure threat. First, unlike threat, challenge produces a greater balance between initiating change, responding to it, and resisting it; it is not predominantly defensive. Second, challenge would close the breach between assertions and action which characterizes threats; usable force should be actively employed and useless force discarded. Third, challenge attempts to make the adversary more changeable, as well as attempting to engender change. Fourth, it puts the emphasis on maximizing gain without inflicting losses on the adversary; it attempts to make the gain of each the gain of all. Finally, it places great value on the method itself, adherence to which will be well worth occasional setbacks in particular conflicts.

The ultimate test of whether any given application of power is constructive or not is in the result. Our knowledge of human behavior should help policymakers anticipate the consequences of decisions. But we must always be prepared to learn and amend if our approach is to merit the term "scientific." An element of judicious uncertainty will itself be a dynamic affirmation of policy-making integrity in a rapidly changing world.

NOTES

1. L. C. Van Atta, "Arms Control: Human Control," *American Psychologist*, XVIII (1963), p. 37.
2. I. Eibl-Eibesfeldt, "Aggressive Behavior and Ritual Fighting in Animals," in Jules Masserman, ed., *Violence and War: Science and Psychoanalysis*, VI (New York: Grune & Stratton, 1963).
3. Richard C. Snyder, *Deterrence, Weapon Systems, and Decision-Making: Studies in Deterrence*, III (China Lake, Cal.: U.S. Naval Ordinance Test Station, 1961).
4. Bernard Brodie, *Strategy in the Missile Age* (Princeton: Princeton University Press, 1959), pp. 272, 393; Bruce M. Russet, "The Calculus of Deterrence," *Journal of Conflict Resolution*, VII (1963), p. 98.
5. Charles Osgood, *Graduated Reciprocation in Tension-Reduction* (Urbana, Ill.: University of Illinois Press, 1961).

7

ARTHUR I. WASKOW

Nonlethal Equivalents of War

The premise of those scholars who have made "conflict research" a growing field of interest, and the premise of those national leaders who have made "general and complete disarmament" a goal of national strategies, is that war is now too lethal to be used without enormous danger. The scholars and the rulers agree that some techniques must therefore be invented for eliminating the possibility of international violence.

Because this premise includes no agreement on the values and interests that might or should prosper in a world without international violence, it may seem to be a minimal premise. It may be heuristically useful, however, to treat it as a maximum goal: to ask what changes would be necessary to eliminate the possibility of international violence, nothing more and nothing else.

If we see a resort to violence in order to settle a conflict as the result of a decision by one or both of the parties—a decision taken at some particular point in time—then the most direct way of preventing a resort to violence would be structuring the conflict system so that there is no one salient point in time at which either party seems to gain by resorting to violence. The reduction of the advantage to be obtained from violence is traditionally achieved among sovereign nations by a threat to inflict unacceptable amounts of violence in return. But this system has proved incapable of eliminating violence among nations in conflict. It is not, therefore, a sufficient means to achieve even the proposed minimum goal.[1]

TECHNIQUES OF SETTLING CONFLICT

Parties in conflict other than nations, and on occasion nations too, have used other means than the reciprocal threat of violent retaliation to eliminate violence. These other means have focused on two general syndromes in which violence is unlikely: Parties in conflict tend to eschew violence at times during their conflict when (1) values or interests held in common greatly outweigh the values or interests in conflict, and (2) an institution other than the parties is (a) made legitimate by these shared values or upheld by shared interests and (b) prepared to use its power to prevent the conflicts from being settled by violence. Most techniques of avoiding violence have therefore tried either to reduce the weight of conflicting values and interests as against common values and interests, or to provide external counterviolent institutions or both.

Changing the relative weight of conflict and community can be accomplished in several ways. The construction of national unity from warring sectionalism has usually been accomplished by weaving ties of joint concern out of economic exchanges, fear of an outside power, and feelings of shared history and a connected future. Somewhat similarly, Gandhian nonviolence has emphasized the common values of a shared humanness, overriding the limited spheres of conflict between the parties. The community side of the balance can also be strengthened for any two parties in conflict if both of them are also allies against other parties on some issues. If the parties and the issues cut across each other, any existing conflicts are less likely to lead to violence because it will never be clear to any one party against which other party violence should be used. Again, if the parties treat conflicts as particular small issues rather than as single great ones, they are less likely to resort to violence, since any existing area of community will weigh more in the scale against particular small issues than against single great ones.

These "noninstitutional" techniques for dealing with conflict can be combined with the creation of new institutions, external to or superior to the parties in conflict, that discourage or prevent them from using violence. Either by monopolizing the means of violence for itself (in the fashion of the state as classically defined) or by deploying sanctions of an economic, spiritual, or other nonlethal sort (in the fashion of the Papacy establishing the Peace and the Truce of God, for example), such an outside institution can reduce the chances that a party in conflict will use violence.

Applying These Techniques

What now confronts scholars and rulers is the question whether these traditional techniques for preventing violence among parties in conflict other than nations can be used in the present world situation to make violence impossible among nations.

The international system with which we will probably have to deal for a considerable time is one in which two coalitions of great states stand opposed to each other's interests and ideals, convinced that the hungry nations can improve their lot only by attacking—or by co-operating with—Western interests and by abandoning—or preserving—the liberal forms of government in which Westerners believe. Each of these coalitions will extend its help to the emerging states in ways designed to advance its own image of the world; each will find willing support in some of these states; and each will attempt with all its energy to block the path of the other. It is hard to see an end to the process within the next generation.

But unprecedented weapons exist *now:* The thermonuclear bomb and the intercontinental missile are the ultimate step in scientific-industrial "productivity," since they give a few men the power to kill many millions in an extremely short time. Although some strategists argue that it is possible to imagine a thermonuclear war that would not destroy a continental power like the United States or the Soviet Union, no one doubts that more than one power now has, or within the next decade will have, the weapons to destroy even a continental state and society.

Grave doubts arise concerning the possibility of the Cold War's withering away before thermonuclear weapons are used in war. We must therefore measure the traditional techniques for preventing violence to see whether they will work, not in some rather distant world, but in the near future, with the Cold War still in existence.

Is it possible within the context of the Cold War to use the traditional means of preventing violence? Can we increase those values and interests held in shared community so as to contain conflict well enough to prevent the parties in conflict from resorting to violence? Can we break up the single great conflict, the Cold War, into manageable smaller ones?[2] Can we create an institution capable of enforcing abstention from violence?

If one assumes the Cold War context, it is hard to see how traditional techniques for preventing violence can be put into effect. The difficulties are obvious if one tries to imagine the operation of the traditional kind of institution capable not only of monopolizing violence and preventing others from using it, but also of deciding political disputes—in short, a world government. One can imagine world disarmament in which controls are vested in a world government, and all nations agree that their disputes will be resolved peaceably under agreed principles of law or by agreed legal-political institutions. World courts, a world parliament, a world executive to control the peace police—all would be essential components of the disarmament arrangements.

But the consensus necessary *in the first place* to agree on legal codes or political assemblies seems not to exist. The provisions of present international law, for example, were developed mostly by Western experience and owe little to Communist notions of law or to the developing codes and interests of the underdeveloped nations. What legal institution could be agreed on beforehand, for example, to deal with a dispute over uncompensated expropriation of private property? In one state and in present international law, the possession of such property may be regarded as a legitimate right that can only be withdrawn upon payment of just compensation. In another state, amassing large corporate properties may be looked on as a species of theft, and expropriation may be regarded as a return of the property to its rightful owners. What court could adjudicate, or commission arbitrate, a dispute on such a point?

Again, what legal code could decide between nations that believe established national borders are just and proper and nations that believe they need to redress injustice by helping to free a colony or by recovering stolen territory? And what government, even if it wanted to join others in giving up military power, would agree to disarmament if it had no hope that such questions as expropriation and border disputes would be settled in its favor?

Nor is world government the only goal that seems impossible to achieve in a Cold War context. How could we make violence less likely by breaking up national confrontations into particular issues, so long as the function of the national governments on both sides of the Cold War is to mobilize the whole national power and energy behind any particular quarrel so as to defeat the other side? Can governments on either side abandon this function so long as governments on the other side persevere in it? What deeper values and more inclusive interests could join societies and governments so bitterly divided on the futures to which they look ahead? What crosscutting alliances can bring particular opponents in the Cold War together in fear of a common foe, so long as the underdeveloped and uncommitted nations are seen not as possible enemies but as prizes to be won or lost?

Isolating the Armaments Issue

There seems to me to be only one answer to these questions that would both fit into the Cold War context and make international violence impossible. That answer would be to treat the armaments, and only the armaments, of the Cold War as a special question; to split off the question of disarmament from all political, ideological, and economic conflicts; to unite both sides on the one question of eliminating the means of fighting wars; to build an alliance between the great powers on the single question of preventing other nations from acquiring nuclear arms; and to build an extranational institution focused on the elimination of arms, and only on that.

But this answer is clearly not the traditional one. The traditional means of eliminating violence has been to do much more than that—to build feelings and institutions of community on a much broader base than the fear of violence in order to end violence. I am here suggesting an attempt to build, on the narrowest conceivable institution and the least possible shared community of interests, the beginnings of an international system for conflict without violence.

While William James, in "The Moral Equivalent of War," proposed harnessing the moral and emotional energy that had previously gone into national wars behind a universal war against Nature, I am assuming the continuance of internation conflicts. What I propose to investigate is the means of redirecting national energies from the conduct of wars with military weapons into what may be called "nonlethal equivalents of war"—efforts at advancing national interests and values without the use of arms.

In order to investigate this possibility, we need to know how narrow the base of community can be and still support the elimination of violence; whether the arms race is merely an instrument for carrying on and managing Cold War conflicts and can be separated from those conflicts; whether, if it is such an instrument, the arms race can be replaced by other instruments; whether it is necessary to improve old nonmilitary instruments for carrying on the Cold War and to develop new ones; and whether we can create an institution strong enough to eliminate arms and international violence without being so strong that it intervenes in the various world struggles over interests and values.

HISTORICAL EXAMPLES

In the effort to work out possible solutions to these problems, it may be useful to review some historical examples of attempts to avoid violence while carrying on intense conflicts of interests and values. Let us examine some cases of attempted avoidance of violence both by nations and by other parties in conflict. This review does not pretend to be exhaustive or systematic, either in terms of the cases in which nonlethal equivalents of war were attempted or in terms of the possible reasons for success and failure in such attempts. But perhaps we can locate some important differences. Let us pay special attention to whether there were acceptable institutions, external or superior to the interests in conflict, able to enforce their abstention from warfare; and to whether either side in the struggle believed that restricting itself to nonlethal techniques would place it at a special disadvantage.

The "Exploration Race"

One historical case of using nonmilitary techniques to pursue conflict is especially interesting now because of its analogies to the Cold War struggle for underdeveloped areas and for control in space. This is the fifteenth- and sixteenth-century "exploration race" among Spain, Portugal, France, England, and Holland. During a considerable part of the period, the conflict over control of the Americas and the Indies was based on the competitive use of geographical and navigational knowledge, diplomatic skill, and the massing of wealth to support the exploratory voyages, rather than on organized warfare among the exploring powers.[3]

The example of the exploration race is especially interesting because controls over it were attempted by a world institution that lacked a monopoly of violence. The attempt failed in part because ideological dissent from the basic values of that institution left its decrees without the force of legitimacy in parts of Europe placed at a disadvantage by those decrees. The world institution was the Papacy; its decrees dividing the discoveries between Spain and Portugal were rejected by the Protestant powers, England and Holland. As the urgency of claiming new territories increased, national interest drew even Catholic France into propounding theories of international law that contradicted Papal claims of power to allocate the new discoveries. But even while the European powers were rejecting the notion of allowing a supranational institution to decide such questions, they were trying to avoid direct warfare over the new territories. They were able to do so for decades at a time, and in 1559 prohibited full-scale organized war in Europe by the negative means of defining "peace" as limited only to that part of the globe east of the prime meridian and north of the Tropic of Cancer. But even the area of "no-peace" continued to be an area of at least half-peace; England's policy in the Americas was "halfway between piracy and settlement," France's a "mixture of trade and piracy."[4]

The peace-in-Europe agreement broke down sporadically, in the absence of an enforcing mechanism. The outbreak in 1568 of open war between Spain and England in the English Channel was one such instance. For lengthy periods in the sixteenth and seventeenth centuries, however, the European powers advanced their conflicting interests in the Americas without fighting major wars. By 1700 the domination of particular areas of the American continents by Spaniards, Portuguese, French, and English was considerably more the result of semipeaceful competition than of outright war.

In assessing the reasons for this mixed record, it is useful to remember that the powers entered no conscious commitment to avoid war, except in Europe, and that there was no supranational institution capable of enforcing even the agreement to keep wars out of Europe. On the other hand, most of the time, none of the contending powers saw any special disadvantage to itself in using brains and money, rather than arms, to compete. It is also instructive that in the exploration race there was no single finish line, no easily determined goal by which the powers could judge failure and success. If there had been such a single standard for winning the race, one power, on perceiving its own defeat, might have more easily turned to military action.[5]

British-American Relations

A more recent example of attempting to carry on intense conflict without war can be found in British-American relations through much of the nineteenth century. Of special interest for research in nonlethal alternatives to war is the careful, conscious effort made by the United States from 1805 to 1812 to find ways of coercing Great Britain that would not require armed attack, and the failure of that effort.[6]

The United States' effort to avoid war with Great Britain from 1805 to 1812 can be ascribed in part to a deep division of thought within the United States as to whether France or Britain was the more culpable in interfering with American commerce and whether France or Britain would be the more dangerous victor in Europe. Unable at any moment to choose against which country to make war, the United States attempted to fight neither but to use nonlethal equivalents of war against both. Since many Americans believed that boycotts of British goods before and during the Revolution had helped to force the British government toward a policy more favorable to America, they proposed similar means for coercing Britain and France in the struggle over commercial rights. An embargo on all American trade, a nonintercourse act forbidding trade with France and England until they changed their policies, and an act reopening trade with both but promising to prohibit it with one if the other would change its policy were successively tried.

Since American trade had been mainly with Britain, and since the Jefferson and Madison administrations had seen British attacks on American interests as the major American grievance, this period of the "Commercial War" emerges largely as a nonmilitary attack on Great Britain. The commercial pressures seem to have damaged British business somewhat, but too slowly to force a change in British policy until it was too late. The United States Congress had already given up on commercial pressures and had declared war.

This decision for war resulted from the belief that American power was not being effectively used in commercial boycotts, which damaged the United States as well as Britain. Congress decided that American power could be more effectively brought to bear through violence. The United States could presumably invade British Canada more easily than the British could defend it. Thus, since Americans believed they were being specially disadvantaged by avoiding violence and since no supranational institution existed to enforce that avoidance, the conflict degenerated into war.

After that war had ended in 1815, most of the conflicts between Britain and the United States centered on relations with Canada. At some times during the nineteenth century, these conflicts seemed to both Britons and Americans part of a long-run struggle for control over the Canadian economy, Canadian political and military arrangements, and Canadian values and ideals. Many Americans may feel that the United States "won" this struggle, since American investment capital has become the major factor in the Canadian economy; the Canadian monetary system is based on the dollar; the Canadian military establishment is closely linked to that of the United States; and Canadian labor organizations are integral parts of American unions. But it is especially interesting that this American sense of "victory" finds little resonance in Canadian opinion. Canadians see their history as a process not of succumbing to either British or American controls, but of establishing a distinct and independent Canadian nationality. In short, the "Cold War" over an "uncommitted" Canada seems, from the Canadian view-point, to have resulted not in "victory" for either contestant but in the emergence of Canada. This process may suggest possible long-run developments in the Cold War over Africa, Asia, and Latin America.

Nonetheless, it is especially instructive to examine how Britons and Americans conducted what seemed to them a struggle over Canada during the nineteenth century. Although the United States had several times attempted to invade Canada during the American Revolution and during the War of 1812, since 1815 the United States has taken no military action in or against Canada. Since the rebellion of 1837, the British have also eschewed military force to preserve their control over Canada or to resist American claims to disputed territory. This avoidance of violence after the War of 1812 has been based on a conscious joint decision of the United States and Britain to pursue their conflicts without violence. The decision against violence was symbolized by the 1818 agreement for naval disarmament on the Great Lakes (although the Lakes were not actually totally disarmed until much later).[7]

The avoidance of war between Britain and the United States was not based on any sudden belief in a community of interest between them. In several major controversies during the nineteenth century—the Maine boundary dispute and the Oregon question, directly involving Canadian interests, and the Alabama quarrel and the Venezuela crisis, into which Canada entered as the exposed flank of British power—there were serious possibilities of war. Each controversy was settled without war, by Britain's diplomatic acceptance of heavy American political pressures. That neither country resorted to war can probably be traced in part to the American belief that the United States could do no better by waging war than it was doing without war, and the British fear that they would do worse because Canada was so vulnerable to American power. Thus, from 1815 through the end of the nineteenth century, the conflicts of Britain and the United States were kept nonlethal, without any extranational enforcement institution, by disproportionate American power and the resultant belief in both countries that avoiding war was not to their disadvantage.[8]

From the Venezuela incident in 1895 to the Alaska-Canada boundary dispute in 1903, however, there were major changes in the style of British and American response. By 1903 increased feelings of a community of interest between the two countries had greatly lessened the chance that they would use military means to carry on conflicts. Though Theodore Roosevelt used vigorous diplomatic and political pressures to coerce the British on the Alaska-Canada boundary question, there was no public threat of war and no real chance of its occurring. An unofficial entente and indeed the beginnings of a defensive British-American alliance had replaced the war-inhibiting effects of a preponderant American power with the war-inhibiting effects of a community of interest.[9]

The Arab-Israeli Conflict

Another case of bitter internation conflict that has been conducted mostly without war is the Arab-Israeli struggle since 1948. The particular issues involved are scarcely necessary to describe, since the quarrels over refugees, territory, use of the Suez Canal, and riparian rights still exist. What is especially interesting for our purposes is that, except for a few weeks in 1956, the conflict has been carried on with little armed violence.

Boycotts, embargoes, propaganda broadcasts, public displays of military potential, espionage, economic aid to other countries, bribery, and subversion have been used by one or another side in the Arab-Israeli conflict. But organized violence has been forbidden by the rest of the world—especially, as the aftermath of the Suez-Sinai crisis of 1956 indicated, by the tacit agreement of the United States and the Soviet Union.

These two powers have acted essentially as a "world state" for the Near East. They have announced their own monopoly—or duopoly—over permission to use force in the area, and have enforced their insistence partly by threatening punishment for using violence and partly by permitting the use of all other techniques for increasing power. This permission to use nonlethal techniques has acted as a safety valve of sorts. Forbidding both lethal and nonlethal conflicts would in effect forbid any expression in international life of real changes in the balance of Near Eastern power. An attempt at total prohibition of change could only result in violent explosion.

While permitting the use of nonlethal techniques, the United States and the Soviet Union have threatened the use of force against Israel when she used lethal means of carrying on the conflict, and the United States has warned that it would use force if one of the Arab states did so.

We should especially note that the geographically restricted Soviet-American "world state" did not require ideological agreement either between the Arabs and the Israelis, or between both of them and the "world state" itself. Nor is it possible to say that interests or values in conflict between the Arabs and Israel have been outweighed at any time since 1948 by the values and interests they hold in common—except their shared distaste for being punished by the United States and the Soviet Union.

Internal Conflicts in the United States

Finally, let us examine a case in which intense conflicts arose not between nations but between groups within a nation, and in which those conflicts were originally settled by pitched wars but later by nonlethal equivalents. The case in point is the United States, a country in which for almost two centuries the private use of violence for private ends was more frequent, and more condoned, than in most nations.[10]

It is important here to distinguish attempts by nongovernmental groups to resist the government, overthrow it, or capture it (which may be called rebellions or insurrections), from efforts by one private group to coerce another without particular reference to the state (which may be called riots). In the United States, the Civil War and the events of September 30, 1962, in Oxford, Mississippi exemplify rebellions. The Homestead battle of 1892 and the Chicago race riot of 1919 are examples of riots. In both these cases, private groups—the Carnegie Steel Company and the Amalgamated Association of Iron and Steel Workers in the Homestead case; white and Negro gangs in the Chicago riots—armed themselves to try to coerce each other. They used their arms until belatedly halted by the intervention of the state. It is this sort of violent conflict—the riot—that most nearly approximates international warfare, and so will be useful to examine.

What is especially interesting about the riot in American history is that we seem to find a watershed around 1940, before which riots were frequent and since which they have been practically nonexistent. Since 1940, the conflicts that were previously fought out with violence have been "fought" instead by the use of political and economic measures. The reasons for this change are most pertinent to the problem of creating nonlethal equivalents of war.

In assessing the legitimacy of private violence in the American system before and after 1940, we must recall two factors of both symbolic and practical importance. The Weberian concept of the state as monopolist of legitimate violence assumes that the state has the means of using overwhelming violence and that private individuals have almost no means of using any. In the United States, however, not until the 1940's did a peacetime standing army exist that could be called an army by Weber's European standards. Conversely, the Bill of Rights specifically reserved to the people the right "to keep and bear arms." Since the arms available to the people were hardly less deadly than those available to the tiny United States Army, it was not until 1940 that the United States could be said in the full Weberian sense to be a "state" with a monopoly of violence.

Indeed, through much of the nineteenth century it was widely agreed that vigilantes on the frontier, slaveowners in the South, Protestants and Catholics in the big cities, were entitled to use violence for ends privately defined; or at the very least, it was not agreed that they were *not* so entitled.[11]

More annoyance was expressed at private violence when it was used by capital and labor and by whites and Negroes late in the nineteenth and early in the twentieth century. Thus in the Homestead affair of 1892, state militia were brought in to stop violence. But although three Pinkertons (armed guards hired by the company) and seven armed workers were killed in a pitched battle at Homestead, it was not until four days later that state militia were sent to the scene.[12] Clearly, the illegitimacy of such private violence was not fully established.

Similarly, the American state acted to end private racial violence only after long hesitation. In 1919, twenty-three Negroes and fifteen whites had been killed in citywide rioting in Chicago, and the rioting had lasted for days before state troops were ordered into the city to halt the violence. Similar hesitation prevented the dispatch of Federal troops to stop rural race riots in Arkansas in 1919 until after about twenty-five Negroes and one white had been killed.[13]

Thus, for a long period in American history, some sort of gray area of legitimacy applied to racial and labor riots, and as a result they continued to occur. The last large-scale labor riot, however, occurred in 1940 at the River Rouge plant of the Ford Motor Company, and the last race riot of any size, in Detroit in 1943. From then till now, for twenty years, no major riot (as distinguished from the Oxford and Little Rock insurrections) has occurred; and in no previous two decades of American history has the incidence of large-scale private violence been so low.

A related group of changes in American society is connected with the end of riots. The symbolic and practical importance of the widespread nullification of the Second Amendment (by means of laws against carrying concealed weapons) and of the creation of a great standing army is not easy to demonstrate in detail, but it is hard to deny.

It is perhaps even more important that the function of governmental armed forces within the nation has since 1940 been much more carefully defined to mean the prevention of private violence, rather than the use of public violence on behalf of one side in a private dispute. Before 1940, the intervention of public forces to break a strike that was being carried out without violence, or to side with whites in incidents of conflict with Negroes, was reasonably frequent.[14] Since then, the neutrality of Federal and state governments in cases of labor and racial conflict has been greatly increased.

In short, since 1940, the state in the United States has followed much more nearly the Weberian model of the neutral institution possessing and enforcing a monopoly on legitimate violence; before 1940, the state in the United States may be said to have followed much more nearly the Marxian model of the institution prepared to use violence on behalf of the more powerful groups in the society, even when their weaker opponents eschewed violence. (Perhaps still earlier, before the Civil War, the state in the United States can be said to have hardly existed at all.)

The effects of the changed attitude toward private conflict and violence can be seen in the fact that conflicts have been recently carried on in intense but nonlethal ways. For labor conflict, this change began with governmental acceptance of the strike as a legitimate weapon during the 1930's. Certainly labor conflicts did not disappear; indeed, in the 1930's they were at least as intense as ever before. But the sit-down strike to deny management both the fruits of the workers' labor and access to its own property was invented as a nonlethal equivalent for head-on violence. Labor used older, nonlethal techniques like the boycott, the conventional strike, and sabotage, and management used techniques like blacklisting, lockouts, and bribery to achieve its ends. Since the 1930's even such heated conflicts as the Kohler strike in Wisconsin, the wave of strikes in 1946–47, and the struggles over organizing migrant farm labor in California have not resulted in violence.[15]

Similarly, the intense conflicts of the 1950's and 1960's between Negroes and whites have not erupted into violence between the two private groups.[16] No major race riot has come in the school-integration campaign. And when a rash of racial outbreaks took place in 1960 and again in 1963 that in many respects resembled the nationwide rash of race riots in 1919, the later outbreaks were by design nonviolent. Much of this can be attributed to the new neutrality of the United States government between the parties in conflict; its possession of a large and effective standing army; and its readiness to prevent either party from using private or semigovernmental violence. Southern police references to their fear of Federal intervention if they took sides against Negro sit-ins, and the symbolic reference of one Southerner, cautioning compliance with court decrees, to "that big atom bomb they have up in Washington," are indications of the effects of the existence of a neutral institution superior to the conflicting groups.

Other factors may have been important in eliminating the riot from American life. The multiplication of national ties across geographical, class, and racial lines since 1940, as well as the almost continuous existence since 1940 of an outside threat and the actuality or possibility of war, has probably intensified American feelings of shared community. This heightened sense of community has probably reduced the likelihood of internal violence. It is hard to separate these factors from those more closely connected with the state monopoly on violence.

PRINCIPLES OF PROHIBITING VIOLENCE

These four instances—the exploration race, British-American and Arab-Israeli conflicts, and internal conflicts in the United States—in which attempts were made to avoid or forbid war as a means for carrying on conflict may suggest some general principles. It would seem that one effective way of prohibiting a resort to violence is to have an institution removed from the conflict, concerned not so much with determining its outcome as with restricting the means used in it. We should note that this institution may be distinguished from a "government," which is supposed to settle the conflict itself. In other words, there is a distinction between (1) decreeing the division of the New World between Spain and Portugal or decreeing the success of the Pullman Company against its workers ("governmental" acts) and (2) forbidding

Spain and Portugal or management and labor to use violence in carrying on their conflicts, while permitting them to use any other means. Only where there is broad ideological consensus, it seems, is a "government" possible; and even then, if it lacks an agent ready to insist on the avoidance of violence, parties in conflict may resort to violence anyway. In fact, it seems possible to have a "government" without a "state" (the Papacy, possessing no monopoly on violence but dividing the Americas) and a "state" without a "government" (the Soviet-American joint policing of no-war rules in the Near East).

In the absence of a "state"—an enforcement agency for prohibiting violence —it seems difficult to keep the techniques of conflict limited to nonlethal means for any long period of time. But it also seems possible that the existence of a "government"—an institution focusing shared values and deciding the outcome of political disputes—is necessary in the long run in order to turn the precarious state of nonwar achieved by a "state" into a stable peace.

In short, our examination of the four cases of conflict suggests that in the context of the Cold War, a reasonable policy might attempt to construct in the near future a world "state" that could not decide political issues but could forbid violence. Such an institution should if possible be set up so that over the long haul it could evolve toward a world "government," if changes in the Cold War context begin to permit the construction of shared interests and values.

Examination of the four cases of attempted nonlethal conflict suggests also that policy oriented to the near future should take into account "unscoreability" of various nonlethal forms of carrying on conflict, the existence of crosscutting alliances and enmities, and belief on both sides that no special disadvantage would be incurred from eschewing violence, as conditions that would all reduce the likelihood of war.

A policy intended to substitute nonlethal equivalents for the present military means of carrying on the Cold War might in the short run attempt to restructure the Cold War so that (1) the outcome of particular skirmishes would be difficult to score as a decisive victory for either side; (2) both sides increasingly believed in the existence of enemies other than the major opponent; and (3) neither side could expect a differential advantage if it resumed using military techniques for carrying on the conflict.

Almost contemporaneously with taking these steps, a policy of moving toward the use of nonlethal equivalents of war would attempt (in the absence of any prospect for uniting the conflicting parties in the Cold War in a more general community of interest) to create an extranational institution capable of enforcing on both sides an abandonment of military techniques and of commanding from both sides acceptance of its monopoly of violence. But no attempt should be made, in light of intense present ideological disagreements, to create a "world government" that would itself settle Cold War issues. These issues would still be fought out directly between the parties by all available nonlethal means.

A CAMPAIGN OF NONLETHAL OFFENSIVES

It may be useful to examine a slightly more concrete model of the world that such a policy might create within the next generation. One can imagine the world as a "disarmed disorder," in which each nation could attempt to advance its interests and defend its ideology without restraints, so long as it did not use violence. The United States, for example, might attempt to free Hungary by explaining to Hungarians over radio the means of quietly and nonlethally sabotaging bureaucratic authoritarianism by using its own red tape against itself; by offering large economic inducements for increased infiltration of ideas and products into Hungary by means of expanded trade; by sending agricultural "county agents" who are experts in the arts of re-vivifying local village politics and improving agriculture; and by judiciously managing educational exchanges. The Soviet Union might attempt to com-munize Mexico by arousing unrest in the peasantry, by demonstrating scien-tific superiority in the race for Mars, and by offering to direct a quick industrial-development program. Some colonial power might use a combina-tion of bribes, control of the schools, and manipulation of the price of key products to continue its domination of a colony. A former colony might use nonviolent Gandhian techniques to infiltrate a neighboring area still under colonial rule. Thus conflicts of states might be settled through economic, political, and psychological equivalents of war that did not involve arms or killing. No state would be subjected to a "world government" that might con-trol its social system.

The main objection to this model of "disorder and disarmament" is that it would not stay disarmed for very long. It is argued that once conflicts were "fought out" by means so threatening, even though initially nonviolent, one or another nation would, in anger, rearm in order to further its ends. And the only punishment for such an action would be rearmament by other nations—a process that reinstitutes the arms race.

The dilemma then is between placing so much emphasis on preserving order in a disarmed world that no nation agrees to disarm, and having so little machinery to keep order that the world cannot be kept disarmed. What is clearly necessary is the invention of some kind of world disarmament-enforcement machinery that is less than government, but more than an inspec-tion corps—a "state" that would be powerful enough to punish an act of rearmament, but not powerful enough to impose a social or legal system on any nation. If such an institution existed, every nation could freely and safely use the techniques of conflict without violence to advance its own interests.

The invention of a disarmament-enforcement institution requires a great deal of thought and research. It is possible to imagine a highly mobile, highly trained police force about as powerful as the police of New York City, and able therefore to arrest individual violators of a disarmament law, or perhaps only to restore the disarmed state of affairs without arresting violators. But in any case the agency would be unable to dictate policy to a government. Still other sorts of institutions could doubtless be discussed. Choosing among them would obviously be a task for international negotiation and agreement.[17]

But deciding on how to conduct conflict by nonlethal means is just as obviously a unilateral matter. Each nation would choose means of advancing its interests and values that were most congenial to its history and most suited to its strengths. Indeed, some nonlethal equivalents of war could be used without waiting for disarmament. The more successful they were, the more pressure they would exert for replacement of the present unsuccessful military means of pursuing conflict; in other words, the use of nonlethal equivalents would itself accelerate disarmament.

The initiation of nonlethal offensives would presumably bring a series of responses of different sorts from different interests in the world. The five distinguishable major interests are those of the developed totalitarian state, the Soviet Union; the largest underdeveloped totalitarian state, China; the emerging Western European group of highly developed, moderately conservative and hierarchical, but libertarian societies, which we may call Europa; the United States; and the large underdeveloped areas in Asia, Africa, and Latin America that have not yet clearly chosen whether they will be seriously attempting industrial development as libertarian or totalitarian states, in friendship with the West or in enmity to it. This last group includes states like India, Brazil, and Nigeria, which still have libertarian governments but have not definitely achieved the takeoff point in industrialization and may be in danger of totalitarian revolutions, and states like Egypt and Indonesia, which are using totalitarian means but have also not achieved takeoff and have one window still open on the West.

We can expect these interests to continue to prosecute both the "East-West" war (the struggle over totalitarian or liberal orientations in the underdeveloped world) and the "North-South" war (the struggle between the rich and the poor over independence, control over resources, and racial distinctions). We can also expect that the two wars will continue to inflame and exacerbate each other, constantly recreating the Cold War in much the present fashion. But the subtraction of armaments and violence from these processes is likely to change the participants—and ultimately the processes themselves.

The two categories of underdeveloped societies—China and the uncommitted group—would be the chief targets of a Western campaign of nonlethal offensives. The campaign could offer the Chinese the opportunity to relax present totalitarian pressures for squeezing capital investment funds out of the peasantry, and insist on permitting Western access to China in return for such aid. Both the aid itself and the conditions accompanying it could be oriented toward liberalizing the Chinese system. To the degree that the Chinese regard totalitarianism not as an end in itself but as a means to speedy industrialization, they should be tempted to accept Western aid.

Meanwhile, the uncommitted nations that had industrialization by any available means as a primary goal would find little to object to in the offers of American aid, even if it were conditioned on the preservation of special privileges for American interests. For the aid would heighten their own strength and bring nearer the time at which they could make their own judgments of what foreign interests to tolerate. Doctrinaire anti-Americans or anticapitalists would have a considerably more difficult time appealing to the anger of the hungry and diseased if their situation were being improved with American aid and if the continuance of such aid and the maintenance of a good international credit rating for further investment were made conditional on respect for private American interests. Even less opposition could be expected if the aid were given on condition of the preservation and expansion of basic liberties, political and economic, for the local citizenry rather than on preservation of American privileges. For in the uncommitted states, totalitarian movements are successful only to the degree that industrial development is not being achieved by nontotalitarian governments.

The Soviet Union, perhaps to a lesser extent than with China but still appreciably, would be compelled to attempt to match Western efforts in the uncommitted world or resign itself to losing influence and power there.

The Soviets would therefore be seriously pressed by a campaign of non-lethal offensives. Their economy is so much more limited than that of the West that they would have great difficulty in competing. In order to do so, they would probably have to decrease military spending, especially on conventional armies that could be growing food or making machinery for export. Thus, on the one hand, the Soviets would be forced to dismantle part of the control machinery necessary to keep their society totalitarian. At the same time, the fears of military attack that haunt them out of an unhappy past would be dissolving as the West reoriented its own expenditures from military to nonlethal operations. Since fears of military attack are the most easily manipulated arguments in favor of the retention of totalitarian controls, the reduction of these fears would ease the task of those elements of Soviet society that have been demanding movement toward a more liberal society.

Since the pursuit of conflict is more likely to remain nonlethal so long as neither party to conflict expects to gain from giving up nonlethal in favor of military techniques, some method of preventing a discriminatory disadvantage would have to operate during the period in which disarmament had not yet been achieved but nonlethal activities were under way. The most useful means immediately available would probably be the achievement of a stable military balance, a "deterrent" that would prevent either side from imagining it could gain an advantage by using force. Under such conditions, for example, the Soviets would be unlikely to respond to a loss of political influence in the underdeveloped world by resorting to military action. Instead, they would probably respond with an increased willingness to negotiate seriously for total disarmament with adequate enforcement, in the hope that relieving their society of the entire arms burden would free it for more effective political and economic action. If they were offered an arrangement for enforcing disarmament that would not impose Western values on them in "world government" style (as present offers do by insisting on compulsory jurisdiction for the World Court and so on), then the Soviets should be even more willing to consider disarmament seriously.

The usefulness in keeping a conflict nonlethal of providing enemies and allies that "crosscut" the parties in conflict would suggest a policy of encouraging non-Cold War alliances and enmities wherever possible. For example, conflicts between China and the Soviet Union and between the United States and emerging Europa might be deliberately accentuated, rather than smoothed over, in the hope of reducing the likelihood of an appeal to violence.

In the period during which the pursuit of nonlethal conflict continued to depend on deterrence rather than on supranational enforcement, the restriction of techniques to nonlethal ones would also depend heavily on the perception by both sides that at worst neither was "losing" badly. In order for this perception to persist on the weaker side, that of the Communists, care might have to be exercised not to overthrow any Communist governments but to change them slowly and subtly, rewarding forces within them oriented to nonlethal activities rather than to the police and military. In short, the conflict would have to be managed so as to be as incapable of being scored as possible, even while victories for libertarian ends and Western power were being won.

This sketch of probable responses to nonlethal equivalents of war raises serious problems. Is mapping the strategy of predictable nonlethal wars any more possible than mapping the strategy of thermonuclear wars? I would argue that thermonuclear strategists are in the position of subjects in a sensory deprivation experiment: that they are unable to check their hyperrational constructions with the real world and hence let their mental pictures run away with them, just as the man deprived of all contact by touch, sight, smell, and hearing of the outside world begins to hallucinate in order to make some sort of world for himself. Is planning nonlethal strategy any more defensible?

A difference is that nonlethal offensives can be tried and checked against predictions without grave risk, whereas predictions concerning thermonuclear wars can be checked out only at the risk of national destruction. In fact, we already have historical evidence—in the cases discussed above and in a myriad others—concerning the effects of using nonlethal equivalents of war.

And if a program of nonlethal offensives were begun, it could be modified as the ongoing events changed our perceptions of reality. Thermonuclear wars are not like that.

There is a final difference, then, between wars of annihilation and nonlethal equivalents of warfare. The one can be researched; the other cannot. A systematic examination of world history, of the kind sketched but not attempted here, would be one form of such research. Another would be experiment or participant-observation with small groups in real conflict, such as juvenile gangs, substituting nonlethal for violent means of carrying on the conflict. Still another would be the careful observation of a full-scale national campaign of nonlethal offensives, with preparations made to change tactics if certain techniques did not work.

The ability to research nonlethal equivalents of war is no mean advantage over thermonuclear strategy. The hallucinating subject of a sensory-deprivation experiment and the astrologer who never tries to check his predictions are men dangerously adrift in the world. Merely imagining the future is no way to build realistic images; it is those men who shape the future and watch it change beneath their hands who understand it.

In the twentieth century, the highly lethal character of war and the ineluctable difficulties of achieving a true peace would suggest that only nonlethal equivalents of war—intense conflict without killing—can give men the opportunity to shape and change their world.

NOTES

1. See Kenneth Boulding, "Toward a Theory of Peace," herein.
2. See Roger Fisher, "Fractionating Conflict," herein.
3. For an overview of the exploration race, see chapters 15 and 16 of the *New Cambridge Modern History*, II.
4. *New Cambridge Modern History*, II, p. 465.
5. On the importance of competing in areas that are difficult to score, see Amitai Etzioni, "International Prestige and Peaceful Competition," in Quincy Wright *et al.*, eds., *Preventing World War III* (New York: Simon & Schuster, 1962), pp. 226–245.
6. See Bradford Perkins, *Prologue to War* (Berkeley, Calif.: University of California Press, 1961), and Julius W. Pratt, *Expansionists of 1812* (New York: Macmillan, 1925).
7. See C. P. Stacey, "The Myth of the Unguarded Frontier 1815–1871," *American Historical Review*, LVI (1950), 1–18.
8. For British-American-Canadian relations through the nineteenth century, see Samuel Flagg Bemis, *A Diplomatic History of the United States* (New York: Holt, Rinehart & Winston, 1950), *passim*.
9. See Howard K. Beale, *Theodore Roosevelt and the Rise of America to World Power* (Baltimore, Maryland: Johns Hopkins, 1956), pp. 82–171.
10. For a more detailed examination of the history of private conflict and violence in the United States, and especially of the racial conflict discussed hereafter, see Arthur I. Waskow, "The 1919 Race Riots: A Study in the Connections between Conflict and Violence," Ph.D. dissertation, University of Wisconsin, 1963.

11. See John Hope Franklin, *The Militant South* (Harvard University Press, 1956);
    John W. Caughey, *Their Majesties the Mob* (Chicago: University of Chicago
    Press, 1960); Ray A. Billington, *The Protestant Crusade* (New York: Holt,
    Rinehart & Winston, 1952).

12. Samuel Yellen, *American Labor Struggles* (New York: Russell & Russell, 1956).

13. Chicago Commission on Race Relations, *The Negro in Chicago* (Chicago: University
    of Chicago Press, 1922); Herbert J. Seligmann, *The Negro Faces America*
    (Harper & Row, 1920).

14. See Robert V. Bruce, *1877: Year of Violence* (New York: Bobbs-Merrill, 1959),
    on the great railroad strike, and Ray Ginger, *The Bending Cross* (New Bruns-
    wick, N.J.: Rutgers University Press, 1949), on the Pullman Strike; concerning
    police tactics before and during various race riots, see Chicago Commission on
    Race Relations, *The Negro in Chicago*; Robert T. Kerlin, *Voice of the Negro
    1919* (New York: Dutton, 1920).

15. The ultimate in conduct of intense intranational conflict by nonlethal means can
    be seen in the British general strike of 1926. Major elements of the British
    working force, three million strong, undertook to stop practically all work in
    transport, power, coal and steel, and construction industries. The strike was
    denounced by business and government as a threat to capitalism, the Constitution,
    and democracy. It was carried out in a mood of "class struggle" and with the
    intent of bringing nearer a "socialist reconstruction" of British society. Yet the
    strike involved almost no violence. The test of strength was almost wholly political
    and economic. Even though the government was not neutral—was in fact one
    of the parties—its police and army were not used to attack or coerce the
    strikers, and the strikers did not prepare for violence.

    See G. D. H. Cole and Raymond Postgate, *The British Common People, 1745–
    1938* (New York: Barnes and Noble, 1961), and Wilfrid Harris Crook, *The
    General Strike* (Chapel Hill, N.C.: University of North Carolina Press, 1931).

16. The Oxford, Mississippi, violence of 1962 was directed not against Negroes—not
    even against the student whose enrollment was being objected to—but against
    Federal marshals. The affair clearly was an insurrection, not a riot.

17. For discussion of possible approaches, see Arthur I. Waskow, *Quis Custodiet?
    Controlling the Police in a Disarmed World* (Peace Research Institute, 1963).

PART III

Developing International Community

8

MORTON DEUTSCH

Producing Change in an Adversary[a]

Public opinion polls indicate that "distrust of the Russians among the American people is about as universal as any feeling could be."[1] Our newspapers repeatedly refer to the "Red menace," "Soviet intransigence," "Communist trickery and deceit." Leading Americans warn of the "Soviet threat to the American way of life" and castigate Communist China as an "outlaw among nations." Many American scholars specializing in the study of Communism hold the view that the Communists are out to impose their system on the rest of the world and will succeed unless we are prepared to face up to a life-and-death competition with them.[2]

I shall, for the purpose of this paper, accept the widely held assumption that the Communists have evil designs on us[b]—that they are out to do us in

[a] The views expressed in this paper do not represent, nor are they necessarily similar to, the views of any organization with which the author is affiliated.

[b] In my opinion, this is a partial truth. It is no doubt true that the Communist leaders are hostile to the United States and would be delighted to see our national power and international influence eliminated or reduced. But our views and theirs, in these respects, are mirror images. Americans would not grieve over the demise of Communism. Each side is correct in seeing the other side as hostile and as being willing to indulge in lawless conduct (i.e., "whatever serves the national interest") to defeat the other. Each side is also notably imperceptive with regard to how its own actions foster and maintain a hostile reaction from the other.

Moreover, as a result of the mutual hostility, each side's view of itself and of the other tends to become rigid and determined by the need to be opposed to the other side. As a result, each side loses its historical perspective and becomes imperceptive of the reality that ideas, men, and societies change; that Adam Smith would not recognize the American "free enterprise" system as his intellectual offspring; and that Karl Marx would not be able to identify Soviet or Chinese "Communism" as his descendant.

by whatever means they can, fair or foul. According to this view, the Communists are seeking to dominate the world and to undermine the United States and other potential obstacles to their goal of world supremacy. Moreover, since this is their objective, one cannot trust them because they will unscrupulously exploit any opportunity to harm us and advantage themselves.

ARE THE COMMUNISTS INCORRIGIBLE OR CORRIGIBLE?

If the Communists are, in fact, an unprincipled adversary out to do us in, what then? One possibility is to consider that the Communists are this way and that they are incorrigible or unchangeable.[c] The conception of the Communists as *incorrigibly* malevolent leads only to the following policy alternatives:

(1) waging a preventive war to destroy them before, presumably, they destroy us;

(2) submitting to the Communists to induce them not to destroy us;

(3) withdrawing into isolation and disengaging ourselves from the complex problems of international relations;

(4) "buying time" through a military policy of stable deterrence and waiting uneasily for doomsday;

(5) attempting to achieve such a clear-cut military superiority over the Communists that they would be rationally compelled to refrain from the use of force to attain their objectives.

The last alternative is sometimes broadened to state that we could use a clear-cut military superiority to prevent the Communists from attaining victories of any sort, military or nonmilitary, while we attempt to weaken them by economic warfare, propaganda, and/or subversion.

I suggest that none of the first four alternatives is tolerable and that each for a different reason is likely to result in a nuclear catastrophe. It is now evident that even a surprise attack on the Soviet Union would leave Russia with a sufficient number of multimegaton weapons to retaliate with a devastating blow. Submission to the Communists would not be psychologically possible for the American people unless we had been hopelessly defeated in a nuclear war. Withdrawal into isolation in the face of an unprincipled adversary is tantamount to surrender; it can only strengthen the adversary and enhance our own sense of desperation.

[c] Psychologists would probably agree that, for most people, it is easier to perceive something by which they feel threatened and which they oppose as *intrinsically* rather than as *conditionally* evil. The perception of intrinsic evil is black and white, it requires less differentiation and integration of experience, it involves less emotional restraint, and it permits unequivocal and uniform moral judgment. Psychologists would also probably agree that quick moral judgment, a black-white picture, an unconditional view of personality and behavior, make it difficult to understand either the determinants of behavior or the conditions for its change.

With regard to the policy of military deterrence, I suggest that a hostile peace will not endure; misunderstanding, insanity, local irresponsibility, or a sense of desperation during a non-nuclear war will ultimately lead to the use of nuclear weapons. The use of nuclear weapons in a war will, in turn, make an all-out thermonuclear war more probable. In effect, there is not enough stability in the "stable" deterrent in a hostile world. However, it is undoubtedly true that the existence of relatively invulnerable nuclear weapons makes war less likely for any specified period of time: it "buys time." But if we "buy time," we must use the time constructively to bring about a change in our adversary before the time runs out. In other words, the policy of military deterrence is not enough in itself; it must be supplemented by a policy which assumes that our adversary is corrigible. Otherwise, we can only uneasily await doomsday.

The Policy of Military Superiority

The fifth alternative—working toward military superiority—is advocated by many influential groups in the United States and it has a surface plausibility. The plausibility, I believe, arises from the reasonable proposition that Western military *inferiority* might tempt the Communists to exploit their military superiority. This proposition, however, does not necessarily imply that the attempt to attain a clear-cut Western military superiority is desirable.[d] Obviously, if the Communists were unwilling to settle for a position of military inferiority, our attempt to achieve military supremacy would only lead to a continuing intensification of the arms race. While an arms race is costly to the Soviet Union and undoubtedly interferes with and distorts their domestic economic development, there is no evidence to indicate either that the Soviet system under threat cannot marshal its population and resources to keep up in an arms race despite the resulting privations or that an intensified arms race will not distort the economy and weaken the democratic institutions of the United States. Thus, there is no reasonable assurance that without turning ourselves into a garrison state (and hence losing our rationale for the effort necessary to defend our no-longer-existing "way of life"), we would do better in an arms race. Moreover, even if we were able to achieve numerical and technological military superiority, the Russians might still be able to do enough damage to prevent us from intimidating them by superior military force. We may get into the position where we can "overkill" them but, even if they can kill us only once, how much of an advantage is this?

[d] The balancing of military power is admittedly a very complex problem since military power includes such diverse elements as geography, weaponry, national will, the state of research, and economic development. In terms of conventional forces, we wish to have clear military superiority to the Soviet Union in Detroit just as they wish to have clear superiority in Magnetogorsk. When I indicate the desirability of equality with regard to military power, I refer to the desirability of both sides being equally capable of preventing the other side from changing the political status quo by the threat or use of military power.

The policy of attempted military superiority also rests upon the assumption that the Communists will rationally accept their inferiority and not do anything that might unleash our military might. If, in fact, we can assume that they will behave rationally in terms of their self-interest when under the threat of our military superiority, can we not assume that they are also rational enough to know that their self-interest would be better served by a peaceful world in which neither side can profit from the use of military force? Evidence and common sense suggest that one acts *less* judiciously rather than more so when an opponent is perceived as trying to attain an intimidating superior force. Would our reaction be one of "rational" acceptance if we believed the Soviet Union were attempting this? Consider only our reaction to the military build-up of Cuba. Would the Soviet Union be more rational than we? Are we to assume that they perceive themselves as villains and perceive us as innocent victims and will then accept as just that they should be humbled by us?[e]

To argue against the reasonableness of the policy of military supremacy does not imply that we should accept a position of military inferiority. As I shall indicate more fully below, we should neither tempt nor encourage Communist aggressiveness by military (or any other kind of) weakness. On the other hand, we do not wish to stimulate the arms race or provoke fears of our aggressiveness (and thus support the most intransigent, militaristic elements in the Communist bloc) by seeking the elusive and possibly non-existent goal of military superiority.

The conception of the Communists as incorrigibly evil, even if it were true, is useless; it does not lead to any reasonable course of action. One loses nothing by assuming that the Communists are corrigible. Such a premise does not imply that we must weaken ourselves in order to influence them to cooperate in building a peaceful world. To the contrary, my discussion later in the paper suggests that we will be more likely to influence them if our own society is strong and thriving and if we are resolute in overcoming our own economic and racial problems. From the assumption of corrigibility, it follows that positive inducement to change, and not merely threats, are appropriate in the attempt to influence the Communists. The shift from a primary reliance on threats may have a salutary effect not only on our adversary but also on ourselves and the uncommitted nations.

Can a Nation Change?

The conception of the Communists as incorrigible is not only useless; it also runs counter to the basic intellectual traditions of science which place stress on understanding the conditions which give rise to and which alter

---

[e] If, in fact, the Soviet leaders feel an underlying guilt about their hostility to the West, they would attempt to defend themselves against this feeling by seeking evidence to justify their hostility. A threatening, superior military capability of the United States would provide ample justification.

phenomena. The scientific tradition insists that evil (if one accepts this view of the Communists) must be understood and not merely condemned. Over and over again, it has been demonstrated that the ability to control and change phenomena which are viewed as intractable depends on the development of understanding. Moreover, history suggests that even aggressor nations may reform.

Americans often forget that as a new nation we were considered bumptious and arrogant by the most established European countries. The United States seized the Floridas from Spain, conquered part of the Southwest after an adventurer's war against smaller and weaker Mexico, and obtained the Oregon Territory by threatening action against Britain. We also tend to forget that American expansion drove the Indian tribes ruthlessly and violently from their lands in a series of wars and broken treaties. During this time, we were stridently anticolonial, encouraging the Latin American peoples to win national independence as we established our own economic and military dominance in the resulting power vacuum. And for many years American slave traders raided the coasts of Africa to supply human chattels to do the menial, backbreaking work of American agriculture. The United States has obviously changed; aggressive, expansionist national policies are not necessarily unalterable.

If the Communists are unprincipled adversaries whose orientation we hope to change, we must ask: How did they get that way? What in their past experiences led them to develop as they did? How did their views of the outside world emerge? What gave rise to their conception of themselves? What functions did their developing internal structure serve? What relationship has our own behavior had to the particular way they have developed? What are the assumptions underlying their current behavior? How do they picture our attitude toward them and toward ourselves? I shall not attempt a detailed answer to these questions. However, a reading of many experts on Communism has led me to the following view.

Communism in the Soviet Union is a child of the West, nourished in the repressive, autocratic, cruel and secretive atmosphere of tsarist Russia. Its development reflects the stresses and strains of its formative environment and the problems of its parentage. I have no need to detail the fact that its formative environment was hostile—consider only the invasion of Russia and Siberia by the United States and other Western nations after the Bolshevik Revolution, the long period of nonrecognition, the initial exclusion from the League of Nations, and the savage destructiveness of the German invasions. It is hardly surprising that they should have developed the motivation to do us in (if, indeed, they have) since their experience led them to believe that this was what we were trying to do to them. Nor is it surprising that they do not agree or adhere to rules of international conduct formulated by us— especially since we, and other nations, have consistently proclaimed and acted on the principle that national interests can never be subordinated to international interests. Is American intervention in Guatemala and Cuba less un-principled than Russian intervention in Czechoslovakia and Hungary, except in minor degree? It is not surprising that they are unwilling to accept a double standard of international morality which is disadvantageous to them. Nor is it surprising that the Communists, having survived and even thrived in a hostile and unprincipled environment, should be confident of their ability to win a competitive struggle with us. They did well when they were weak. Shouldn't they do even better now that they are strong?

THE COMMUNIST ORIENTATION

To state that Russia's hostile, competitive orientation to the West has had realistic defensive functions in terms of past experiences does not, of course, minimize the problem in bringing about a change in this orientation. Let us examine some of its central features so that we may better understand the task confronting us.[3]

(1) It is a central Communist belief that Russia's enemies ("the West") strive not merely to contain Communism but to destroy it. Thus, whether the atmosphere of international relations is superficially harmonious or tense, the basic question remains, "Who will destroy whom?"

(2) While the goal of Communism is victory over its enemies, the operational tactics of Communism must be flexible and must be rationally responsive to the opportunities and dangers characterizing specific situa-tions—advantages are pushed to their limit, retreat is made when neces-sary, and adventurist or risky or emotionally-based actions are avoided.

(3) The style of Communism is that of rude belligerence and its posture is one of unyielding resistance toward the West. By appearing brazen when they are deeply apprehensive, the Communists attempt to convince the enemy that they expect attacks and are prepared to meet them confidently. A defiant attitude not only hides their sense of inferiority from the enemy, but also protects them from their own fear of helplessness in the face of the enemy. Further, their belligerence and rigid resistance serve to remove any temptation to succumb to the enemy by helping to unmask the hostility which lurks beneath his occasional surface friendliness.

(4) The Communists attempt to limit contact with the West and to main-tain a sharp rather than fuzzy demarcation between themselves and their potential enemies. They do so because they believe their enemies will attempt to use "the smallest crack" for espionage and will use friendly contacts and false promises to subvert and seduce their populace, tem-porarily undergoing hardships. The limitation of contact and the emphasis on secrecy express their fear of being vulnerable to external enemies who are out to destroy them.

(5) The Communists believe that the tide of history is on their side and that their side has a noble, humanistic objective: the creation of a world-wide society in which no man exploits another, in which the fruits of man's labor are freely available to all according to their need. They see this objective as appealing to all but the exploiting classes and those who are confused and misled by the propaganda of the exploiters. Thus, they perceive a fundamental split between the people and the leaders of the enemy nations. The enemies of Communism are the leaders of the West (the "Wall Street clique") and not the people.

(6) The enemies of Communism are viewed as being highly rational, intelligent, and effective, even though they are fighting a losing battle. Their power is never to be underestimated. Their continuing, basic hostility is always to be taken for granted and, in that sense, their hostility cannot be provoked; they believe the enemy unceasingly aims at the annihilation of Communism. The ruling group of the enemy camp derives its policies from sober calculations of the relationships of forces rather than from feelings or from considerations of prestige. It acts in terms of its own self-interest; agreements are made not to promote friendly feelings but simply to represent the existing balance of forces.

There are several things to be noted in this description of the Communist orientation to the West. First, it is based on an image of a life-and-death struggle: Communists will be annihilated unless they annihilate their opponents. Their image of the enemy is, in a sense, an evil version of themselves. Second, there is the pervasive sense of vulnerablity so that they must constantly be on their guard against the enemy. Third, mechanisms built into the orientation make their image partially immune to counterevidence or refuting experience. Also, their behavior, determined by their image of the enemy, is likely to produce reactions from their opponents which will make them feel that the image is true.

CHANGING A HOSTILE ORIENTATION

How can we change such a self-perpetuating, hostile orientation? Obviously, it is a difficult task and, with our present level of knowledge, success is by no means certain. Nevertheless we must try. Drawing on analogies from psychotherapeutic experience, I suggest that there are four critical tasks involved in producing such a change.

First of all, there must be some motivation to change—the gains the Communists derive from a hostile orientation must not be so great as to outweigh the anxieties and difficulties engendered by the present situation.

Second, they must be made aware that the experienced anxieties and difficulties are causally connected with their competitive, hostile orientation.

Third, the current environment must not provide substantial justification and support for the continued maintenance of the defensive, hostile orientation appropriate in the past: new experiences, convincingly different from their past experiences, must indicate a genuine interest in their well-being.

Fourth, they must perceive that they will gain rather than suffer, have less anxiety rather than more, if they adopt a new orientation.

I do not list these tasks in order of importance or priority. They are all necessary and they must all be worked on if change is to occur.

The Motivation to Change

There is some evidence that progress on the first task—motivation to change—has been made. The leaders of both the Soviet Union and the United States are, I believe, deeply anxious about the present world situation; neither group believes that a competitive victory is possible through war. The new doctrine of peaceful coexistence consistently and repeatedly espoused by Khrushchev, despite bitter internal opposition, is a sign of this. Similar statements by Kennedy and Eisenhower, including their denunciations of right-wing extremists, can also be viewed as evidence that our leaders realize that nuclear weapons no longer permit victory through war. The existence of H-bombs is thus, in a perverse way, a force for change. Moreover, the economic burden of ever-increasing armaments, the increasing pressure from neutral nations who feel threatened by the arms race, and the increasing discontent with the arms race within the populations of the superpowers also work in the direction of change.

What are the gains from a competitive, hostile orientation? They are of two types—internal and external. Ample evidence suggests that a hostile, competitive orientation to the outside world fosters internal cohesiveness and permits Soviet leaders to justify and exert repressive controls to inhibit internal dissidence and challenge to their leadership. On the other hand, there is considerable reason to think that the present Soviet leaders believe that many internal stresses and strains are the indirect effects of the enormous costs of the arms race and that, without these costs, they could rapidly improve the lot of the Soviet people and could afford to lessen these repressive controls. Moreover, the process of de-Stalinization, initiated by the present leaders of the Soviet Union, indicates their realization that repressive controls have serious limitations as a means of motivating enthusiastic support for the goals set forth by the Communist party. In addition, the denunciation of Stalin and his paranoid despotism constitutes a repudiation of some aspects of the Soviet Union's past. In effect, the present leaders have attempted to dissociate themselves from the irrational suspiciousness and the brutal, homicidal acts connected with Stalin. In so doing, they have made it more difficult to reinstitute such despotic policies. Internally, almost all observers agree, the

Soviet people have responded gratefully to the lessening of suspiciousness and tyranny.

Externally, it is apparent that the Soviet Union has made some gains by a competitive, hostile orientation to the West. It has gained political and economic influence in underdeveloped areas by being hostile to the remnants of Western imperialism. However, to the extent that we become more active in helping the peoples in these areas to achieve independence, freedom, and a higher standard of living, and to the extent that we free ourselves of racial prejudice, the Soviet Union will have little to gain from hostility per se to the West. The revolutionary changes which are sweeping through Africa and Asia and which are beginning to be felt in Latin America were not instigated by Communism and cannot be controlled by Soviet military power.[f] Moreover, there is already some indication that the Soviet Union's criticisms of the West are not, in themselves, the Open Sesame to the affections of the newly emerged nations of Africa and Asia.

In effect, the Soviet Union is now being faced with the task of offering something positive—something more than the financial aid, technical assistance, and so on being offered by the West—if it wishes to compete for influence among the new nations. It has already entered this competition and has begun to find that it is an expensive competition with no easy and quick gains for the Communist bloc.

Another manifestion of change concerns Soviet military power which has, of course, been used to maintain control over Eastern Europe. A widely held view is that the Soviets will use their military power to gain political control whenever they can get away with it. This conception presupposes that political and economic imperialism would be viewed as a profitable course of action by the Soviet leaders even in a world where they perceived no military threats to their national security. Or, in other words, that the Soviet leaders would force a nonthreatening, non-Communist nation to become Communist and subservient if they could not convert it to their viewpoint. There is, of course, some evidence to support this view—consider only Czechoslovakia and Hungary. However, there is another side to this picture. Despite its military power, the Soviet Union has discovered that it cannot simply impose its will on other Communist nations to obtain unquestioning obedience to orders from Moscow. There is a growing diversity and independence of decision within the Communist group of nations. Yugoslavia, Poland, Rumania, China, and Albania diverge in different respects from Soviet doctrine.

---

[f] Our military power vis-à-vis most of these areas is considerably greater than that which the Soviet Union can bring to bear. Our tendency to view the Communist threat primarily in military terms has led us to give arms to backward, unpopular governments, enabling the Communists to identify us with reactionary military cliques while they attempt to identify themselves with popular unrest and the groups advocating progressive social change. It is encouraging that the Alliance for Progress places emphasis upon the need to identify with popular aspirations for social reform rather than upon military aid.

The changes that have taken place within the Communist world reflect a growing relativism in the Communist ideology and may contribute to an erosion of the rigidity of the Bolshevik doctrine. The image of a utopian world Communism has been tarnished by the reality of conflict and diversity within the Communist bloc; the changing image may yet suggest that diversity among nations cannot be abolished by power or by superficial ideological similarity. This realization may weaken the readiness to run risks and to make sacrifices to establish a Communist domination over the world.

However, the erosion of the ideological base for militant Communist expansion has not yet proceeded far enough to warrant a lack of concern about the aggressive potentials of Soviet military power. The fact that Soviet military power has been used to establish and maintain unpopular Communist governments in Eastern Europe suggests that prudence requires the West to develop and maintain military forces sufficient to insure that the Soviet leaders fully understand that military aggression, or the threat of it, will be unrewarding to them. We have to press for agreements that would end the arms race, that would stabilize and reduce the military forces of both sides, and that would eliminate military elements from areas of intense international conflict (Central Europe, Southeast Asia, Middle East).[g]

Similarly, we must be prepared to deter subversion and indirect aggression against ourselves and other independent nations so that these courses of "unfair competition" become unrewarding to the Communists. We do not want to tempt them by indifference and lack of response to violations of civilized standards of international conduct. On the other hand, we do not wish to justify illegal behavior by emulating it. Nor can we reasonably assert the right to use military force (such as extensive military aid and the intervention of American troops) to support unpopular dictators who are threatened by internal revolutionary movements led by Communists. Since we cannot allow the Communists to claim the moral right to overthrow non-Communist nations, we cannot claim the moral right to preserve the status quo simply because it favors us.

Increasing Their Awareness of the Effects of Their Behavior

If my analysis is correct, the Soviet Union has made important internal and external gains from a competitive, hostile orientation to the West. But these gains have diminished considerably and are being overshadowed by the

[g] We should, of course, seek reasonable verification of compliance. However, since the Soviet leaders apparently view secrecy as necessary for their internal security, we should anticipate little immediate progress in obtaining agreements that require the Soviet Union to "open up" its society to external inspection. This is particularly likely to be the case when the agreement offers them no major economic saving. We may be more successful in obtaining disarmament agreements if we concentrate on agreements that do not require open access to Soviet territory by human inspectors—i.e., on agreements that can be monitored by nonhuman sensors or on agreements relating to areas outside of both the U.S. and U.S.S.R. which are potential areas of military conflict.

anxieties and difficulties associated with the arms race. However, I do not believe they are yet sufficiently aware that the arms race is partly stimulated by our reaction to their orientation toward us. They, of course, see the causal arrow pointed in the opposite direction—*their* attitude is determined by our hostile, threatening orientation to them. I doubt that the Soviet leaders are sensitive to how we react when they say, "We will outlive you" or "Your grandchildren will live under Communism." I doubt that they are aware that their own actions and words lead us to react in such a way that their view of a hostile world is confirmed.

How we can help the Russians to become aware of the relationship between their actions and our reactions is a difficult problem for which I have no pat solution. Obviously, encouraging more and more of their leaders to visit the United States and to talk informally with congressmen, administration officials, businessmen, and others, may enable them to realize that many of our most influential citizens do, in fact, perceive our orientation as defensive and determined by their hostile, threatening orientation. We should encourage these visits whether or not they are willing to reciprocate. Philip Moseley[4] has pointed out, "In comparing the 1931 level of [Soviet] knowledge about the West with the level of 1961, I have to say that the 1961 level is about two percent of the 1931 level." We must change this horrifying situation by providing their leaders with as many opportunities as we can for informing themselves about us. (I place stress on "leaders" because one may suspect that their subordinates here in the United States tend, as do most subordinates, to frame their communications in ways which do not challenge the prejudices and stereotypes of their superiors.)

In addition to fostering frequent contacts among leaders, we should attempt to institutionalize a direct process of communicating accurate interpretations of the actions and utterances of each side. We should have some regularized way of holding up a mirror to the Soviet leaders so they can see how they look to us when they act in a certain way, and vice versa. Possibly, alternating every other month, the President might give a talk to and expose himself to questions from the Politburo, and the Soviet Premier might do the same for leading officials in our government. There is no doubt that the technical problems of arranging direct but restricted communication from nation to nation could be solved. I suggest that the communication be restricted to the leaders rather than made available to the public in order to reduce the temptation to propagandize. However, neither side is sufficiently disinterested and free of manipulative desires to be able to portray without bias their image of the other.[h] It may well be that we each need a neutral mirror to interpret

---

[h] Thus, for example, if American leaders interpret Khrushchev's statement headlined as "We will bury you" to mean "We will destroy you" rather than "We will outlive you," the misinterpretation may be a deliberate distortion to make the statement seem more hostile than it was. In Russian, Khrushchev's statement implied that American capitalism would die because of its comparative inefficiency while socialism would continue to flourish.

communications so that they are unlikely to be misinterpreted by either side. It would not, I imagine, be impossible to set up a group of competent statesmen and social scientists from neutral nations which might perform such a function. The record of each side in predicting the reactions of the other side is pitifully poor and suggests the need for some such procedure.

Providing New Experiences to Facilitate Change

While increased social and self-insight is helpful in bringing about change, the most important strategy in inducing it is to act and react in a way which is inconsistent with the other's expectations. One should, of course, anticipate that when this is done the other will be disconcerted and will attempt, initially, to provoke reactions which will justify his original expectations. The great difficulty in executing this strategy is in resisting the trap of being provoked to actions which will confirm his expectations. Thus, if we wish to change a hostile orientation, we must see to it that the current environment does not provide justification and support for its continued maintenance. The Communists must have new experiences with us which are convincingly different from their past experiences—new experiences which, on the one hand, indicate that we have a genuine interest in their well-being and which, on the other hand, indicate self-respect and an unwillingness to be abused.

In the paper "A Psychological Basis for Peace,"[5] I have attempted to spell out some of the policies and actions we might adopt that might lead the Soviet Union to change its orientation. These policies include giving up the quest for military supremacy, establishing continuing joint military and technical groups to lessen the dangers of war and to work for disarmament, showing an active concern with what the Russians regard as important, accepting the viability and legitimacy of their system for them, conforming to the standards of international conduct we wish them to conform to, developing a genuine interest in their internal successes rather than failures, expressing in action and words our desire for a rapid improvement in their standard of living, recognizing and honoring their achievements, welcoming whatever assistance they may be able to give us, expanding mutual trade, fostering cultural and educational exchanges, establishing co-operative programs of research and advanced studies, and institutionalizing international competitive contests in diverse fields to encourage peaceful competition for international prestige.

Perceiving Gains from a New Orientation

In sum, I suggest that a policy which combines *both* firmness and friendliness, a policy of *friendly strength*. This is the surest way of helping the Russians to perceive the gains they can achieve by a change in orientation. We should attempt to establish an international atmosphere amicable enough to permit nations with diverse internal systems to engage in mutually rewarding, co-operative endeavors.

To create such an atmosphere, we shall have to launch a *sustained* program of *massive reconciliation* in which we try to express and maintain a willingness to co-operate with the Soviet Union when it is to our mutual advantage. We should not expect that our offers of co-operation will be received with gratitude, or will be reciprocated fully, or will be frequently accepted. Even so, we should persist in offering to co-operate whenever we see opportunities which will profit *both* sides. Our underlying attitude must be sufficiently self-confident so that we do not feel threatened by the fact that they, as well as we, will profit from co-operation, or by the possibility that, because of our greater affluence, they may on occasion profit relatively more than we.

Obviously, the Communists will have no incentive to co-operate unless they stand to gain rather than to suffer, unless they become more secure rather than less, as a result of co-operation. It is, of course, these very gains from co-operation which will create a web of interdependencies that give each side a positive interest in the other's well-being. However, Russia's legacy of sustained suspicion is such that it will take continuing good will, sustained offers of genuine co-operation, and a persistent readiness to accept their offers of reasonable co-operation on our part, before their underlying image of a competitive struggle for survival is replaced by a sense of interlaced common interests.

CHANGING OURSELVES

Here, let me turn briefly to the question of how we can influence ourselves to sustain a policy of massive reconciliation. In other words, how can we change our own hostile orientation to the Soviet Union, especially since their actions often provide a justification for our orientation? This is an extraordinarily difficult question and most of us evade it. Many of those trying to change Russia's orientation do not face up to the social and political functions which it serves. The analysis I have sketched above might be politically disastrous unless there were a concurrent change in the American orientation.

Roots of American Defensiveness

In examining the question I have raised, I suggest that we must begin to understand the roots of our own defensiveness. I use the term "defensiveness" to indicate that our conception of the Communists is determined, not only by what they are actually like, but also by our own internally generated needs and anxieties. I would suggest that we must confront three major internal problems, three roots of our defensiveness, before we can lose our obsession with Communism.

First, historically, the United States has been able to have things pretty much its own way. Prior to World War I, our geographical isolation permitted this. After World War I, and especially right after World War II, we were the strongest power on earth. We were not able to remain isolated nor are we likely to remain the supreme power. The future suggests that we will have to accommodate ourselves to the fact that we will be a strong power among other equally strong powers in a highly interdependent world. In a sense, we have to adjust ourselves to a loss of unique power, to a loss of unique status. Loss of status for a proud people is always difficult to accept. We must investigate previous historical examples of such loss—for example, England—to learn as much as we can about coping with this difficult national situation.

A second root of defensiveness lies in the careers, skills, special privileges, jobs, and financial interests which have been developed in relation to a hostile world. These vested interests will naturally feel threatened by a change in our orientation unless they are given the strongest assurance that they will not lose by such a change. I suggest that the president urge Congress to adopt, as as a declaration of national policy, a statement to the effect that scientists, the military, employers, industrialists, and investors will be compensated for any losses they suffer as a result of the curtailment of defense activities. This statement must, of course, be buttressed by the development of meaningful and detailed plans, at the local as well as the national level, for enabling the people and industries involved in defense to play a significant and profitable role in a peaceful world.

A third root of defensiveness lies in a lack of confidence in ourselves—a lack of confidence in our ability to maintain a thriving, prosperous, and attractive society that can be morally and intellectually influential among nations without a preponderance of military power. Obviously, we must work to overcome our problems of racial prejudice, economic instability, and lack of dedication to common purposes. To the extent that we have a thriving society coping successfully with its own internal problems, we will have less ground for the fears and less need for the hostilities that interfere with international co-operation. Unless we can make democracy work in Mississippi, what reason is there for believing that we can influence the underdeveloped nations to adopt the social reforms and political practices necessary to prevent international turmoil and strife?

Speaking to Both Audiences Simultaneously

My discussion has emphasized the fact that our own defensiveness may make it difficult for us to adopt an orientation toward the Soviet bloc which might lead to the end of the Cold War. Any change will require vigorous political effort by the diverse groups who see the present state of international relations as perilous. In addition, it may require pressure from friendly, influential nations (for example, in Europe and in South America) who are not as obsessed as we with the nightmare of Communism. However, not all courses of constructive international action are likely to provoke equal amounts of defensiveness. It may well be that our most important intellectual task is to uncover courses of action which will be reassuring to the Communists and which will challenge our own defenses least. The problem is to define programs of action sufficiently close to our own national identity which still deal positively with the Communist world. These actions must serve constructive functions for both the internal and external audiences, each of whom is highly defensive.

How do we convince both audiences[1] that their fears are unwarranted? The answer to this dilemma lies, I believe, in the policy of *friendly strength* which I have described above. Both audiences must be persuaded that the military strength of either side cannot overcome the other and that the resort to military force will be mutually destructive. Public statements of our own military capability should always be accompanied by clear recognition of Soviet military strength. Expression of our own determination to resist military aggression should be coupled with acknowledgment of the Soviet determination to do the same.

Explicit recognition of mutual military power (and, hence, of the impotence of military power to resolve conflicts of interest) should be accompanied by open recognition that the internal achievements of the two societies will not affect the ultimate military balance of power. On the contrary, our public statements to both audiences should demonstrate an awareness that internal difficulties and failures make a nation with nuclear arms more rather than less dangerous. Neither we nor the Soviet Union have any reason to gloat if internal problems or external loss of face strengthen the primitive, repressive, and belligerent elements in the other nation. We would do well to affirm repeatedly our real interest in a prosperous and thriving world, in which all nations (including those in the Communist bloc) are coping successfully with their internal economic, social, and political problems.

The promotion of the positive goal of a peaceful world, composed of thriving, independent, and co-operating nations, rather than the negative goal of containing Communism, provides a potential meeting ground for both audiences and a potential avenue for co-operation. Undoubtedly, the "meeting" will initially be on the safest grounds (for example, the adoption in the United States of ingenious Soviet-developed surgical staplers which join severed blood vessels and nerves, or the widespread use of American-developed polio vaccines in the Soviet Union). When there has been a successful encounter, however, it should be given the widest public recognition.

Even when the grounds for co-operation are least secure, when there is reason to believe that the other side is seeking to obtain a competitive advantage—for example, in attempting to use the vulnerabilities of underdeveloped nations to spread anti-American Communism—there is nothing to

---

[1] There are, of course, more than two audiences. One has to consider one's allies, the uncommitted nations, and so forth. However, if one can speak constructively to both the Soviet and American power-holders, it seems likely that the difficulties with other audiences can be surmounted.

be lost by proclaiming and pursuing a positive goal which is not oriented to, or determined by, the Cold War. On the contrary, a policy of aiding under-developed nations which is oriented to their need for prosperity and in-dependence rather than our fear of Communism is more likely to produce attitudes favorable toward us. Such a policy is not only likely to be more effective in preventing the spread of anti-American Communism but, in ad-dition, it leaves open the continuing possibility of co-operation with the Communists to achieve the mutually acceptable objectives of reducing poverty and instability among nations.

More generally, one can state that the reduction of international tension requires that the leaders of the United States and Soviet Union be constantly aware that their words and actions have implications for the two audiences. Neither audience is likely to attribute evil intentions to itself nor altruistic motives to the other, nor are they likely to accept a position of military inferiority. Statements or deeds which rest on the claim of moral superiority or of superior power can only incense the external audience, even though they may please the internal audience. On the other hand, the announcement and pursuit of positive goals which can contribute to the welfare of both sides, and to which both may contribute, enhance the possibility that co-operation will occur sooner or later.

For purposes of discussion, throughout this paper I have accepted the widely held assumption that the Soviet Union can be viewed as an un-principled adversary. A Soviet reader, if he felt this were a more apt char-acterization of the United States, might apply the reasoning in this paper to the problem of changing the United States.

NOTES

1. From Samuel Lubell (well-known public-opinion expert), "Internal Divisions on Dis-armament in the U.S.," unpublished paper.
2. See, for instance, Philip E. Moseley, "The Soviet Challenge," paper given at the Institute for World Affairs Education, University of Wisconsin, summer 1961.
3. I draw the following description largely from Nathan Leites, *A Study of Bolshevism* (Glencoe, Ill.: The Free Press, 1953). Leites's description is, I believe, an excellent depiction of the official American view of the Soviet orientation; it may not be an accurate view of the actual orientation of the leaders of post-Stalin Russia. My own view is that the characterization of only one of the parties in a two-sided conflict, without characterization of the interaction between them, tends to be misleading. It is somewhat like knowing that a wife condemns her husband to neighbors, opens his mail, takes money from his wallet, and does other nasty things. Knowing this about the wife may be misleading unless one also knows whether the husband is a habitual drunkard and adulterer or a generous and reasonable man.
4. Moseley, *loc. cit.*
5. In Quincy Wright, William M. Evan, and Morton Deutsch, eds., *Preventing World War III: Some Proposals* (New York: Simon & Schuster, 1962).

9

URIE BRONFENBRENNER

Allowing for Soviet Perceptions

". . . [S]ince wars begin in the minds of men, it is in the minds of men that the defences of peace must be constructed." So reads the preamble to the charter for UNESCO to which both the United States and the Soviet Union are signatories. It is a sobering fact that among the millions being spent today for research on national security, almost nothing is being expended on systematic studies of what goes on in the minds of the Russians, their perceptions, fears, yearnings, and modes of thought.

Under such circumstances, even a crude assessment, limited by imperfect data and methods, can serve a useful purpose, if only to call attention to the kinds of results that might be obtained and the importance of their implications. Such is the nature and the aim of this paper. It draws on field observations, made in the course of recent visits to the U.S.S.R., in order to shed some light, however dim, on the Soviet image of American acts and intentions and on the motives and modes of thought most influential in producing that image. Such perceptions and predispositions are of the utmost importance. What influences Soviet policy toward war or peace is not our acts and intentions as we know them but as they appear in Soviet eyes.

METHOD

Before turning to substantive matters, a few words are in order about the technique employed for obtaining the data. On the surface, the procedure seems hardly worthy of being dignified as a "method," since it consisted simply of conversations with Soviet citizens. Nevertheless, the conversations did involve some special features which distinguish them from the typical discussions engaged in by Westerners in the U.S.S.R. These features differed somewhat in each of two visits I have made during the past few years.[a]

Open-ended Conversations

During the first visit, which occurred in May and June of 1960, the following practices were followed:

(1) Traveling alone without a guide;

(2) Wherever possible, departing from the Intourist trek; for example, eating in public restaurants instead of the large hotels, going about on foot or using public transportation, going to parks, places of recreation and other locales frequented by the general public;

(3) Taking the initiative in striking up conversations rather than waiting for others to do so;

(4) Insofar as possible, choosing persons to talk with at random (for example, before going into an eating place, deciding in advance to sit at the third table on the right with whomever should be there);

(5) Beginning a conversation with open-ended leads rather than with pointed questions or positions;

(6) Presenting myself in the role of interpreter between East and West rather than as a militant proponent of the American view or as a Soviet sympathizer;

(7) Not taking notes in the presence of the informant;

(8) Keeping a record of informant's age, occupation, ethnic origins, and so on, for subsequent analysis;

(9) Using feedback to verify my perceptions (namely, asking my Soviet companion to listen to a restatement of his views and correct any omissions or distortions).

A Pseudo-Experiment

During the second visit, which took place in November and December of 1961, the open-ended conversations were supplemented by procedures intended to maximize, as far as possible, conditions favorable to communication. The procedures, worked out with a group of social science colleagues at Cornell[1] following the first visit, are derived primarily from recent theory and research on social perception and communication. The underlying prin-

---

[a] After writing this paper, the author made a third visit to the U.S.S.R., this time as an exchange scientist for a period of three months. Although no systematic observations were made on this occasion, the general impression gained during this longer sojourn lend further support to the evidence and interpretation here presented.

ciple can be stated succinctly as follows: Effective communication is most likely to occur if carried out in a context in which there has been prior recognition and, where possible, acceptance of some values cherished by the other party. Concrete examples of how this principle might be applied to improve our communications with the Russians (without compromising our own values) are provided in the report cited.

Although originally developed for the Soviet case, the approach is presumed to have general validity. Accordingly, we undertook to pretest it first in the reverse direction—that is, in communicating with Americans about the Soviet Union. One of the specific techniques employed was the presentation of extended excerpts from the conversations collected during my earlier visit. Since these conversations typically involved a dialogue between an American and a Russian, the dissonant Soviet view was systematically balanced and offset by statements of the American position.[2]

This technique was used exactly in reverse during my second visit to the Soviet Union. I presented to the Russians excerpts from my conversations with Americans in which I had attempted to communicate the Soviet view, and my fellow countrymen had of course responded with statements of our own position and with counterargument. Actually, the sets of conversations used in the two countries were strikingly comparable, since, as has been documented elsewhere,[3] Soviet and American perceptions of each other are in many respects mirror images.

Use of similar materials in the two cultural settings made it possible to compare Soviet and American responses to analogous stimuli and to gauge the extent to which each group could be made to understand and accept dissonant information about the other.

The Sample

Over the course of the two visits, extended conversations were conducted with approximately one hundred Soviet citizens in different walks of life, including unskilled laborers, clerks and technicians, factory managers, scientists, and party workers at the city, *oblast,* and republic level. Despite the effort to interview a random group, the sample was of course biased. Proportionate to the total Soviet population, there was an over-representation of urban residents, scientists, students, and those most likely to have contact with the visitor from the West—Intourist personnel, other travelers, speculators and the disaffected.

SOVIET PERCEPTIONS OF WESTERN INTENTIONS

The open-ended interviews and structured stimuli yielded a wide range of data about Soviet perceptions and motives affecting the Russians' image of the United States. We shall first examine certain generalized attitudes bearing most directly on the issue.

Russian Fears of Western Attack

Such fears were the most salient and recurring feature of the Soviet conversations. Several lines of evidence point to the conclusion that they represented no mere perfunctory parroting of a propaganda line, but were genuine, intense, and virtually universal. First, the signs of fear were evident not only in what people said but in the way they said it—in physiological reactions, voice quality, deterioration of speech pattern of the type associated with high levels of anxiety, and so forth.

Second, the expectation of Western aggression was evident even among the relatively few Russians who voiced criticism of the regime. Without exception, all of them expressed the fear that the United States, spurred on by West Germany, would attack the Soviet Union.

It is important to recognize that, incredible as it may seem to us, the evidence for Western aggressiveness appears from the Soviet point of view consistent, continuing, and overwhelming. To Russians it is as plain and incontrovertible as Soviet aggression is to us. The major elements in the pattern include Allied intervention in 1918–20, the subsequent hostility of the outside world toward Communist Russia, the failure of collective security in the thirties, the horrible fulfillment of Soviet fears of attack from the West represented by the German invasion, the establishment of NATO, encirclement by Western bases, and the rearmament of West Germany. They see recent signs of our renewed aggressive intent in the U2 incident; the Cuban affair; the arms build-up under the Kennedy administration; the Supreme Court's decision against the American Communist party, which was disillusioning and apparently quite disturbing to many Soviet citizens; public statements by such leading American scientists as Teller and Libby, such congressmen as Senators Goldwater and Dodd, and by members of the Birch Society, whose license to speak is interpreted by the Russians as evidence of tacit government support; warlike pronouncements in the press —for example, articles from the *Army and Navy Journal* and *Time*'s map showing arrows from Polaris locations to Moscow, Leningrad, and other large Soviet population centers; and of course, most recently, our emphasis on inspection. To the Russians, an intent on our part to carry out espionage seems obvious and inevitable. As a deputy to the first secretary of an *oblast* in the virgin lands explained it, "First you tried to fool us with your 'open skies' policy. When we wouldn't be taken in, you did your spying anyway with U2. Now that we've put an end to that, you need a new entry. So you try to trick us again the way the Germans did before World War II. They too deceived us into agreements so that they could wander about our country, spy out our defenses, and prepare their attack."

The Threat of West Germany

The last remark illustrates the saliency of West Germany in Soviet fears. It is here that Soviet perceptions depart furthest from objective reality. The belief that West Germany is dominated by Nazi elements and, in turn, controls Western policy is widespread. There is the conviction that Americans are deliberately encouraging the resurgence of German militarism and are using West Germany as a base for anti-Soviet activities of espionage and subversion.

The "Incredibility" of Deterrence

Perhaps the most disturbing aspect of the Russian image of the West revealed in the conversations was the Soviet failure to "get the message" intended by the strategy of deterrence to which our present policy is committed. It is not that the Russians fail to understand that we will retaliate if attacked. This they readily, and spontaneously, acknowledge. What is not getting across is the crucial part of the message: that we would never attack without provocation. When I tried to explain to Soviet citizens our purpose in shifting to "hard" and mobile missiles located away from centers of population, there were two common reactions. The first and less intense was to see the strategy as a ruse: "It is all part of a trick to get us off our guard while you secretly prepare for attack. Besides, you don't really mean it, because if you did, you wouldn't be doing all those other things." And once again the speaker would inundate me with talk of U2, Kennedy's arms build-up, and militant statements by leading figures in America and West Germany.

The second reaction to my explanations was both more common and more violent: "How can you even think this way! It is monstrous and inhuman to be so cold and calculating. You Americans just do not understand the horror, death, and destruction of modern war on your own soil. To talk of such a strategy as a way to peace is sheer madness." In short, it is not that our strategy of deterrence was noncredible; it was simply incredible.

A similar response of reluctance even to discuss the subject was elicited when I sought to explain to more sophisticated Russians, such as scientists or members of peace study groups, the kind of research that was being done in the United States on arms control and related problems: for example, game theory, simulation techniques, and probability sampling for zonal inspection. The reaction was almost one of shock. It was as if applying such technologies to peace were to profane holy ground.

IMPLICATIONS OF SOVIET PERCEPTIONS OF THE WEST

Before turning to still other Soviet orientations, it is important to examine possible limitations and implications of our material on Russian attitudes toward the West.

The "Reality" of Perception

In presenting Soviet views of the outside world, I am of course not imply-
ing that they are valid in the sense of being in accord with objective facts.
Nevertheless, they are valid at another level. In the words of one of the
pioneers of American social psychology, W. I. Thomas, "Situations defined
as real are real in their consequences." Thus the Russians are likely to act in
accordance with their picture of the world, even though that picture may be
grossly distorted. Because of this psychological fact, if we are to be realistic
ourselves, we must treat Russian perceptions as if they were real and consider
their implications for Western strategy.

Communist Leadership versus the Russian People

Granting that the rank and file of Soviet citizenry have irrational expectations of impending aggression from the West, can we really conclude that
similarly distorted perceptions and fears animate the Soviet leaders? After all,
for the Russian people at large, the fears are fed by government-inspired
propaganda. The leaders know this and, in addition, have other sources of
information, including first-hand experience with Westerners both within and
outside the U.S.S.R. Are their views as unrealistic as those of the general
population?

The data available to me permit no definitive answer to this question. Unfortunately neither Comrade Khrushchev nor any other member of the Central
Committee turned up in my random sample. Nevertheless some indirect evidence may be relevant.

First, studies of other modern societies typically show substantial continuity in the views of the outside world held by the leadership and by the
population at large. This relationship is enhanced by the tendency of the
leaders to believe their own propaganda.

Second, most of the men who are today leaders of the Soviet state held
positions of responsibility immediately prior to and during World War II.
They were exposed, perhaps even more than the average Russian, to the full
impact of the deceit, destruction, and death wrought by the aggressor from
the West. Such an experience is likely to increase rather than diminish susceptibility to irrational expectations of treachery and sudden attack.

Finally, although I met none of the Communist inner circle, some of my
informants were not far removed from this group. On one occasion, after
listening to a lengthy exposition from a fellow passenger, I commented that
I had heard many ordinary Russians speak along similar lines but wondered
about the rulers of the country, high-ranking members of the party; did they
feel the same way? "Well," my companion replied, a smile on his lips, "after
this hour's conversation you are in a position to judge for yourself." He
then explained that he was a member of the Supreme Soviet in his own

republic and assured me that similar views were held by members of the Central Committee of the All-Union Communist Party.

The Importance of Context

If the Soviet leaders do share with their people an irrational fear of Western treachery and attack, what are the implications for American strategy on arms control and prevention of war?

We must recognize at the start that any Western proposals will take their meaning for the Russians from this larger perceptual context. So long as the context remains unchanged, the likelihood is that any specific proposal will be viewed in such a way as to confirm the established image of American deceitfulness and aggressive intent.

It is important to recognize that the forces driving the Russians to invidious interpretation are of the most powerful kind. They derive not only from historical and political factors, but from compelling psychological factors as well. Over the past ten years, a substantial body of research has accumulated in the behavioral sciences, demonstrating that human beings exhibit a strong tendency to maintain consistency in their perceptions, particularly when these perceptions are shared by their fellows. New events are apprehended in such a way as to be compatible with previous experience and expectation. The tendency is so powerful that facts which, on objective grounds, seem incapable of any but a contradictory interpretation are reorganized so as to maintain consistency.

Soviet citizens and their leaders are certainly as susceptible to this mechanism as any other group. Indeed, as we shall show later, there are grounds for supposing that they may be especially vulnerable. In any event, with specific regard to American arms control proposals to date, the Russians have for several reasons found it very easy to perceive confirmation for their worst expectations. First, as we have already noted, prior experience seems to them unequivocal and compelling. Second, we give virtually no thought to the larger context of action by the United States and the West which may precede or accompany the presentation of the proposal. Third, we typically do little to "immunize" the proposal itself against invidious interpretations in line with Soviet expectations. And once the Russians see the meaning of our proposal in their terms (for example, inspection equals espionage), it becomes part of the cumulating evidence confirming American treachery and aggressive intent.

The preceding considerations lead to an important operating principle: *Any concrete proposals we wish to make must be prepared for by prior and simultaneous actions in other spheres which enhance the likelihood that the particular proposal will be seen in a new and less threatening context. In addition, the proposal itself must, insofar as possible, be "immunized" against invidious interpretations.*

The Problem of Seeing through Soviet Eyes

Paradoxically, if American strategists were to take the unlikely step of adopting the foregoing principle and seeking to apply it, the results would probably be ineffectual, if not disastrous. Soviet behavior is determined by Soviet perceptions, Soviet fears, and Soviet modes of thought. Any attempt to predict how the Russians would react which is based solely on considerations of strategy, deductive reasoning, and the assumption (usually unrecognized) that Soviet thought processes are similar to our own, is doomed to miss the mark. Given our necessarily limited perspective, we cannot arrive at an appreciation of the springs of Soviet action solely through the power of logical analysis, no matter how rigorous, or of creative imagination, no matter how ingenious. As the essential starting point for our estimates, we need first to obtain and analyze data which can instruct us about the nature of Soviet perceptions, motives, and fears. Moreover, if the assumption of continuity in cultural attitudes has any validity whatsoever, we need not wait until we can install wire taps in the Kremlin or get Khrushchev on the psychoanalytic couch in order to have relevant information.

The following are two examples from the range of investigations which could be carried out.

(1) *Analysis of Soviet writings on disarmament*—Soviet reactions to American proposals for arms control appear in Soviet newspapers and specialized journals. Such reactions include reviews of Western books and articles on the subject, as well as Russian translations from these, in part or in full. These materials need to be analyzed systematically, not from the point of view of military or political strategy, but for what they reveal of Soviet motives, needs, and tendencies to distorted perception. Particularly instructive in this connection is the choice of material presented, omissions in a translated text, and so on. The technology for carrying out analyses of this kind already exists.

(2) *Study of the Soviet image of German behavior*—If it is correct that Soviet views of the West become most distorted when associations with Nazi treachery and invasion are aroused, it is important to avoid any explicit or chance similarity to past Nazi practices. This, in turn, requires that we become familiar with the nature of German activities with regard to the U.S.S.R., especially in the period of the Nazi-Soviet pact and, of course, during the invasion itself. Such studies should focus major attention on Russian sources, since they provide the basis for current Soviet attitudes.

What Follows from Fear?

Implicit in the preceding analysis is the assumption that development of strong Soviet fears of the West decreases the possibility of agreement on measures for arms control and, more generally, constitutes a danger to the security of the United States. But a contrary view exists. There are those who maintain, for example, that it is precisely fear of the West which convinces the Russians of the necessity of arms control. The more ominous the danger, the more likely they are to realize the necessity of coming to terms. Indeed, the strategy of deterrence, on which our whole policy is based, relies on fear as the inhibiting force to Soviet aggression. If we allay Soviet fears in the interests of increasing Soviet receptivity to proposals for arms control, we may at the same time be undermining the major barrier to Communist expansion.

This line of reasoning also rests on certain assumptions, and it is useful to make these explicit. First is the expectation that an American build-up of arms will lead the Russians to fear American military might. As we have seen, this expectation appears to be fully justified.

Second is the assumption that if we shift to hard and mobile missiles, move rocket sites away from cities, and explain what we are doing, the Russians will be convinced by such action that we would never attack unless provoked. Hence, the only thing they have to fear is their own aggressive initiative. But if we are correct in expecting some continuity between the perceptions of the Soviet people and their leaders, the evidence cited above raises a question about the validity of the preceding assumption. This is especially true so long as a substantial portion of the other "messages" coming from the West to the Soviet Union communicate quite a different intent.

Third is the assumption that, as the United States becomes objectively stronger than the Soviet Union, the latter will feel weaker and more vulnerable; hence will become more tractable and less likely to initiate aggression.

Finally, implicit in the entire argument is the assumption that the Soviet Union will appraise its own situation rationally and will adopt the course of action indicated by logical analysis of the strategic considerations involved.

The last two assumptions go beyond Russia's image of the United States; they deal with the Soviet Union's conception of itself and with the manner in which Soviet society is likely to respond to situations of threat and conflict. We turn next to a consideration of these topics in light of such evidence as is available from my Soviet conversations.

THE SOVIET SELF-IMAGE

Next to fear of the West, the most salient feature of the conversations was the Russians' preoccupation with their own national image. This preoccupation manifested itself in a number of ways: in expressions of Soviet righteousness in international affairs, invincibility, pride, and extreme sensitivity.

The Russians' View of Soviet Aggression

Perhaps the remarks of Soviet citizens most dissonant to Western ears are those relating to what we regard as flagrant examples of Communist aggression. With only a few exceptions, the Russians with whom I spoke appeared to view with genuine approval the actions taken by their rulers in Czechoslavakia, Poland, Germany, Hungary, and elsewhere around the globe. Specifically, they saw their government as having given deserved assistance to forces of progress and due warning and rebuff to impending aggressive moves by the West. A case in point was the reaction of Soviet citizens to Russian resumption of nuclear testing, which had occurred only a few weeks before my 1961 visit. While acknowledging the dangers of escalation and fall-out, all the Russians with whom I spoke uniformly approved Khrushchev's decision. They believed it had been forced by what they viewed as signs of increasing American belligerence and preparation for a first strike.

The Conviction of Invincibility

Paradoxically, in the same breath with statements of their fear of attack from the West and the horrors of war, Russians would cock their heads and speak defiantly of ultimate victory. I recall two ballad singers performing in a public square. The first song was "Do the Russians Want War?" ("Ask my mother, ask my wife"). Then, directly after, came a melody in martial beat ending: "But if imperialists come in, look out! Our habit is to win!" The audience shook their heads earnestly to the first song and nodded proudly to the second. I pressed one Soviet citizen for the basis of such convictions. His reply: "We shall beat you, not because we are superior militarily, not because we have a sounder economy, but because we are stronger morally."

Soviet Pride and Sensitivity

Coupled with a sense of national righteousness and invincibility was an inordinate pride in Soviet achievements in all spheres—educational, economic, scientific, artistic, and social. People were constantly pointing out, not only to the foreigner but to each other (especially to children), that this or that was first, newest, largest, or best. At the same time, their sensitivity to criticism was acute. Russians were quick to interpret casual words or actions as slurs on the national honor. For example, to take photographs of anything but the very ancient or the very new was to risk public censure. An unfavorable comment about a building, play, or administrative procedure was interpreted as a reflection on the entire Soviet society.

The most significant feature of these reactions was their irrational quality. In speaking of achievements, Soviet citizens—including persons holding positions of considerable responsibility—often made statements about products and performances that were patently untrue and denied inadequacies visible to the naked eye. Moreover, the accompanying gestures, tone of voice, and physiological reactions were of a kind which suggested that they were engaging, not in calculated misrepresentation, but in involuntary distortion born of inner tension. In other words, at least at that moment, they believed what they were saying; they were deceiving themselves.

In the same measure that criticism evoked violent defense, denial, or counterattack, praise of one or another aspect of Soviet society elicited equally disproportionate reactions of enthusiasm and personal warmth. The hunger for praise and prestige was impressive. Of particular interest in this connection was the effect of praise on communication. Ideas which previously seemed not to be understandable were now comprehended and even half-accepted.

In order to examine the implications of these national attitudes and reactions for American policy, we must first place them in the larger context of the general pattern of response to conflict situations in Soviet society.

MODES OF ADAPTATION IN SOVIET SOCIETY

We have noted that in the sphere of international and national behavior, Soviet citizens tend to see the West as the source of all evil and their own nation as "the best of all possible worlds." Any defects in the latter are either denied or described as vestiges of capitalism (and now, of Stalinism). Thus vice and virtue are conveniently separated geographically and politically—all, of course, to the benefit of the Soviet image.

Patterns of Response in Everyday Life

Curiously enough, during my visit, I first became aware of this mechanism not at the international level but at the mundane. In observing individual Russians confronted by everyday problems, mistakes, and personal differences, I noted repeatedly a ready resort to these same mechanisms of denial and displacement. A store clerk, unable to find her pad of receipts would immediately accuse her working companion, and, even when the object was found on her own desk, would insist that the other had taken and surreptitiously replaced it. Or a person who had failed to keep an appointment would accuse his companion of having failed to appear. In like manner, mistrust, self-righteousness, and sensitivity to criticism were manifest in many spheres besides the patriotic. Reactions of this kind can of course be observed in any society. Moreover, one is more likely to notice them when traveling in a country that is seen as a potential enemy.

For this reason, the results of the pseudo-experiment described earlier are particularly important. The experiment, it will be recalled, required that in both cultures, analogous stimuli consisting of dissonant material be presented in an acceptable context. Unfortunately, since I was not altogether certain of

the procedures for eliciting and recording responses, they were not kept
constant. But the differences in reaction in the two settings were sufficiently
great to override these limitations. It proved far easier to get an American
to change his picture of the Soviet Union than the reverse. Although
showing some capacity for change, Soviet citizens were more likely than
Americans to cling to their stereotypes and to defend them by denial and
displacement.

It is of course true that in this pseudo-experiment the stimuli were always
being presented by an American, who was recognized as such in both settings.
During the past year, however, I had a recurrent opportunity of observing
American reactions to statements made by Soviet students living in the
United States. Although these statements were not made in a context as acceptable as mine had been, the American reactions to the Communist source
were very similar to those observed in the pseudo-experiment.

In short, I am persuaded that a comparative study of modes of adaptation
in American and Soviet society would reveal a stronger predilection in the
latter for black-and-white thinking, moral self-righteousness, mistrust, dis-
placing of blame to others, perceptual distortion, and denial of reality.[b]

[b] This does not mean, however, that such reactions are not prevalent in our own
society. Quite the contrary. In response to my efforts to tell fellow Americans about the
Soviet Union, instances of resistance, distortion, denial, and displacement were common
occurrences. Here are some examples:

(1) In order to bring some of these matters to the attention of the general public, I
prepared a popular version of my article on the "mirror image" in Soviet-American
relations. The article was accepted for publication by one of our leading weeklies
with a circulation in the millions. (There was even to be a fullpage photograph showing
the Capitol and the Kremlin both reflected in mirrors!) In due course I received a
handsome check and was informed that the article would appear in the forthcoming
issue. When the appointed time came, I went so far as to buy a copy. But my article
was not there. Instead, there was a piece by Herman Kahn on the advantages of
deterrence. When I wrote the editor for an explanation, I received the following reply:
"We regret that recent developments on the international scene make it impossible for
us to publish your fine article. We hope that the Russians will soon take the heat off
Berlin so that we can take the lid off your excellent piece."

(2) In a subsequent article on Soviet secrecy, I had asked explicitly that sensational
illustrations be avoided. We finally agreed on a picture of the Kremlin wall. But when
the issue finally came out, two line drawings had been added. One showed a hand
holding a pencil poised for writing; gripping the hand and firmly guiding it was a
uniformed arm. The second sketch depicted a Westerner walking a Russian street
and behind a wall, stealthily observing him, a man in a dark overcoat, his hands
in his pockets, with the right pocket bulging.

(3) Recently I gave a public lecture on the excellent facilities the Russians are
providing in their nurseries for young children. In the course of my remarks, I
mentioned that such institutions had long waiting lists of parents who wished to
have their children enrolled. The next day, the leading metropolitan newspaper
headlined: "Khrushchev Takes Three-Month Babies from Parents to Be Raised by
State," and the article quoted me as having stated that "Russian attempts to mold
men like machines are succeeding." Both statements represent gross distortions of
what I actually said.

Individual versus Group Psychology

It was formerly thought that people who distorted reality were sick, and their illness, if not hereditary, was the product of a unique personal history of trauma, especially in early childhood. No doubt such early experience can lead to serious disturbance. In the past twenty years, however, considerable research in social psychology has demonstrated that perfectly healthy persons, when placed in certain kinds of social situations, experience perceptions and exhibit behaviors which are quite inappropriate when judged against objective standards.

As an example, we may cite the effect first shown in a set of experiments by Solomon Asch, known as the "Asch phenomenon."[4] In these experiments, the subject finds himself in a group of six or eight of his peers, all of whom are asked to make comparative judgments of certain stimuli presented to them —for example, identifying the longer of two lines. At first the task seems simple enough; the subject hears others make their judgments and then makes his own. In the beginning, he is usually in agreement with them, but then gradually he notices that more and more often his judgments differ from those of the rest of the group. Actually the experiment is rigged. All the other group members have been instructed to give false responses on a predetermined schedule. In any event, the effect on our subject is sometimes dramatic. At first he is puzzled, then upset. But soon he conforms, and begins to report the stimuli as they are described by his fellows.

---

(4) In Moscow, I asked an American newspaperman if he was aware of the degree of commitment to the Soviet way of life exhibited by many Russians. "Sure, I know," came the reply, "but when a Communist acts like a Communist, it isn't news. If I want to be sure that it will be printed back home, I have to write about what's wrong with the system, not its successes."

(5) During another talk to a class of fifth and sixth graders mostly from middle-class professional and faculty families, I was showing some slides of scenes in Russian villages. A hand went up: "Why do they have trees planted along the road?" A bit puzzled, I turned the question back to the group: "Why do you suppose?" The answer came quickly: "So that people can't see what they're doing behind the trees." A girl had a different idea: "It's to make work for the prisoners." I asked why some of our roads had trees planted along the side. "For shade." "To keep the dust down."

So long as such mechanisms of distortion exist in our own society, they threaten our security on three counts. First, we may mistakenly misinterpret an act of the Russians as aggressive and thus precipitate a nuclear war. Second, and more likely, if the war stays cold, our predilection for black-and-white thinking may lead us to underestimate the enemy's assets and overestimate our own, as we did so tragically in the case of Cuba. Third, and most likely of all, we may fail to recognize or respond to a genuinely constructive step should the Russians ever make one. Even if our leaders were to perceive the Soviet move for what it was, American public opinion might not permit them to take the necessary next step of accepting the Russian action in good faith. In this manner, the present level of popular prejudice against the Soviet Union restricts the Government's freedom of constructive initiative or response.

Conditions Fostering Distortion and Denial

Experiments like these have demonstrated that the fear of social deviance can be a powerful force in determining what one perceives or does not perceive. It can lead both to distortion and denial. Other investigations have identified additional factors which contribute to such perceptual tendencies. These include the following conditions:

(1) Exposure to pressure for achieving excessively high or unattainable standards of performance;

(2) Situations in which deviation or failure implies moral culpability or weakness and entails public disapproval or ostracism;

(3) Situations in which criteria for objective comparison are minimal or absent;

(4) Identification with a social group that is striving for upward mobility from a relatively inferior status.

It is noteworthy that all four of these conditions are met in present-day Soviet society.

The Impact of Historical Experience

But in addition to these contemporary pressures, the Soviet people are constrained by psychological forces deriving from their national history which also predispose them to exaggerate their achievements and to deny internal defects. These forces have been discussed in greater detail elsewhere,[5] and may be summarized by the following quotation:

The deprivation, oppression, suffering, and unceasing labor that the Soviet people have had to bear over the last several decades could be endured only in the name of some almost superhuman goal. To question the effort or the accomplishment is to make this anguish all in vain. Hence the sensitivity, defensiveness and pride of Soviet leaders and citizens alike, especially when their aspirations and achievements are called into question.

The Dynamics of Distorted Perceptions

The preceding analysis leads to the conclusion that instances of Soviet distrust, distortion, and denial are motivated by much more than purely strategic considerations. They are not so much products of logical analysis and deliberate decision as expressions of deeply internalized, powerful emotional needs that have become part of an enduring cultural pattern. It is these needs which underlie the distorted perceptions we have described as characteristic of Soviet society.

It is therefore a matter of some interest to inquire how such distorted perceptions are affected by and in turn affect objective events. What happens, for example, when such images are directly challenged by contradictory evidence? Or when they are given confirmation by events in the external world? Do either of these conditions serve to dissipate the distorted picture? If not, are there other forces that can be invoked to this end? Finally, under what circumstances do people act in accordance with their distorted perceptions, and how, if at all, can such action be forestalled?

Unfortunately, the behavioral sciences are as yet far from definitive answers to these questions. Some knowledge does exist which, though crude and tentative, may foreshadow the general outlines of future research results. For example, there is evidence to suggest that when distorted perceptions are directly challenged instead of being dispelled they are defended even more forcefully by more radical means. There are also indications that a similar reaction occurs when irrational fears and expectations are confirmed by reality. In short, any objective event which increases internal anxiety enhances resort to perceptual defenses. It also increases the likelihood of tension release through overt behavior responsive to the *perceived* threat. Conversely, the likelihood of distorted perceptions and irrational behavior is reduced as sources of anxiety and threat are removed. For example, in the Asch experiment, the presence of a single confederate who reports objectively almost eliminates the experimental effect; the subject is again able to see what is actually there.

In light of this analysis of the dynamics of perceptual distortion and defense, we are now in a position to return to a consideration of the major focus of this inquiry.

IMPLICATIONS OF SOVIET PSYCHOLOGY FOR AMERICAN POLICY

If the preceding analysis of modes of adaptation characteristic of Soviet society is valid, it raises serious questions about the consequences of any American strategy which (1) seeks to communicate our intentions primarily through the building up and selective deployment of weapons, and (2) assumes that Soviet action will be determined through a process of rational weighing of and decision among possible outcomes. On the contrary, the evidence suggests that a strategy of this kind is likely to enhance irrational fears, thereby increasing tendencies to distortion, distrust, denial, and displacement. Particularly with respect to the Soviet Union, if pressures from without coincide with internal crises, such as agricultural failures or economic shortages, we risk the possibility that the Soviet Union will return to an era of regimentation and paranoid nationalism.

Such a conclusion should not be taken to imply that militant Communism is merely a product of psychological forces. There can be no doubt that Marxist ideology, with its injunction to further the inevitable triumph of Communism, the fervent belief in its own perfection, and the frightening vision of implacable capitalist hostility, strongly reinforces, and in turn is strongly reinforced by, the psychological processes we have been describing. But our concern is to identify the most *alterable* of the conditions which, on the one hand, are likely to magnify the total complex of forces to dangerous proportions, and, on the other, to strengthen whatever potentiality for liberalization exists in contemporary Soviet society.

With this twofold objective in view, it is useful also to examine the implications of our analysis within the more restricted area of measures for arms control. Here our line of reasoning suggests that any procedures which confront the Russians with their own deficiencies and self-delusions are likely to arouse the strongest resistance. Indeed, one might hazard the prediction that, even if the Russian leaders were to agree in good faith to the kind of inspection procedures we have been insisting upon, they would ultimately be forced to renege.

A Counteractive Approach

Certainly the outlook is not sanguine, at least in the short run, but neither is it as hopeless as might appear. The very psychological characteristics which make the Russians susceptible to irrational fears, distortions, and displacements also present opportunities for encouraging their movement in other directions. For example, we have already referred to the Soviet craving for recognition and prestige and the disproportionate positive reaction which response to this craving elicits. Needs of this kind could be responded to in order to counterweigh other, more obstructive tendencies, such as the Soviet penchant for secrecy.

It is difficult to give actual examples, primarily because we have so seldom availed ourselves of such opportunities. One instance, however, does come to mind: granting an interview with the president to Mr. Adzhubei, with the understanding that the text of the interview would be published in the Soviet press. I had the opportunity of observing that the Russians kept their part of the bargain even in such faraway republics as Kazakhstan. For the first time, the views of an American president were presented in full to the Soviet people.

This single example suggests how much might be accomplished if we took occasion more frequently to acknowledge genuine accomplishments and achieved status in the Soviet world.[c]

---

[c] An even more dramatic and effective example of this kind occurred during the author's most recent visit in the spring of 1963. President Kennedy's speech at American University, which exhibited many of the features advocated in the present discussion, was printed in full in both *Pravda* and *Izvestiya* and evoked enthusiastic reactions from Soviet citizens in all walks of life.

Incentives to Positive Response in Soviet Society

But recognition of achievement and acknowledgment of prestige are but two of many modes of behavior by a Westerner that evoke in Russian citizens a positive response all out of proportion to the stimulus. In the Soviet conversations, topics which had a similar effect included discussions of Soviet suffering in World War II, of education, science, poetry, children, and—especially —peace. In fact, a good guide to Soviet psychological hungers is what one reads about in their own newspapers.

There is one important exception to the preceding generalization. Paradoxically, the Russians are remarkably responsive to expressions of American idealism. Unfortunately, the key concept here is not the one we have been using. For ideological reasons, the word "freedom" has for Soviet citizens a connotation of irresponsibility and license. The traditional American value that has unambivalent appeal is *human dignity*. To the Russian, this quality is perhaps best symbolized in the person of Abraham Lincoln, who, surprisingly enough, is something of a national hero in the U.S.S.R. (In 1959 a sesquicentennial celebration of Lincoln's birth was held, involving national ceremonies, special editions of his writings, and a new biography prepared for general use in the schools.) A reaffirmation, in our dealings with the Soviet Union, of our commitment to Lincolnian ideals, might contribute in some measure to evoking less antagonistic responses.

Finally, at the most general level, perhaps the greatest contrast suggested by the results of the pseudo-experiment was the different power in the two cultures of exposure to facts versus feelings. In general, American respondents were influenced most by being presented with objective evidence about Soviet society; any feelings I may have had on the subject, including antagonistic ones, were best kept in the background. Quite the opposite was true with the Russians; if I wanted to convey something of the American outlook, I had to rely on emotion to carry the message. Communication was most successful when one spoke in the name of ideals and feelings rather than invoking evidence and logic. The lofty principle had to come first; only then could facts be introduced, and even so, preferably as inevitable deductive necessities, rather than as empirically independent observations.

In short, the Russians take attitudes and emotions much more seriously than do we. This explains their overreaction to American demagoguery as reflected in our public media. At the same time, we could turn this sensitivity to our own account by drawing more heavily on our own rich idealistic traditions.

The Persuasive Effect of Modest Commitment

A recognition of Soviet fears and motives does not exhaust the possible contributions of a psychological approach to American policy. For example, it is a common observation, confirmed by research, that people ordinarily believe themselves safe in making small concessions, since they can always stop short of the next step if they so desire. Actually, psychological studies on persuasion indicate that commitment to one step has the effect of changing attitudes toward the next. This means that it may be to our advantage to involve the Russians in agreements which we do not regard as fully adequate (provided, of course, that such agreements do not seriously endanger our own security). Once committed, the Russians may be more likely to take what we regard as a truly consequential step.

The Place of a Psychological Approach

In urging adoption of a psychological perspective in considerations of American policy, I am not arguing for the elimination of other more traditional considerations. Were American decisions to be guided substantially by psychological concerns to the neglect of military, political, economic, and other factors, the outcome would be tragic indeed. But it is the major thesis of this paper that the converse of the foregoing proposition is equally valid. To base our arms control and disarmament policy primarily on considerations of strategy and rational analysis is to court disaster just as surely. It is true that we know less of psychological realities than of military and political ones. The assessments offered above regarding Soviet perceptions and motives and their strategic implications are at best hypotheses. But the means for checking these hypotheses and arriving at better ones are at hand. The required research is admittedly difficult, but it is possible. And until our information becomes more firm, we can, at the least, give serious consideration to the dangers and possibilities suggested by existing theory and knowledge. For the most likely and most disastrous error the United States can make is to misjudge Communist perceptions and predispositions to action.

NOTES

1. "A New Approach for Communicating with the Russians." Report prepared by a working group of Cornell faculty members. Available from the Cornell University Center for International Studies.
2. For other, quite different applications of the general principle in the American context see Urie Bronfenbrenner, "Secrecy: A Basic Tenet of the Soviets," *New York Times Magazine* (April 22, 1962), p. 7; idem, "Possible Effects of a Large-Scale American Shelter Program on the Soviet Union and Other Nations"; report prepared for submission to the Armed Services Committee of the House of Representatives, May 1962; and idem, "The Mirror Image in Soviet-American Relations," *Journal of Social Issues,* XVII (1961), pp. 45–46.
3. For some concrete examples see Bronfenbrenner, "The Mirror Image in Soviet-American Relations." This report also discusses other methodological problems bearing on the validity of the material obtained.
4. S. E. Asch, "Studies of Dependence and Conformity: I. A Minority of One against a Unanimous Majority," *Psychological Monographs,* LXX (1956), 70 pp.
5. Bronfenbrenner, "Secrecy: A Basic Tenet of the Soviets," *loc. cit.*

10

AMITAI ETZIONI

Atlantic Union, the Southern Continents, and the United Nations

If the historian, writing with the hindsight of the twenty-first century, shares some of the follies of his predecessors, he will like to quote a specific date at which the United States intention to form an Atlantic union was revived. He will probably choose Kennedy's address in Independence Hall on July 4, 1962. There, he will state, a current notion was given a new life and presidential prestige. After one and a half years in office, the Kennedy administration seemed to have reached a crucial decision; it decided to enter into a partnership with a united Europe, to be registered as the Atlantic union. Our historian might add that the inclination to form such a partnership can be fully explained in the political context in which it was made; the question that could be speculated upon but not answered in the early 1960's was what the long-run repercussions of this union would be.

Political decision-makers tend to take into account more contingencies than most people, but to limit their examination to the near future. Experience has taught most politicians that the long-run future is utterly unpredictable and hence decisions based on specific assumptions about the future are hazardous; that it is harder to gain the support of voters and fellow politicians for long-run than for short-run moves; and that the next elections might bring into office another man, thus largely removing the future-after-the-next-elections from their control. Politicians hence tend to focus on the near future.

The typical intellectual, viewing decision-making from the outside, tends to see fewer contingencies than the politician, but often follows them more deeply into the future. (He is better equipped to speculate, and a mistaken analysis is much less consequential; he will lose neither his right to speculate nor his job.) Thus the difference in viewpoint between the intellectual and the politician is neither accidental nor undesirable, and the interaction between the two probably makes decisions more realistic and deeper in time perspective. The decision to form an Atlantic partnership is no exception; we here report first its political context, then speculate about its long-run repercussions, which leads us to examine alternative modes of international organization.

THE POLITICAL CONTEXT

The Economic Aspect

The Atlantic union is desired in part as an instrument for relocating the economic burdens of the West. The United States wishes that Western Europe would contribute more funds to the development of emerging nations and the cost of various international institutions and that it would increase its share in financing Western defenses. (While the United States spends 11.2 per cent of its national income on defense, France spends only 7 per cent and West Germany, 3.2 per cent.)[1] This wish is the result of both increased European prosperity and American economic and fiscal difficulties. Recent years have seen rapid economic growth and full employment in Western Europe; in America, at the same time, efforts to accelerate the growth of the economy and significantly to reduce unemployment have not succeeded. Industrial production was 52 per cent higher in the EEC countries in mid-1959 than it was in 1953. Even Britain's production rose in this period by 19 per cent. That of the United States rose by only 14 per cent.[2] Figures for 1960–62 show similar discrepancies. On the fiscal side, while the extent of gold drainage has been reduced, the danger to the dollar is far from overcome.

The relationship between European affluence and American economic troubles is close. The modern machinery of European industry was bought in part with American reconstruction funds. The European economic miracle is in part a consequence of American financing of Europe's military defenses, especially those of West Germany. At the same time, the United States paid much of the costs of the United Nations and provided most of the Western foreign aid. Were it not for American financing of these Western commitments, the American balance-of-payments would be highly positive, since the United States exports more than it imports. Its deficit is a direct result of its contributions to the free world and the United Nations.

Now, as Europe's economic assets mount and the American dollar crisis continues, the United States wishes to shift to Europe some of these commitments. The United States recognizes that if the junior partners are to be expected to provide more of the funds, it is necessary to raise their status. To increase Europe's representation appears the best way to increase its "taxation." This tendency—the sources of which are economic—to change Europe from an area subject to American hegemony to a full partner is enforced by pressures of political origin.

A Political Aspect

Recent years have brought some concern on the American side of the Atlantic that the Europeans might be becoming less committed to the West. While the extent of the shift is limited, the trend seems to be clear and its sources evident. Ever since the Russians launched the luniks in 1958, the United States' omnipotence has been questioned. The debate about the missile gap did not help to reassure the Europeans. The new-look emphasis on the use of conventional arms as the first counter to a Russian attack on Western Europe is often viewed as an American effort to limit the conditions under which Europe is protected by the American nuclear umbrella. Many Europeans question whether the United States would, under any conditions, risk an all-out war for Europe's sake. Again and again the junior partners toy with the idea of going into business on their own. DeGaulle's France is trying to build up an independent nuclear deterrent, talking freely of a Europe *from* the Atlantic Ocean to the Urals, omitting the United States from the European picture. West Germany, to which unification is dear, is not averse to considering "greater flexibility" in its international orientation. Similar trends can be recognized in other NATO countries. Only in Britain, the most loyal American ally, is this so-called neutralist viewpoint limited chiefly to the left wing of the Labour Party.

The United States is thus confronted with the possibility that the stronger and the more united Europe becomes, the less it will be inclined to follow what the United States sees as the best policy for the West. A way to alleviate this political problem seems to parallel that of relieving the economic one: increase and formalize, strengthen and institutionalize the American-European ties and grant Europe more power in running the union to increase its sense of participation and responsibility. Hence the United States is anxious to have its most trusted ally enter the core of Europa, the expanding European Economic Community (EEC).[3] The United States initiated the reorganization of the OEEC into the OECD (Organization for Economic Cooperation and Development), designed to be the organization through which Europa, together with North America (United States and Canada became full members), will channel aid to the less developed countries. To further tie the United States and Europa economically and to symbolize the political ties, the administration initiated and Congress approved the 1962 Trade Expansion Act. To lessen Europe's fears about being left unprotected in case of a major showdown, the United States has, since 1957, given Europeans more information on American strategic planning and has more regularly consulted them through the NATO Council.[4] To top all this comes the vision of an Atlantic union—a great united military, economic, and political power—presented in several speeches by Kennedy and his staff. This would be a union in which the United States would view Europa "as a partner with whom we can deal on a basis of full equality," as Kennedy put it.[5] The patronage would become a partnership if only the Europeans would agree to share fully in the responsibilities.

The Military Aspect

Central to these political considerations are military ones; and most central to the military ones are those of nuclear policy. The United States strongly desires to keep its monopoly of Western nuclear power and to prevent France and West Germany, or Europa, from developing their own nuclear deterrent. The United States motivation is multifold. The proliferation of nuclear weapons increases the danger of nuclear war by accident or by unauthorized action; it makes identification of the attacker almost impossible; it is likely to bring these weapons into the hands of governments much less responsible than those of the United States or the U.S.S.R. Moreover, being inadequate of itself, a European nuclear force would serve as a "trip wire," involving the United States in a nuclear war when Europe desires.

The tightening of European-American ties and the reconstruction of power relations is expected to remove Europe's desire for an independent nuclear deterrent. By making the two one, the United States would have to view an attack on, let us say, Denmark as one on New Jersey. By sharing the power of control, the Europeans would participate in commanding the shared nuclear power. Moreover, much money would be saved, because building up and maintaining a nuclear deterrent is prohibitively expensive. The union would enable specialization, with Europa building up conventional forces for the defense of Western Europe, and the United States holding the nuclear umbrella. How far the United States is really willing to share control of the nuclear trigger, and whether the prospects of an Atlantic partnership will really bring Europe to give up its dreams of nuclear independence and glory, are questions that have to be answered in the context of assessments of the long-run repercussions of the Atlantic union.

THE ATLANTIC UNION: LONG-RUN QUESTIONS

The Basic Features

There is no Atlantic union. At the moment it fulfills a role in political speech-making and is a vague expression of fairly clear political needs, needs served in part by talking about a union rather than by forming one. President Kennedy, probably worried about the reaction of the conservative majority to implied loss of sovereignty, was careful to emphasize in his Philadelphia speech that the formation of the union is a goal that is "premature" to discuss now in any concrete detail.[6] He stressed on another occasion that such a union is just an aspiration, not a plan or a grand design.[7] Among other things required, Kennedy emphasized, is a united Europe. The United States cannot be expected to view each one of the numerous West European nations as full partners; if they united, however, their combined population, area, market, and military potential would command the respect of the United States and entitle them to full say. But Europe has far to go before it will be united.

Still there is a need to speculate on what repercussions an Atlantic union would have. For one, it is rather evident that some form of tighter international organization is both called for and evolving. But is the envisioned union the one that best serves our needs? If not, what better unions are feasible? Second, the conception of the Atlantic union as a symbol that indicates intentions and directions, even if no reality will ever emerge from this image, influences the present and is even more likely to influence future international developments.[8]

The Atlantic union is far from a clear conception, with regard to both its membership and its structure. This lack of clarity is not accidental; in part it reflects the general political wisdom of not making any decisions or commitments before they are absolutely necessary.[9] Vagueness about membership avoids offending those who might like to be in but are likely to be excluded; vagueness about structure keeps some of the conservatives, who fear any loss of sovereignty, from fighting the union. Some features of this union, though, do seem relatively evident. The Atlantic union will be a bloc organization resting on two regional bases, a united Europe and a North American one. Who will be included in each is not clear. The core of the European region will in all likelihood be the six members of the EEC, plus whatever other countries would join it as full members. This will probably include most European NATO members, especially the United Kingdom. Neutralist countries—Sweden, Switzerland, and Austria, as well as Finland—are now expected to be left out of the political union of Europa. On the American side, Canada is expected to join the union, but prospects for regional integration between the United States and Canada seem at the moment dim.[10] To the preceding list, Australia and New Zealand as well as Japan are sometimes added.

The partnership is to have a military facet (a revised, possibly nuclear-armed NATO), an economic facet (removal of trade barriers and OECD), and a co-ordinated foreign policy, with regard to both the Communist bloc and other nonmember countries.[11] This is hoped to be accompanied by changes—to more commitment to the Atlantic union—in the political identifications of the citizens of the member countries and some lessening of their commitments to their respective nation-states. The eventual formation of a confederation or federation is not excluded, but constitutional formalization is probably unimportant. The tendency is to work through flexible, informal arrangements—committees, conferences of heads of state, and functional organizations—rather than to tackle frontally the question of sovereignty and to form supranational institutions.

Proponents of the union often emphasize that countries that are not members, especially the developing countries, will benefit from the union, since its increased economic strength will allow the West to increase its foreign aid. Kennedy stated, "The Atlantic partnership of which I speak would not look inward only, preoccupied with its own welfare and advancement. It must look outward. . . ."[12]

The relationship between the Atlantic partnership and the other free world countries will take several forms, but most nonmember countries will be tied to one of the members, recognized as its sphere of responsibility. Twelve African countries, all former French colonies but Guinea, already have such a tie-up with the EEC and France. They are allowed to import their agricultural products into the EEC without paying the tariffs other outsiders have to pay. France informally represents these countries in the institutions of the EEC and is also their chief source of credit and foreign aid.

A similar relationship exists between Britain and many Commonwealth countries. While some of these ties will have to be reduced before Britain will be allowed to enter the EEC, negotiators at Brussels agreed that if Britain will enter, some extra ties to the Commonwealth countries will be maintained. Ghana, the West Indies, Nigeria, Rhodesia, Kenya and others will still be viewed as part of the British sphere of responsibility. In an Atlantic union, the United States would have a similar role with regard to the Latin American and Central American countries, as well as Formosa and the Philippines. It is already their special patron in international investments, loans, tariff reductions, and price controls. Other members of the Atlantic partnership will probably also have some nonmembers that they "take care of," as West Germany does, for instance, its ex-colony, the Cameroons, and Italy, Libya.

Thus member countries will maintain spheres of influence that have grown out of their imperial past, with little interference from the others. True, some countries have been or are a source of competition over patronage among various Atlantic countries. Thus, Iran shifted from the British to the American sphere, as did Indochina from the French to the American as part of the general increase in American overseas commitments after World War II. Other countries, such as India, will continue to be cosponsored by several Atlantic nations. Only a few potential outsiders have no clear sponsor.

Basic Questions

An assessment of the long-run effects of the crystallization of the Atlantic union can hardly be acquired by staring into the crystal ball. We shall attempt to benefit from examining the effects of formation of the EEC, the international organization closest to the envisioned union, and draw on general theoretical considerations.

The formation of the Atlantic partnership and similar international organizations enables nations to act together more intimately. Often such an increase in international co-operation requires some pooling of sovereignty; thus not only is the relationship among nations changed, but also a new superior collective is created. The specific questions one faces in trying to evaluate a new political collective are:

First, *how many levels of international organization make for most effective co-operation*—one (a global organization, like the United Nations), two (a regional organization, such as the EEC, and a global one), three (a regional one, a multiregional one, and a global one), and so forth?

Second, *what is the most effective division of functions among the various levels* (effective in terms of the goals of those that set up the collective)? Is, for instance, defense to be regional (as in NATO, SEATO, and so on), or multiregional (as SAC is), or global (as an international police force would be)? The same question has to be asked about the division of authority. Control of the services of one functional need can be divided among the various levels. Regulation of the economy can, for example, be divided at least temporarily among a bloc organization for mutual reduction of tariffs; a regional one for free flow of labor; and a national one for issuing currency. Finally, citizens' loyalties to these international organizations tend to distribute themselves in varying fashions; for instance, over the past five years the regional EEC has gained and the member states have lost some of these loyalties. While it is hard to control, or even to predict, these shifts, they affect the degree to which functions and authority can be shifted to higher levels; hence any analysis of international collectives that excludes the assessment of the changing distribution of loyalties is incomplete.

The relationships among units on the same level—let us say among nations in a regional organization, or among regions in a multiregional (bloc) organization—are in part determined by interlevel division of functions and authority, and in part set by the composition of the units on each level (for example, the degree of homogeneity) and the distribution of power and assets among them. The third question is: *Which interunit relations are more, which less, in line with the purposes of a particular international collectivity? How restrictive is hegemony by one country or group of countries?*

Finally, *the effects of different kinds of regional and bloc organization on global organizations and on that of other blocs* must be evaluated, since the ability of any one international organization to carry out its goals is much affected by the courses taken by others like itself and by the global organizations. Those, in turn, are affected not only by the action taken, but by the very nature of the organization they respond to.

THE ATLANTIC UNION: LONG-RUN PROSPECTS

We turn now to outline the modes of international organization that recommend themselves on the bases of theoretical considerations and past experience. When we assess the Atlantic union in view of these recommended modes, we find that it is rather adequate from two viewpoints; that one cannot clearly assess where it stands on a third one; and that it has two rather severe defects. This leads us to present, in the closing sections, an outline of an alternative organization.

The Merits of Multilevel Organization

The designer of international organizations has to decide whether to arrange for *direct representation* of all nations on the top level, as in the United Nations, or *indirect representation*, in which nations are grouped in regional or other subunits, which then send representatives to the top level, as the Russian troika system implies. (Still another possibility is to leave the full control of some functions to lower levels of organization, for example, regional, and the full control of others to the top level; such functional differentiations are discused in the next section.) Observation and analysis of other political structures suggest that large and diverse groups or organizations reach a higher degree of consensus and co-operation in structures of indirect representation.

The political process is one in which groups whose members differ in belief and interest work out a shared policy. This is in part a process of mutual concession and compromise, but it is also a process in which the sides become more responsive to each other, grow closer in outlook and interest, and develop some new shared sentiments and needs. As a rule, the larger the number of participants in an organization, the greater the differences of belief and interest among them, and the more difficult such consensus-formation becomes.[a] This holds for student groups in social-relation laboratories, for executives in industrial conferences, and for politicians in national government. Increasing the number of participants in a group may make it so heterogeneous that one of two things will happen: either the group's ability to form consensus will break down or a new consensus-formation structure will be formed.

An examination of international relations shows that here too consensus-formation of heterogeneous units requires indirect representation.

The United Nations is probably best characterized by lack of consensus, which arises from the deep cleavages in interest and belief among many of its members. But when we review those rare and relatively unimportant decisions where an over-all consensus was reached, we see the same multilevel structure in operation.[13] Representatives of various groups of nations "caucus" to work out their shared position; then their unofficial spokesman

---

[a] This is not a necessary relationship since new members might be like old ones, but in most cases increase in numbers increases heterogeneity. The degree of increase is, of course, not proportionate to the number of participants added. The marginal heterogeneity will tend to decline as the number grows.

makes contact with those of the other caucuses or blocs, to work out a general compromise that, in turn, is brought to the United Nations floor for discussion or acclamation.[14] Bloc decisions themselves are frequently reached in a two-level process. The conference of 25 unaligned nations in Belgrade reportedly had three factions: neutral-neutrals, pro-Western neutrals, and pro-Communist neutrals. The African "bloc" seems to have at least two groupings, though their degree of cohesion is as yet hard to assess: that of the Casablanca group, led by Nasser and Nkruma, and that of the Brazzaville group, led by the Ivory Coast Prime Minister, Houphouet-Boigny.[15] The two groups frequently vote *en bloc* in the United Nations.[16]

While blocs in such international organizations as the United Nations—particularly in conferences like the Belgrade Conference—are highly fluid, subgroupings of potential supranational unions seem to have a higher degree of permanency. The Benelux countries constitute such a subgrouping in the EEC, though by no means with regard to all issues; Australia and New Zealand seem to constitute such a subgroup in the British Commonwealth of Nations; and the EEC and the EFTA played such a role in GATT.

Thus the process of forming consensus on the international level seems to be quite similar to that in national ones. Here, too, indirect representation (or, a multilevel structure) is a more effective way of consensus formation than direct representation of all participants on the same level. This suggests that the commonly held image of a global organization in which all 120-odd states are directly represented, with no intermediary bodies, is not the best way to structure any large-scale international organization.

There is not much to say about the envisioned Atlantic union from this viewpoint, except to make the crucial observation that, whatever the details of membership and structure, it surely will fully satisfy the need for inter-level differentiation. Some fifteen to twenty national governments are expected to provide the lowest organizational level; several regional ones, the second level. At the moment projections favor the dumbbell shape, which would consist of two regional organizations, a North American one (the United States and Canada), and a Western European one (the thirteen European members of NATO). Other alternatives are discussed, such as viewing Canada as part of the European region because of its special ties to Britain and its reluctance to form closer ties to the United States. Another possibility is that Britain and Canada might join the United States to form one regional organization, with continental Europe forming the other one. Whatever the number of regional organizations and their composition, the third level would be one of a bloc organization, the Atlantic union itself.

Whether the top-level representation would be limited to regions or would include all member nations, or for some purposes regions and for some others nations, depends largely on the division of functions and authority among the levels—our next question.

Interlevel Division of Functions

When international relations are limited to one level, the question of division of functions obviously does not arise (though one might inquire which functions are best left to the nation-state and which "internationalized"). But when there are two or more levels of international relations, the question of what functions are allotted to each level is important.

International organizations and unions differ in the number of societal functions they serve. Some are monofunctional; they deal only with labor issues, or health issues, or postal services, or aviation. Other international organizations serve two or more functions (as does, for instance, the Nordic Council which serves political, economic, educational, and cultural needs of the member nations). *The broader the functional scope of an international organization, the more consensus-formation required; hence, the fewer the number of nations at each level (or more precisely, the lower the degree of heterogeneity*[b]*) it can tolerate without loss of effectiveness.* Thus it is not surprising that the typical monofunctional organizations have from seventy to one hundred and ten members, all directly represented, while typical multifunctional unions have only three to eight members. The Nordic Council, for instance, has only five members; the Eastern European Community (with two major organization tools, the Warsaw Treaty Organization and the Council for Mutual Economic Aid) has eight members; the EEC has six.

Even more important than the number of functions encompassed is the nature of the function that is internationally served, in terms of its articulation with other functional needs of the same society. Several authorities in the study of supranationalism have pointed out that internationalization of one function tends to spill over into others. Haas, for instance, shows in his study of the integration of coal and steel industries in West Europe how the ECSC spilled over into integration of atomic research (Euratom) and later, into general economic integration, the EEC.[17] This, in turn, seems now to spill over in the political direction. Some experts have also suggested that various functions differ in their spill-over potential.[18] On the basis of various sociological considerations that cannot be discussed here,[19] I would order the spill-over value of various functions—from low to high—as follows: (1) international organizations that deal with such services as postal services, allocation of radio frequencies, police co-operation, and so on, usually referred to as functional organizations; (2) tariff unions; (3) military organizations; (4) economic unions (common markets); (5) political unions.

Initially, higher spill-over functions will have to be left to the lower level of new international collectivities, since those require much consensus-formation, which is best attained in small, homogeneous units.[c] On the other hand,

[b] On the relationship of size to heterogeneity, see footnote [a], *supra.*

[c] High spill-over functions do not require more consensus-formation in themselves, but by definition they draw more matters into the "internationalized" sector, and hence increase the need for consensus-formation.

the lower spill-over functions can be delegated to higher, more encompassing levels.[d] Thus one would expect economic integration initially to be limited to such small, regional units as the European Economic Community, the Nordic Council, and the Central American Union. One would also expect tariff reduction units, such as GATT, to be larger; and to leave such "technical" functions as allocation of radio frequencies to such higher-level, encompassing organizations as the specialized agencies of the United Nations.

The preceding analysis thus suggests that in order to gain and maintain consensus *it is not enough to differentiate decision-making among two or more levels, but it is also necessary, at the initial stage, to limit the functions delegated to higher levels to those that have a low spill-over value and hence a low consensus-formation need.* Attempts initially to delegate other functions to the higher level would make the structure ineffective because of inability to agree on one policy. The League of Nations and the United Nations Security Council are prime examples.

While it seems next to impossible to start with a structure in which higher spill-over functions are carried out at the top level, we should note that differentiated, multilevel international structures tend to *transfer upward* functions, authority, and loyalties. The history of the United States Federal government vis-à-vis the member states is a typical example. First a confederation was transformed into a federation; then gradually, military powers were transferred from state to Federal level. The authority to regulate the economy was upgraded only in the last generation.[20] Parallel to this upward transfer of functions, the authority of and loyalties to the president and other Federal institutions has increased and that of states has declined. We might in the next years witness the beginning of such upward transfer in the EEC, with the growing functions and powers of the Economic Commission, the formation of new supranational political institutions, and a parallel decline of the national functions, authority, and normative appeal. *Thus initial limitation of the top level does not prevent it from later gaining functions, authority, and loyalties.*

It is, of course, impossible at this stage to foretell which functions will be carried out at the various levels of the Atlantic union, what the allocation of authority will be, and how the citizens' loyalties will redistribute themselves. It seems safe, though, to expect that there will be interlevel differentiation, and that its general pattern will be to keep high spill-over functions initially low in the structure and delegate only lower spill-over functions to higher levels. At least initially, most political decisions will still be made on the national level. Many economic decisions and some military ones will be regional. Other military decisions and regulation of matters concerning

---

[d] Higher levels of organization might include fewer representatives than lower ones, but the consensus to be reached still has to cover the full range of members' positions; it is in this sense that it is more encompassing than that of lower levels. The interlevel differentiation of consensus-formation, at least initially, only eases the procedure and somewhat reduces but far from eliminates the basic differences among the members.

tariff will be blocwide. Technical functions could be carried out on a bloc level or higher by the United Nations or other global organizations, a point to which we return below.

While this is likely to be the initial functional distribution, one would expect the process of upward transfer to set in. NATO and the OECD already provide the forerunners of the Atlantic bloc organization; strengthening of their authority and increase of their functional scope vis-à-vis the national and regional organizations might be next steps in the upward transfer. One would expect the development of additional Atlantic institutions—for example, a regular meeting of heads of member states—that would indicate the upward transfer of new functions. Whether this will lead to an Atlantic confederation or federation, one cannot suggest, even in this speculative discussion.

In short, on this score too the envisioned Atlantic union meets this criteria of effective international organization both in the way the division of functions and authority is expected to be initially arranged and in its potential for upward transfer, at least to the bloc level.

Interunit Relations

The central question here is that of distribution of authority on each level—that is, who controls whom? There are at least three major possibilities:

(1) All members—nations in a region, regions in a bloc—might have equal power and status. While such a structure is never completely realized, it is approximated by highly integrated systems. The United States Federal government might be somewhat more influenced by the larger states than by the smaller ones, especially in the House of Representatives, but in general it is an independent power unit, not identified with any one state. This is a politically *egalitarian* structure.

(2) The opposite extreme is one in which the system is controlled by one unit. Most *empires* were organized in such fashion, including the Roman, Ottoman, and British empires. So was the Communist bloc up to 1953.

(3) The third type is an intermediary one, in which one unit (or a few) has more power than the others, but is highly responsive to the other units, tries to share decisions as much as possible and make its leadership as nonarbitrary as possible. We refer to this type as a *commonwealth* organization. The British relationship to its colonies changed from an empire to a commonwealth. France now has a similar relationship with most of its former colonies in Africa. While the early gunboat period of the United States–Latin America relationship is rarely referred to as imperial, and the present one as a commonwealth, actually the Organization of American States is a Western Hemisphere commonwealth with United States leadership. The Communist Eastern European community is changing from a highly imperialist one, which it was under Stalin, to one that moves toward being a commonwealth.

The reasons why empires either crumble or change to commonwealths are many. In part, the spread of nationalism, education, and democratic ideals made the blunt control of an empire obsolete; the interbloc struggle made an imperial relationship a Cold War liability.[e] In part, it results from increased liberal influence within the imperial powers themselves.

The transition from empire to commonwealth is analogous to the entrance of the middle and working classes into political society. It involves an increase in equality, through reallocation of three major assets: wealth, political power, and status.

Wealth is reallocated by reduction or elimination of various exploitive practices of the imperial powers in the colonies, and by granting foreign aid and loans to the ex-colonies. *Political power* is reallocated by the removal of imperial military and police units from the colonies, and by foregoing the threat to re-employ them. While empires can force compliance, common- wealths have to convince their members or "buy" their co-operation. Re- allocation of political power and *status* takes place when the former colonies are granted independence and full representation in global and regional organizations. National status is an important source of psychological grati- fication for most citizens. Hence the importance attached to attaining the various status symbols associated with political independence and representa- tion—from a national flag to a seat at the United Nations. That economic reallocation and development far from erase the deep differences between "have" and "have-not" countries and that attaining full political independ- ence and representation does not provide equality of political power enhance demands for the equal allocation of status symbols.

While the envisioned Atlantic union meets well the requirements of inter- level differentiation of representation and functions, its interunit distribution of wealth, power, and status is not so satisfactory. It raises two problems, one with regard to United States' relations to the less developed countries, and one with regard to the relations between the United States and Europe.

The major difficulty of the Atlantic union lies not in its bloc organization, but in its semi-imperial relationship to the less developed countries. These nations are not full members of the new union, nor are they to be com- pletely excluded.

Historically, the United States, in its nonisolationist periods, oriented itself chiefly toward Europe, with Latin America as a secondary focus. After World War II, when Britain, France, and Germany were very weak, especially when the interbloc struggle shifted to the southern continents, the United States' commitment to Asia and Africa was built up, and its global power and leadership extended to all continents and races. But with the continued suc- cess of the EEC, the American gold crisis and other factors discussed above,

e This holds not only for the present Cold War. The change from the British Empire to the British Commonwealth of Nations was accelerated by the two world wars. The major shift in the American orientation to Latin America came after 1933, as the United States tried to counter the spread of fascism and fifth columns in the Western Hemisphere.

a reorientation to Europe set in. The Atlantic union would be a strong expression of this reorientation; it would be an alliance of the "have," ex-imperial, white countries, to exclude the "have-not," ex-colonial, colored countries.

The Union and the Semi-Empire

The Atlantic Union is likely to have some less developed members, such as Turkey and Greece, and to exclude some developed countries, such as South Africa, Sweden, and possibly Japan, Australia, and New Zealand. The differentiation line will, however, be crystal clear and highly visible. Inside the union would be most non-Communist industrial countries, and most of the members would be highly industrialized. The majority of the nonmember countries would be less developed, often mainly exporters of one or two agricultural products or raw materials.

We refer to the relationships of various members of the Atlantic union to their wards, as well as that of the union as a collectivity to the aid-receiving countries, as "semi-imperial" because, while some of the extreme forms of economic exploitation as well as the use of coercion, are removed, some economic exploitation and much paternalistic treatment remain, especially in the exclusion of these countries from the decision-making process.[f]

The division between union members and wards has many correlates and consequences. The average literacy rate in the union would be low, in the semi-empire, high. The average growth of population would be slow in the union and rapid in the semi-empire. The average per capita income in the union would be about seven and one-half times higher than in the semi-empire—about $1,500, compared to $200.[21] Almost all the Western aid-granting countries would be in the union; almost all the receiving ones in the semi-empire. The union would be all, or almost all, white; the semi-empire, racially mixed.

Economic implication—The forming of the Atlantic partnership would, among other things, remove economic barriers to the movement of goods, labor, and capital among the members gradually forming a common market. The first steps toward such a goal are taken in the EEC. Next, additional NATO members are expected to join. The American trade bill of 1962 is generally expected to lead to a reduction in the tariff barrier between the EEC and the United States. Since eventually the economies of the members of the Atlantic partnership will be at least as intimately related to each other and as sharply separated from outsiders as the EEC economies are now,[g] the effect of the integration of the EEC on nonmembers is highly relevant to our question.

The success of the EEC generated deep anxiety, which led either to urgent pleas for membership, or to great hostility to this union, or to both. Even such

---

[f] These points are elaborated below.

[g] For one possible exception, see below the discussion of universal liberation of trade of some products.

comparatively powerful economies as those of the United Kingdom and the United States found it inadvisable to be excluded by the EEC tariff walls. United Kingdom, Norway, Denmark, and Ireland asked for membership; Greece, Turkey, Spain, and Portugal for associated membership;[22] Austria, Sweden, and Switzerland for a new neutral associate member status. Many other countries requested some form or another of a most-favored status, i.e., one that will allow them to circumvent the tariff barriers. All this while the EEC has eliminated only 50 per cent of its internal barriers, has regulated only one-third of its external tariffs, and includes only six countries. It is easy to imagine what the impact of the fully integrated economy of the Atlantic union would be when it includes fifteen to twenty countries, among them the United States.

Theoretically this problem could be solved by granting membership to all countries that desire it. But the Atlantic union intends to limit membership mainly to industrial "have" countries.[23] What the status of the less developed countries will be is far from clear. The 1957 Treaty of Rome granted the French colonies a special status for five years, and gave them tariff preferences for their export of tropical agricultural products to the EEC.[24] Now the privilege granted to the colonies, which have meanwhile gained independence, is about to expire, and the question of their status is reopened. At best, the special status of those that remained within the French commonwealth will be extended. One can imagine that in the Atlantic union, countries that are wards of one member or another will be granted a similar status. Thus Nigeria and Ghana, which are now out and complain bitterly, will be in as British wards.[25] Similarly, Latin American countries, which now pay high tariffs on their products, will be in as American wards.[26] Countries that have no patron might conceivably become wards of the union at large.

The outsiders are assured that they will benefit from the Atlantic partnership because the enhanced economic growth that unification will bring about for its members will enable the union to grant more foreign aid and credits to less developed countries than in the past, and the members of the Atlantic partnership will support global price-control schemes to protect these countries' exports from wide price fluctuations. This often sounds to the less developed countries as if the rich first cousins console the poor second cousins, concerning their exclusion from the rich uncle's will, that the inheritance will allow the first cousins to give more charity to the second ones.

A more radical solution that is sporadically discussed is to eliminate altogether the new union's external tariff wall, at least for those products of which 80 per cent or more are produced by member countries, as many important industrial products are.[h] Such reduction of the outside walls would

[h] The EEC, plus its five prospective members and the United States, export the following percentage of the free world exports: aircraft, 97 per cent; cars and trucks, 91 per cent; metal-working machinery, 86 per cent; organic chemicals, 82 per cent; inorganic chemicals, 81 per cent; office equipment, 81 per cent; industrial machinery, 81 per cent; and electrical machinery, 80 per cent [*Newsweek*, 59 (March 26, 1962)].

reduce the economic damage the union causes to outsiders, but it is doubtful that the problem can be solved in this fashion. To the degree that these reductions are limited to some products, the problem is somewhat eased, but far from eliminated. Even if tariffs on all commodities were fully removed, limitations on movement of capital and especially of labor are likely to remain to prevent mass immigration from the "have" to the "have-not" countries.

Any large-scale reduction of the outside walls would undermine the ability of the Atlantic partnership to employ Keynesian control of its economy. As national regulation of unemployment, deflation, or inflation is given up, it will have to be taken over by regional and bloc authorities. If Atlantic bloc controls are weakened by removing the external walls without a provision for new walls of a still larger union, the first economic crisis will drive the countries back to national or Atlantic regulations. Including all the less developed, often neutral, countries in the union would create such a different structure that it would be Atlantic in name only. We examine below the merits and demerits of such a wide union; presently we continue to explore the effects of the Atlantic union, limited in membership mainly to "have" countries, as envisioned by its designers.

The relationship between the Atlantic partnership and other free countries is thus confronted with a dilemma: If the wall is maintained, nonmembers will suffer considerable economic deprivation; if the wall is eliminated or largely reduced, an economic crisis is likely to shake the whole structure or to restore the wall. But even if one makes the unlikely assumption that a combination of a reduced wall with a large-scale foreign aid program would eliminate all economic disadvantages to outsiders (other than the Soviet bloc, which is intended to be negatively affected), an Atlantic union would still have a highly alienating effect on the nonmember countries.

The political status aspect—The global struggle between the "have" and the "have-not" countries is one over the reallocation of power and prestige, not simply of wealth. Like the lower classes entering political action in industrial society, demanding not only higher wages but also political representation and acceptance as first-class citizens, so the new nations seek their full share on all three counts. The achievement of national independence, of seats in the United Nations and in other global organizations, desire to be heard before decisions are made, being "in" rather than "out," all play a large role in their political life. Not a small part of the attraction of the Communist bloc, in addition to its promise of rapid industrialization, is that it never treated *these* countries as colonies, i.e., as inferiors, and that a nonwhite people obtained a first-class status within the bloc.

The central alienating effect of Atlantic union is that it is likely to strengthen and focus the anti-white, anti-imperial, anti-European feelings in the Southern continents; that, again, a small group of countries holds the rest of the world as second-class citizens. It is illuminating to compare the course the United States follows in these matters with that chosen by Britain when it was confronted with a similar problem.

The British example—The British overseas system started as an empire in which there was one power and many colonies. When these colonies threatened to follow the American example, Britain preferred to keep them in by gradually reallocating economic rights, political privileges, and member status so that by 1918, four white countries—Canada, South Africa, Australia and New Zealand—had full membership status in the Commonwealth. While the ministers' conferences took place in London, and while Canada had more influence than New Zealand the fact that all members had formally equal status strengthened their commitment to the Commonwealth and to Britain. After World War II new colonies gained independence, but these were quite different, including such countries as India, Ghana, Malaya, and Ceylon. They were not white, not Protestant, less developed, and high in illiteracy. Still, the Commonwealth was enlarged to include all of them as full members. When the strain of increasing membership with societies of different natures reached a breaking point, the country forced to quit was white racist South Africa, not any of the nonwhite new nations. Actually, the developing nations now hold the majority in the Commonwealth. This is not to suggest that all these countries have the same influence in London, but they are all fully recognized partners whose representatives sit in when the ministerial conference meets, when the monarch is crowned, and so on. Such equal participation and status-sharing does not solve all problems, but it has much symbolic value and effect. We can best appreciate its scope if we imagine that Britain declared, following World War II, that it was going to form a union with the four white dominions, to be called the First Commonwealth, which would bring its decisions to the attention of the other ex-colonies, which would constitute the Second Commonwealth. Whatever promises Britain could have made in the name of the First Commonwealth to the Second, there is little doubt that these proud new nations would have been most deeply alienated from the Commonwealth if they had stayed with it at all. This is almost surely the reaction the Atlantic union will face. Some of it is already coming in, though the union is now much more a symbol than an international reality.[27] The envisioned union is going to please most European members and the more submissive ex-colonies. Most Brazzaville countries seem not to mind the ward status. The majority of the new nations, though, seem likely to be alienated wards or to reject this semimember status altogether, as Guinea did to the French commonwealth and as Ghana has already announced it will do to the EEC if Britain should join.

Those who follow the *realpolitik* school are likely to make a triple mistake here. They may feel that the sentiments of the developing nations are not a real force; that so long as the West continues to award them large-scale economic aid, they will know where their interest lies. They may feel that even if alienated, these countries have little if any real power;

hence as long as Europe is with us, their alienation is of little real significance.

We feel that the sentiments of these countries are as important as their economic interests in affecting their decisions. Most of these countries demonstrated this when they preferred the symbolic gratification of national independence and nationalization to the administrative and economic patronage of the imperial powers. Sentiments are a force a *realpolitik* analysis has to take into account. Second, some of these countries are likely to become quite important powers—Brazil, for instance. Moreover, for the past decade, and in all likelihood for the next ones, the struggle between the East and the West has focused over the minds of the people in these Southern continents. The more stalemated weapon systems become, the more important symbolic issues become. Further alienating the three underdeveloped continents might well largely undermine the very goals for which the Atlantic union is formed.

Global and Interbloc Organization

Whatever the relations within a regional or bloc organization, it operates within the context of more encompassing global organizations and in relation to other regional and bloc organizations. Moreover, the interaction of any particular regional or bloc organization with others of its kind is affected by its relationship to the global organizations, since the latter seek to regulate the interaction among the lower-level units.

Relationship to global organizations—Theoretically, a global organization might be as broad and encompassing as a society, or as narrow in scope as a functional organization dealing with technical matters. Moreover, the fact that a regional or bloc organization is an instrument of international co-operation with regard to one, some, or all social functions (economic, military, and so forth) does not exclude the possibility that the same functions will be served in part by a global organization, just as service by a state government does not preclude a federal service. The global organization might simply come in as a higher level of organization—one with more encompassing membership and superior authority—with regard to the same functions or as co-ordinator of regional or bloc operations. Actually, we have seen that the existence of such intermediary levels assists consensus-formation on the global level. Thus, regional and bloc organizations might not only avoid hindering global organization, but enhance it.

Moreover, the process of upward transfer of functions, authority, and loyalties might occur between the bloc and the global levels as it does between lower ones. The United Nations might be originally used only for technical matters; later it might also co-ordinate foreign aid and global tariff reduction. This might be followed—if the process is to be continued on this level—by a gradual build-up of an international police force and binding courts and, eventually, gradual economic and political integration.

Regional and bloc organizations should therefore not be judged *a priori* as anti-United-Nations or as undermining other global organizations. They might be steppingstones to a global community. The main question is not whether there are initially intermediary bodies or not, but what orientation they take toward global organization. Do they see the bloc organization as the ultimate superior body, and are they jealous of its functions and power? Or do they orient positively to the more encompassing global structure? Do they attempt to block, to slow down, or to accelerate the process of upward transfer to the global level? It is important to pose this question in the right context. At the present stage of the upward transfer process, all nations, regional organizations and blocs refuse to transfer the control of their armed forces to the United Nations or to give its assembly and executive the right to make binding decisions. But at the present stage, the process does not call for such delegation.[i] The central question now is whether the various bloc and regional organizations are willing to allow the United Nations and other global organizations to take over or keep those technical functions and, before long, those matters concerning co-ordination of development, space exploration, and some global tariff reduction, which the process of upward transfer of functions seems ready to accommodate. A bloc can be viewed as anti-United-Nations at this stage only if it tries to block *these* transfers. At a later stage, military, economic, and finally, political functions—which the regions, not to mention the blocs, have not as yet acquired—might be extended to the global level; *then* the test of upward co-operation will change accordingly.

Nothing in the present image of the Atlantic union or existing plans allows one to answer this question. There is no reason to believe that the union will deprive the United Nations or other global organizations of the largely technical functions they now carry out. Whether this union will in the future allow upward transfer of functions higher in spill-over value cannot be derived from the structure as now envisioned. One finds among the Atlantic spokesmen both those that see it as a steppingstone toward a stronger United Nations, and those that hope that it will replace the United Nations.[28]

Interbloc relations—The preceding analysis suggests that, assuming a continuous growth of international co-operation, regional and bloc organizations are likely to grow first. Only after control of central functions, such as military and economic ones, has been shifted to these levels can one expect

[i] Some readers may feel that while the process might not call for such transfer, the international situation does. Our point is that whatever the needs may be, one cannot realistically expect the United Nations or other global organizations to jump into community or statehood, to skip all the intermediary stages of the process. The process might be accelerated, but the United Nations will not be granted—or if it would, it would not be able to fulfill—the more central functions of economic, military, and political regulations unless it is gradually built up through the exercise of "lesser" functions. That is, functions that put less strain on the consensus-formation mechanisms till the intermediary plateaus of regional and probably bloc organization are more firmly established.

their control to be gradually transferred to the global level. It would follow that a jump into global community and world government is extremely unlikely.

The question arises of how the different modes of intrabloc organization affect the interbloc relationship. This is a particularly crucial question, since the stability of the international system will largely depend on interbloc orientations, at least for the near future.

Many authorities believe that a multibloc system, or two blocs with a large number of uncommitted countries, is more stable than a polarized system. In a polarized system, the sides cannot make further progress through regrouping of blocs (which is possible if there are more than two) or by attracting uncommitted countries. A complete stalemate ensues in which the two sides, especially if they are hostile to one another, are likely to seek each other's destruction.[29]

We point out below that the world might actually be moving toward bipolarity, and that a bipolar world might well be more stable than a multipolar one, because nuclear duopoly avoids many of the dangers of the Nth-country problem. We suggest here that the discussion of the effect of polarization often overlooks an important dimension independent of the number of blocs—the degree of *fluidity* of the blocs. All blocs exert some pressure on members and supporters to maintain their bloc affiliation, but they differ greatly in the degree to which such pressure is exerted and in the means used. International stability is largely endangered by rigidity (i.e., low fluidity) when countries that join a bloc are not free to leave it and military force is used, if necessary, to prevent their secession. Thus, if all or most countries joined a bloc and shifts were not tolerated, this would have consequences often attributed to a mere bipolar system, even if there were three or more blocs. On the other hand, a bipolar system in which countries (or regions) are free to shift, even if some economic or status loss is involved, could be as stable as a multibloc system, if not more so.[j] We should also point out that a bipolar system is highly unstable not only when both blocs are rigid, but also if only one of them is. If countries are free to leave one bloc but not the other, this might create a trend of accumulation of countries in one bloc, which might frustrate the other into violence. One of the first political functions the United Nations might acquire, or that a bilateral bloc agreement might establish, is the freedom of countries to shift from bloc to bloc, into third blocs, or into neutrality. Freedom to shift does not require that the sides will not try to make their blocs seem ideologically or economically attractive, but that no military force will be used to prevent shifting.[30]

Viewed with this in mind, the envisioned Atlantic union is a means to strengthen one bloc organization against the other, and to improve its chances

[j] A fluid bipolar system is surely more stable than a rigid tripolar system, in which a coalition of two blocs against the third would be likely, and there would be no room for further peaceful gains, other than changing the coalition pattern.

to attract, if not to control, uncommitted countries in the competition with the Communist system. The short-run aspirations are, to use Waskow's terms,[31] international "stability"; the long-run goal is "victory" over the other bloc. This could be attained either by waiting for the Communist bloc to liberalize internally; by breaking away, one country after another, from the Communist bloc to become neutral or to join the West; or, as some seem still to expect, by destroying the other bloc by the use of force. But there is nothing "Atlantic" about these aspirations; they are very much the kind of aspirations any hostile bloc is likely to have toward another, especially if no reconciliation or building of a superordinated community is expected. The only relevant "Atlantic" feature is that the hard core of this union will be NATO, a military alliance, and the nuclear striking force of the United States. It differs in this sense from the EEC, the Nordic Council, the British Commonwealth, and most other transnational organizations whose bases are economic, cultural, or political rather than military. But the increase in scope of the Atlantic union, the addition of a common market, and possibly the growth of a political organization and even a community would serve to submerge, not to emphasize, the military foundations of this union.

Summing Up the Union's Characteristics

In sum, the envisioned Atlantic union fully answers the need for differentiation of consensus-formation among two or more levels; within its own limits it clearly builds the kind of interlevel division of functions that is likely to succeed, i.e., keeping initially high spill-over functions to lower levels and delegating lower spill-over ones to higher levels, and at the same time supporting the upward transfer of functions to the bloc level. It is less clear what the union orientation to top-level, global organizations is. Until now there have been few plans for a transfer of additional functions to the top level; in fact, some resistance to such plans might be detected. But these plans might be formulated and gain more support as the bloc organization is firmly established. It is in this context that we must view the relationship to the Communist bloc; now it is antagonistic, but there is little if anything in this union that would prevent it from serving as a steppingstone to the building of an interbloc community. The most alienating effects the union is likely to have, especially as its design becomes more clear and its institutions established, are in Asia, Africa, and Latin America. In part, the source of alienation will be economic, but more crucially it will be the result of status and political factors, for the Atlantic union is going to be a "closed, restrictive, exclusive"[32] white club that will implicitly treat all these countries as second-class citizens, to be given grants but not seats in its councils and to be guided but not to share in the formulation of policies that directly affect their fate.

While there is hardly a point of no return, the restructuring of the Atlantic union to include the less developed nations raises the question: What would the union be like if they were included to begin with, just as they are in the United Nations or the British Commonwealth? Since this seems to be one of the major shortcomings of the Atlantic union, we devote the following discussion to a brief analysis of a Western union, the Commonwealth of the Free, that is similar on several counts to the Atlantic one, but differs on this crucial dimension: It is not exclusive to "have" countries; it includes "have-nots" as well.

THE COMMONWEALTH OF THE FREE

A Multilevel Structure

The Commonwealth of the Free[k] would be a multilevel organization like the Atlantic union. Like the union, it would provide for more international co-operation in a bloc organization above national and regional ones. The main point of difference would be that the commonwealth would include a much larger number of regions, such as the Western European Union (a somewhat enlarged EEC), the Nordic Council (Scandinavian countries, possibly including Britain), the Central American Union, the South American Union, the North American Union (the United States, possibly with Canada), various African regional organizations, and others. The United States would not join any regional organization other than possibly the North American one, but would remain free to serve as the regulating and balancing power among the various regional units, a point to which we return.

All nations and region members of the commonwealth would be equally represented in its annual conference of heads of state and various blocwide organizations. Puerto Rico might provide the capital for the commonwealth, to symbolize the wider-than-Europe orientation of the organization, the role of the United States in it, and successful application of a Western way of development.

Interlevel Division of Functions

On the commonwealth level one would expect first the development of functional organizations, such an organization in which mutual tariff reductions are negotiated (similar to GATT, but one that would include all member countries). This could become a commonwealth-wide common market at a later stage, as the commonwealth political institutions developed enough to be able to carry the regulatory functions such economic integration requires.

Although many projects of economic development would possibly continue to be regional, much co-ordination, such as price stabilization and planning of interregional division of labor and funds, could be commonwealth-wide. The European-American OECD would be replaced by an organization in which

k We refer to it in this section, to save breath, as the commonwealth, not to be confused with the British Commonwealth.

both the granting and the receiving nations would be represented, as they are now in the International Monetary Fund. Similarly, many of the defense systems, such as those of NATO, SEATO, CENTO, ANZUS, and the Rio Treaty, would continue to be regional, but they might be supplemented by some central co-ordination, standardization, and strategic reserves. Some co-ordination of foreign policy, especially regarding the other bloc and the United Nations, could be developed along the lines suggested by Buchan for NATO only.[33] While almost all political unification would be initially regional, the development of central values, symbols, and institutions, such as the annual meeting of the heads of states, might enhance the upward transfer of political identification.

In general, we expect the process to be one of upward transfer of functions, authority, and loyalties. As the integration of regional units partially replaced the nations as the units of action, the commonwealth would partially replace the regional units. This upward transfer would be accelerated if contributions by the "have" countries were made to the commonwealth and then allocated by its central bodies, in which all members were represented, or by regional ones. The main point is to avoid economic patronage of one country by another, especially if the former is much inferior in its bargaining power. Such patronage is too much like the old colonial relationship; sooner or later it produces alienation that undermines both the relationship and the system relying on it. The Colombo Plan and the five-country consortium for India set precedents for wiser multilateral relationships by avoiding a one-to-one tie between a "have" and a "have-not" country.

Removing the special ties between an aid-granting and an aid-receiving country might weaken the willingness of "have" countries to contribute to the foreign-aid program. While being a patron often has some economic advantages, much of the reward is psychological. The British taxpayer is more willing to finance grants to the West Indies than to Brazil, and the French taxpayer to the Ivory Coast rather than to Pakistan because of rewards they obtain for looking after "their" dependents. But, as the American experience shows, these rewards can be generalized from a specific country (for example, the Philippines) to the free world. Eliminating patronage ties by first pooling the aid available, then allocating it through the central commonwealth or regional institutions in which the recipient countries are represented, would do away with much of the alienation foreign aid generates. It is like replacing the grant of a rich man to his poor cousin with welfare services financed by progressive taxation.

A decision implicit in this structure should be made explicit: a commonwealth structure would make the developing nations much more committed to the commonwealth and the Europeans less committed than they would be to the Atlantic union. This is expected since the Europeans would have, at least formally, the same status in the commonwealth as other members, and their semi-imperial relations to their ex-colonies would be further weakened. But it seems that the weaning of Europe from older habits is essential for the success of the West in a nonviolent competition with the East over the Southern continents. And as the experience of the United Nations and of the British Commonwealth show, the European countries can learn to accept equal status with the new nations.

Interunit Relations

What would be the United States' position in the new commonwealth? First of all, it would be a regional member, because of its size, assets, and power. Second, it would participate, like other regional members, in the various commonwealth-wide organizations. Third, it would transfer to the commonwealth organizations many of its overseas obligations, to be administered by organs in which all members were represented and which they all financed, each contributing according to his assets. One per cent of the gross national product for development is, for instance, considered an acceptable levy.

The United States' special role in the commonwealth would be to throw its weight, as it did often in the past, on the side of the "have-not" countries, to counterbalance the latent imperial tendencies of the "have" countries. Thus the United States would continue to press for larger contributions by all "have" countries, especially those that are now laggard on this score, to developing nations, and for a more rapid liquidation of the remainders of colonial regimes, as it did with the Netherlands over New Guinea, with Portugal over Angola, and with Belgium over Katanga.

Which side needs more support—the emerging nations or the established ones—is the central choice implied in choosing between forming an Atlantic union or a Commonwealth of the Free. For the United States, joining an Atlantic union would entail a further strengthening of ties to the established nations, the building up of an already strong commitment, and the weakening of a lesser commitment—that to the emerging nations. On the other hand, a membership in the commonwealth would *not* imply that the United States was joining the new nations to the neglect of its more powerful and traditional allies; rather, it would be trying to find a new balanced union in which both could be placed. The proposal also recognizes that the European countries are not monolithic societies. Within them are, on the one hand, liberal forces that desire to open a new page in their relationship with the new nations, and on the other, conservative forces that romantically dream about the empire days. Initiating the Commonwealth of the Free, as outlined above, would strengthen the liberal forces.

The Commonwealth and Outsiders

The formation of the commonwealth would constitute more an institutionalization of the present Western bloc than a radical break from it. Still, this reorganization might have some deeper repercussions. These depend on what the criteria of membership in the commonwealth would be; how much pressure, if any, would be put on countries to join it; and finally, if the formation of an institutionalized commonwealth would lead to a bipolar world of a rigid or nonrigid type.

Membership in the various regional organizations could be open to all countries that met certain minimal standards. Those might include some economic conditions, such as agreeing to remove, at a certain pace, barriers to international trade and movement of capital and labor, or co-operation in the regional development plan.

Second, some minimal political entrance standards might be set. The exact specification of these would have to be carefully considered, but the broad guidelines clearly suggest themselves. On the one hand, if the West insisted on accepting only fully established democracies, there would be extremely few members in the commonwealth. Many European countries would not qualify, not to mention most new nations. On the other hand, it would be morally wrong and politically unwise to allow tyrannies of the right or the left to join. Such members make the West support the kind of regimes it has set out to counter, and undermines its appeal to the people of most countries who desire a world that has more freedom and social justice.

Where exactly one draws the line is not so important as that one recognizes that nations, like people, are free to choose their company. There are certain minimal standards to which the West would not force anyone to adhere, but it need not associate or share its assets with those who do not adhere to them. Setting such standards is not unprecedented. The Kennedy administration from time to time set a standard, for instance, in the Alliance for Progress (development) and for the Dominican Republic (democratization). But unfortunately it was not consistent in pressing for these standards. We would favor making such standards a minimum requirement for membership in the Commonwealth of the Free. It should also be able to expel members whose regimes deteriorate. The expulsion of Cuba from the OAS in 1961 sets both a procedural and a substantive example.[34] If Haiti, Nicaragua, and Paraguay had been expelled too, this precedent would be of course much more potent.

While surely one should not force any country to join any union, there is nothing morally or politically wrong in making membership attractive. Thus, for instance, one should not force Colombia to join a Latin American union, but one might limit foreign aid to countries that democratize, develop, and co-operate with their neighbors, as was an explicit condition in the Marshall Plan. What countries object to is having aid contingent on joining a military alliance that they believe benefits the aid-granting country but not themselves. Making democratization or regional co-operation a prerequisite would be viewed as much more legitimate and would be much less alienating, if not to a particular government, at least to its people and those of other nations.

Countries that have a Communist regime, such as Yugoslavia, should be confronted with the same conditions for membership as other countries. If Spain and Portugal are expected to abolish police brutalities before they can join the commonwealth, so must these countries. When free elections become a membership requirement, they should be required for Communist countries as well.

Thus every country should be free to join, not to join, or to leave any regional union and the commonwealth, but at the same time efforts should be made to make membership both attractive and in line with the basic norms of the Commonwealth of the Free. In this way, one of the most important missions of the West would be fulfilled: the commonwealth would provide a model of international organization in which nations were encouraged, but not forced, to grow both economically and politically.

If this system were successful, many countries would join the commonwealth and few if any would leave it. Could this not, in the long run, largely reduce, if not eliminate, the pool of uncommitted countries, and lead to an unstable world?

We should, first of all, point out that polarization would not necessarily occur, even under these conditions. At least some countries, on the periphery of the commonwealth, would probably prefer to play the two blocs against each other without committing themselves to either side.

Second, nothing in the system advocated here would prevent countries from leaving one regional union or bloc to join the other, or to become neutral, or to form a bloc of their own. It is true that the more integrated countries become, the more difficult such mobility will be. But if the countries have voluntarily entered such marriages, why should this not limit their "individual" mobility? Of course, they could still move in and out of blocs. Such moves would inflict some losses—the more bloc or regional integration, the larger the loss—but this would be by no means impossible, nor would the loss be intolerable.

We should also point out that there is no way of preserving a multibloc system once there are two superpowers, unless the other countries wish it. One can hardly expect the U.S.S.R. to force countries to stay neutral if they wish to join their bloc. Actually, as we have seen, it is not so important for international stability to have two, three, or four blocs as it is important that membership is free to come and go.

Finally, the bipolar world is—next to a monopolar system—the best system for the handling of the Nth-country problem. It is much easier here than in a multibloc system. So long as there is no nuclear disarmament, many countries, quite likely at least one in every bloc, will strive to have a nuclear striking force, if only to deter the others, and as a symbol of hegemony within their bloc. This means that, the larger the number of blocs, the larger the number of nuclear countries is likely to be. In a bipolar world the danger of not being able to identify the nuclear attacker is almost eliminated, while in a tripolar—not to mention a larger system—this problem becomes almost insoluble. Thus, at least from this viewpoint, a bipolar world is more stable than a multipolar one, even with the same degree of rigidity in both.

In sum, the Commonwealth of the Free, like the Atlantic union, would group nations into regional organizations and a bloc structure. It too would satisfy the requirement for a multilevel structure of decision-making, and it too would leave high spill-over functions to the lower levels of organization and delegate low spill-over functions to higher levels. In both bloc organizations, the process of upward transfer is likely to occur, though in both it might stop at the bloc level rather than continue to the global one. The main difference between the two is the scope of membership and the relations among them. The Atlantic union would be an exclusive, rich, white, ex-imperial and semi-imperial organization. The commonwealth would include, on equal footing, the "have" and "have-not" nations, white and nonwhite nations, ex-empires and ex-colonies. Second, the role of the United States would be quite different. In the Atlantic union, its ties to Europe would be strengthened and those to other countries outside the club weakened. In the commonwealth, the United States would be first among equals, not tied particularly to any regional organization, free to influence the distribution of assets in the historical direction of greater equality of wealth, power, and status. The commonwealth would also have more leverage than the Atlantic union to encourage new nations to develop and democratize, since by fulfilling these conditions they could gain membership, a reward lacking in the exclusive Atlantic union. In the long run, the global level of organization will have to accumulate functions, authority, and loyalties to a degree that will enable it to limit conflicts among blocs to nonviolent competition.[35]

Blocs must ultimately be judged by their relationship to the global level of organization. Do they serve as steppingstones, as an intermediary stage in the process of upward transfer, or do they prevent this process? The Atlantic union and the Commonwealth of the Free might both serve as blocs of either type, though the large number of new nations—less committed to the Cold War—that would be members of the commonwealth makes it more likely that it, rather than the Atlantic union, would facilitate the upward transfer to the global level of organization, the build-up of stability that rests on one world and the United Nations.

NOTES

1. These figures are for 1958. The German expenditure has since somewhat risen. See Alastair Buchan, *NATO in the 1960's* (London: Wildenfeld & Nicolson, 1959), p. 39.
2. *Loc. cit.*
3. Emile Benoit, *Europe at Sixes and Sevens* (New York: Columbia University Press, 1961), pp. 255–257.

4. Buchan, *op. cit.*, p. 104.
5. *New York Times*, July 5, 1962.
6. *New York Times*, July 5, 1962.
7. Speech before the National Association of Manufacturers on December 6, 1961.
8. On the role of image in general and in international relations in particular, see Kenneth Boulding, *Conflict and Defense* (New York: Harper & Row, 1962), pp. 96 ff., 156–157.
9. This point was much stressed by Richard Neustadt in *The Presidential Power* (New York: John Wiley & Sons, Inc., 1960), which is reported to have impressed President Kennedy.
10. On the prospects for a United States-Canada regional union, see S. F. Kaliski, "United States Trade with Canada," *Current History*, XLIII (1962), pp. 75–76. On discussion of the Atlantic union and various membership lists, see Karl W. Deutsch *et al.*, *Political Community and the North Atlantic Area* (Princeton: Princeton University Press, 1957); various books by Clarence Streit, especially his *Freedom's Frontier* (New York: Harper & Brothers, 1961); George Catlin, *The Atlantic Community* (London: The Macmillan Co., 1959).
11. For some interesting suggestions, see Buchan, *op. cit.*, Ch. 4.
12. *New York Times*, July 5, 1962.
13. See Leland M. Goodrich, *The United Nations* (New York: Thomas Y. Crowell Co., 1959), pp. 65 ff.
14. Private communication with UN officials and participant-observation in a UNESCO Conference in Montreal, in 1959.
15. Immanuel Wallenstein, "Background to Paga-I," *West Africa* (July 29, 1961), p. 819.
16. See Thomas Hovet, Jr., *Bloc Politics in the United Nations* (Cambridge: Center for International Studies, M.I.T., 1958).
17. Ernst B. Haas, *Uniting of Europe* (Stanford: Stanford University Press, 1958).
18. Ernst B. Haas, "International Integration: the European and the Universal Process," *International Organization*, XV (1961), pp. 366–392.
19. This point has been elaborated in my "The Epigenesis of Political Communities at the International Level," *American Journal of Sociology*, XVIII (1963), pp. 407–421.
20. This is illustrated by the increase of Federal participation in labor-management negotiations and the formation of nation-wide unions and manufacture associations. This point was stressed by C. Wright Mills, "The Power Elite: Military, Economic and Political," in Arthur Kornhauser, ed., *Problems of Power in American Democracy* (Detroit: Wayne State University Press, 1957), pp. 145–172.
21. These rough estimates are based on figures provided in Max F. Millikan and Donald L. M. Blackmer, eds., *The Emerging Nations* (Boston: Little Brown, 1961), pp. 150–151.
22. *New York Times*, September 15, 1962.
23. See footnote 10, *supra*. The fifteen NATO countries are most often listed.
24. See Arnold Rivle in "African Problems of Trade and Aid," *Current History*, XLIII (1963), pp. 31–32.
25. The EEC was variously referred to in these countries as "colonialist" and "imperialist." *Ibid.*, p. 32.
26. The losses to Latin America are so far not in absolute terms, but in the shrinking proportion of the EEC market Latin America provides. This is the case because the general demand of the EEC market has increased, so that it made up in part for the losses due to higher tariffs imposed on Latin American products. This still means, in net, that Latin America is lagging behind as long as it is not "in." On these points see Walter J. Schwitz, "A Common Market for Latin America?" *Current History*, XLIII (1962), pp. 2–4.
27. Fears and bitterness were expressed in a meeting of the United Nations Economic Commission for Asia and the Far East in Tokyo in March, 1962 (*New York Times*, March 8, 1962); by Latin American countries at a meeting about coffee prices in the United Nations in New York (*Time*, LXXX [August 13, 1962]); by Tito and Nasser in a statement in Cairo, in February, 1962 (*New York Times*, February 12,

1962); by Nehru and other leaders of the British Commonwealth during the Conference of Prime Ministers (*New York Times*, September 9, 1962).

28. Senator J. W. Fulbright, referring to "building a cohesive community of free nations," stated: "This objective should be pursued as far as possible within the United Nations. In large measure, however, it must be pressed outside the UN, through instrumentalities that reflect a limited but real community of common interests." See his "For a Concept of Free Nations," *Foreign Affairs*, XL (1961), p. 1.

29. See Morton K. Kaplan, *System and Process in International Politics* (New York: John W. Wiley & Sons, 1957). Cf. Amitai Etzioni, *Winning without War* (Garden City: Doubleday, 1964).

30. The conditions under which such shifting can be safeguarded by more than treaties are spelled out in my *The Hard Way to Peace: A New Strategy* (New York: Collier Books, 1962).

31. See, in this volume, "Nonlethal Equivalents of War."

32. Lippmann uses these terms to refer to the EEC and to plead for the admission of Britain into it, not noting that its admission would hardly change these qualities of the EEC or the Atlantic union. See his *Western Unity* (Boston: Little Brown, 1962), p. 38.

33. Buchan, *op. cit.*, Ch. 4.

34. Tad Szulc pointed out that "There is no convincing reason why the inter-American system should not have a machinery to police its own behavior, particularly at a time when a departure from the minimal standards of democratic conduct could lead to a complete political and ideological breakdown." Address, Latin-American Colloquium, Georgetown University, Washington, D.C. (June 28, 1962).

35. This point is elaborated in Part III of my *The Hard Way to Peace*.

PART IV

Constraints on Decision-Making

11

ANATOL RAPOPORT

Critique of Strategic Thinking

Instead of defining "strategic thinking" at the outset, we shall rely on the entire discussion to convey its essential features and flavor. Moreover, we shall not be concerned with the merits of specific policy recommendations dominated by strategic thinking. Critical analyses of such recommendations are undertaken elsewhere in this volume and in other writings of the authors represented here. Our concern will be with the general framework in which strategic thinking occurs. Specifically we have in mind the underlying, frequently implicit but sometimes helpfully explicit, assumptions on which rest the arguments of the numerous proponents of various deterrence policies in the present global conflict. The output of the RAND Corporation contains a wealth of examples of this approach. An especially revealing specimen, in which the emotional as well as the intellectual props of the strategic orientation are alarmingly apparent, is Herman Kahn's much-discussed volume, *On Thermonuclear War*.[1]

We shall be referring to the exponents of strategic thinking as "the strategists," and it will appear at times that "the strategists" are being accused of shortsightedness, callousness, and other faults. It should be clear that these accusations are leveled not at individuals but at idealized representatives of a mode of thought. In practice it would be impossible to point out "the strategists" as a sharply defined group. All of us at times think strategically. Indeed, strategic thinking is only a variant of rational thinking, and so is a part of the heritage of science. We could easily resign ourselves to the conclusion that the evil by-products of strategic thinking represent a part of the price we pay for being civilized. On the other hand, we could accept the responsibility placed on us by civilization to apply the methods of analytical critique to self-appraisal. If, as some strategists maintain, thinking in strategic terms is no more than a dispassionate appraisal of realities and potentialities, the same is true of the critique of strategic thinking. Of necessity, however, such a critique, being a critique of *thinking* rather than an appraisal of military or political situations, must depend to some extent on intuitive and introspective methods and so must bring in concepts foreign to strategic thinking.

Our critique will be made from two points of view. From one, it will appear that there is an inherent tendency in strategic thinking to simplify the analysis of a situation in order to make a decision problem more tractable. Decision problems can be cast into several models, which can be arranged in an ascending order of complexity. The more complex the model, the more problematic becomes the estimation of data required to solve the associated decision problem. Accordingly, pressure is constantly operating on the strategist to simplify the situation, either by casting it into a simpler model or by skirting around the estimation problem. The concomitant danger is in the omission of possibly the most essential features of the problem.

From the other point of view, the dangers inherent in strategic thinking are even more serious. They lie in the tendency not merely to oversimplify problems but to misrepresent them. This happens when a decision problem cannot be solved at all within the framework of strategic thinking, even if exact data are available. We shall give examples of such problems, which have no "best" solutions in the context of strategic decisions. Such problems can be solved only if we invoke extra-strategic considerations, which must of necessity be couched in terms foreign to strategic thinking, such as social norms, trust, empathy, and so forth. Ironically, it is rigorous strategic analysis that has brought these extra-strategic concepts to the forefront. Nevertheless, when we assume the role of strategists, we tend to avoid introducing these concepts into our analysis. We shall offer conjectures on why this is so and will argue the necessity of overcoming this blindspot.

THEORY OF RATIONAL DECISION

We shall begin by examining the elements of the theory of rational decision, which serves as the alleged rigorous basis of strategic thinking. In particular, the theory of games, in many ways the most advanced and sophisticated branch of decision theory, has had a pronounced influence on strategic thinking.

As strategists, we do not, of course, always or even frequently represent situations as formal decision problems or as schematized games. Our expositions and recommendations rest, for the most part, on verbal arguments, frequently spiked with rhetoric. To the extent, however, that strategic thinking can lay claim to a "scientific" foundation (a claim often made in various guises), the support for this claim must come from an analysis of situations and problems in the methodological framework of rational decision theory.

It will be useful to distinguish three kinds of decision theory: formal, prescriptive (or normative), and descriptive (or empirical). The formal theory is purely deductive. Like mathematics, of which it frequently appears as a branch, formal decision theory does not depend on data. The axioms of the theory, as well as all the pertinent variables in any problem, are always assumed given. The task of the theory is confined to constructing a deductive apparatus to derive logically necessary conclusions from the given assumptions.

Prescriptive theory, on the other hand, is concerned with the determination of *optimizing* decisions. The existence of such "best" decisions does not by any means imply that real people are always or predominantly guided by them. Thus discrepancies between the prescriptive theory and observed behavior do not refute a prescriptive theory. Such a theory says how people ought to act, not how they do act.

A descriptive theory seeks to find principles that guide real people's decisions. It must therefore rely on behavioral data. Such a theory accomplishes its aims if it can say (and support the statement with empirical evidence) something like this: "People make decisions *as if* they were guided by the following decision rules. . . ." Since the decision patterns of different people may be different, the descriptive theory will rely in part on classifications, typologies, and other groupings of decision-makers.

It follows that formal decision theory (which includes the mathematical theory of games) is most closely related to the deductive disciplines (logic and mathematics), prescriptive decision theory to applied science (engineering and operations research), and descriptive theory to the behavioral sciences. Obviously, recommendations based on the deductions of the formal theory imply the application of prescriptive theory. But as we shall see, applications are often powerless without the knowledge of actual decision processes. Thus rational decision theory can provide a useful guide to action only if all three of its sources are drawn upon.

DECISION UNDER CERTAINTY

The simplest example of a decision problem involves the choice of one of several courses of action, where the outcome of each course is uniquely determined. If the choice is between actions $A_1, A_2, \ldots A_n$, leading respectively to outcomes $O_1, O_2, \ldots O_n$, and if O_i is the most preferred outcome, then the decision to Choose A_i is called a rational decision.

Already in this simplest problem we can see the distinctive features of the formal, prescriptive, and descriptive approaches. The formal theory does no more in this context than *define* the rational decision. Prescriptive theory must prescribe. It can therefore be applied only after the most preferred outcome has been determined, which may require no more than an introspective "scanning" on the part of the decision-maker. Descriptive theory, on the other hand, must relate many people's preferences to their decisions, which requires the examination of many preference schemes and many decision schemes. It is by no means certain that such comparisons will immediately enable the investigator to organize his data into a theory, that is, a set of general propositions consistent with observed facts. In short, it is not certain that a descriptive theory of rational decisions is at all possible. To assume that it is possible is to affirm the basic faith inherent in the scientific enterprise.

The "minimal axioms" of a rational decision theory (whether formal, prescriptive, or descriptive) can be illustrated in the context of our example. They are generally taken to be

(1) *Consistency:* If O_i is preferred to O_j, then O_j is not preferred to O_i.

(2) *Transitivity:* If O_i is preferred to O_j, and O_j to O_k, then O_i is preferred to O_k.

(3) *Instrumentality:* If A_i leads to O_i, and A_j to O_j, and if O_i is preferred to O_j, then A_i is chosen in preference to A_j.

In the context of formal theory, these "axioms" are no more than definitions. In the context of prescriptive theory, they are rules for ordering preferences and choosing actions. What role do the axioms play in descriptive theory? Clearly they cannot be general descriptions of our gross observations of how people order preferences and choose actions. Violations of these principles are all too common, as the following examples show.

(1) A man prefers meat to fish at one time and fish to meat at another, apparently violating the consistency axiom.

(2) Among three oranges, a man prefers O_1 when he must choose between O_1 and O_2; O_2 when the choice is between O_2 and O_3; O_3 when confronted with O_3 and O_1. Here the transitivity axiom appears to be violated.

(3) A man knows that A_1 will lead to O_1 and A_2 to O_2 and prefers O_1 to O_2 but nevertheless chooses A_2, apparently violating instrumentality.

One possible conclusion is that such behavior is not "rational." But of course we can do better than that. We can often redefine the situation so as to remove the violations of the axioms. For example, it may appear on closer examination that the man prefers fish to meat only on Fridays. We can then list four choices instead of two: (1) meat on any day but Friday, (2) meat on Friday, (3) fish on any day but Friday, (4) fish on Friday. In this context, consistency is not violated.

In the second example, we may discover that the man compares oranges according to three criteria—price, appearance, and flavor—and that in each paired comparison a different criterion dominates the choice.

In the third example, the man may have realized after comparing O_1 and

O_2 that not only O_1 would be the consequence of choosing A_1, but also some cost associated with A_1 itself, which was not compensated by the difference between O_1 and O_2.

Such investigations belong to descriptive decision theory. They are undertaken with a view to establishing a consistent and transitive preference ordering among a set of outcomes. Prescriptive theory, on the other hand, assumes such an ordering already established. Thus if each action leads to a certain outcome, application of the instrumentality principle makes the decision problem trivial.

DECISIONS UNDER RISK AND UNCERTAINTY

Choices of action cease to be trivial in situations in which actions do not lead to unique outcomes. The simplest possible case of this sort is that of two actions, A_1 and A_2, of which A_1 may lead either to O_1 or to O_1', while A_2 leads to O_2. A real decision problem arises if O_1 is preferred to O_2, which, in turn is preferred to O_1'. Does (or should) the "rational man" prefer the certainty of O_2 to the risky choice between O_1, which is better, and O_1', which is worse?

Common sense dictates the relevant considerations. What are the relative likelihoods of O_1 and O_1'? How much is O_1 preferred to O_1'? In short, how big is the risk, and is it worth taking? We note that two new elements have been introduced into our view of rational decisions—degree of preference and likelihood of occurrence. In the context of *certain* outcomes, likelihood of occurrence was clearly irrelevant. Nor was it necessary to assume degrees of preference. Only an *ordering* of preferences was required. With the introduction of outcomes whose likelihoods influence decisions, both of the above-mentioned new concepts enter *per force*.

If the outcomes are uncertain, we can distinguish two limiting cases: (1) the likelihoods can be assigned as numerical probabilities; (2) nothing is known about the likelihoods. (Intermediate cases involving partial knowledge of the likelihoods will not be discussed here.)

The notion of a calculated risk (to the extent that this phrase is not simply a label used to justify a dangerous policy) depends essentially on the possibility of attaching numerical values to likelihoods of events, as is done in the theory of probability.

In our example, suppose the probabilities of O_1 and O' are known—p and p' ($p + p' = 1$)—and suppose the worth (utilities) of the three outcomes can be expressed *numerically* as u_1, u_1', and u_2 respectively. Then if the optimization principle is to maximize the expected utility, the decision-maker is told to choose the risky action $A^{1'}$ provided $pu_1 + p'u_1' > u_2$, and the certain action A_2 otherwise.

On what basis is such a decision called rational? The most convincing rationale usually offered is that based on the law of large numbers proved in the theory of probability. The law applies if the utilities are additive; that is, the utility of N outcomes O_1 is Nu_1. Then the law states (roughly) that if the risky choice is made many times, the odds become so overwhelmingly large that the average gain *per choice* will be very nearly $pu_1 + p'u_1'$. Thus the situation is reduced to one where the choice is between (nearly) certain outcomes, namely between $pu_1 + p'u_1'$ and u_2 per choice. For instance, if a man rolls a die many times in succession and receives two dollars every time a 4 appears and pays one dollar when it does not, he can expect after 1,000 throws to lose very nearly fifty cents per throw ($\frac{1}{6} \times 2 + \frac{5}{6} \times (-1) = -\frac{1}{2}$). His choice is between this amount and nothing per throw, which results if he refuses to play. The gamble clearly does not pay. It pays, however, to the gambling house, which operates on precisely this principle, as do insurance companies and all businesses that base their policies on actuarial calculations.

If the expected gain principle is a rational one, at least where money gambles are involved, why do people make risky choices that do not pay? In particular, why do people gamble in casinos? The usual common-sense answers are either that gambling addicts are stupid or that they derive other satisfactions from the gambling situation, which compensate them for the monetary losses.

Neither of these explanations is satisfactory in the context of buying insurance. Clearly, the buyer of insurance (say fire insurance) accepts a risky choice with a negative expected money gain (positive to the insurance company). But few people would call him stupid on that account or guess that he gets a thrill from the gamble. A possible explanation is that people buy insurance because "this is the thing to do." This may very well be. It is easy, however, to construct an example removed from customary practice, in which the acceptance of a risky choice with even a large positive expected money gain will seem exceedingly unwise.

Suppose a man is asked to stake his life savings ($10,000) on a draw of a single card from a well-shuffled deck. If the deuce of spades is drawn, he gets a million dollars; otherwise he loses his $10,000. The probability of drawing a particular card is $\frac{1}{52}$. The expected gain is therefore ($\frac{1}{52} \times 1,000,000$) — ($\frac{51}{52} \times 10,000$) = $9,423.08, a very substantial positive expected gain. Yet most would agree that the man would be foolhardy to accept this offer.

Utility theory was originally invented to circumvent this difficulty. James Bernoulli argued in effect that to most people a million dollars is by no means "worth" one hundred times more than $10,000. It might, for example, be worth only ten times as much. If utility values of money amounts instead of the money amounts themselves were used in the calculation of expected gains, it would turn out that many gambles with positive expected money gains have negative expected utility gains and vice versa. Thus the expected gain principle would be saved as a rational decision principle.

Let us now see how our risky decision rule reads: In risky situations assign numerical utilities to outcomes (whose probabilities are presumed known). Choose the action that leads to the greatest expected utility return.

As always, we must keep in mind that a decision theory may be viewed as either prescriptive or descriptive. The rule as stated is a prescriptive rule. The verbs are in the imperative mood. In a corresponding proposition of descriptive theory, the verbs would have to be in the indicative mood: "For every person, each of a set of outcomes has a numerical utility, whose expected gain the person seeks to maximize." To validate this proposition, one should actually exhibit a "utility function," which governs each person's decision.

If the theory is prescriptive, the problem arises of how to apply the rule. For example, the decision-maker might ask, "How do I assign (my own) utilities to outcomes? I have a good idea about my order of preferences, but I am at a loss how to assign *numerical* values to the outcomes."

If the theory is neither prescriptive nor descriptive but only formal, these problems do not arise. The utilities, like the probabilities, are simply assumed given. The translation of the general principle (of maximizing expected utility gains) into specific cases involves nothing more than calculations of these expected gains. Since the calculations are sometimes difficult, the problems associated with risky outcomes may be by no means trivial (as they are in the case of certain outcomes where only an inspection and a comparison of magnitudes is involved). Still these problems remain, in the context of formal theory, straightforward problems (*problèmes bien posés,* to use Henri Poincaré's expression). One always knows how to solve them in principle. The problems associated with prescriptive and descriptive decision theories, on the other hand, become serious methodological problems as soon as risky outcomes are introduced. Whereas the determination of a simple preference order could reasonably be considered a simple task (at least in simple contexts), a method of determining utilities (introduced to preserve the expected gain principle) is by no means a straightforward problem.[a]

To summarize, the introduction of risky choices into a decision problem

---

[a] The theory of utility we have just outlined is based on ideas introduced by Bernoulli in the eighteenth century. Later this theory lost most of its appeal, mainly because there seemed to be no way to determine utilities either objectively or introspectively. In their *Theory of Games and Economic Behavior* (Princeton: Princeton University Press, 1955 [rev. ed.]), Oskar Morgenstern and John von Neumann reintroduced utility theory on a different basis. In their formulation, the utilities of outcomes of any decision-maker can, in principle, be determined if the decision-maker has consistent and transitive preferences among all risky choices. The utilities so assigned are then automatically such that the choices reflect decisions to maximize expected utility, and this optimization principle need not be introduced as an additional principle of rational decision [cf. R. D. Luce and H. Raiffa, *Games and Decisions* (New York: John Wiley & Sons, Inc., 1957), Chapter 2]. This stratagem virtually reduces decisions under risk to decisions under *certainty,* since each choice now leads certainly to a (possibly risky) outcome, which is not distinguished from any other kind of outcome. In this way, the prescriptive theory of decision under risk is reduced to triviality. The problems of descriptive theory remain (and possibly become aggravated), because of the difficulty of determining consistent and transitive choices among risky outcomes. Formal theory, however, is helped immensely by this "tautological" definition of utility, since the maximization of expected utility now becomes a logical consequence of its definition and so prescriptive aspects can be sidestepped. This solution has enabled Morgenstern and von Neumann to build their *formal* theory (decisions in conflict situations) on logically sound foundations.

complicates the task of a formal decision theory only moderately, in that it necessitates a numerical calculation instead of a simple comparison of magnitudes. But it complicates the task of a prescriptive theory substantially, because it poses the problem of how to assign utilities to events. It complicates descriptive theory severely, because it poses the problem of determining how *other* people assign utilities to events (especially since different people may do so in different ways). This uneven rate of increasing complexity in the three types of theory persists as the decision situations become more and more complex.

Our next step is to pass from choices among risky outcomes to those among uncertain ones. These are outcomes whose probabilities are unknown. In addition to assigning utilities, the decision-maker must now also assign probabilities to events. The behavioral scientists correspondingly must ascertain how people assign probabilities to uncertain events (if they do). Formal decision theory bypasses this problem. Indeed, if probabilities were assumed as given, the problem would be reduced to the risky choice problem. To distinguish the uncertain choice problems, formal decision theory has introduced assumptions not based on probability considerations and has thus continued the line of development that links elementary decision theory with the more advanced theory of games.[2] We shall not pursue this development here, although we shall examine the theory of games in its own characteristic context—the conflict situation.

PROBABILITIES OF EVENTS

Let us now look at the problem of assigning a probability to an event. Such assignments can be made on three kinds of grounds—empirical, logical, or intuitive. To illustrate the first, suppose we are given a coin that is said to be biased and are asked to estimate the bias. A reasonable way to proceed is to toss the coin many (say 1,000) times. The observed frequency of heads is a good estimate of its probability. If such repeated experiments cannot be performed, we cannot estimate probabilities on empirical grounds.

Early workers in probability theory argued that probabilities can be assigned on logical grounds. In order to do so, it must be possible to list a set of events among which "there is no reason" to suppose any one is "more likely" than another. For instance, in the case of a perfectly symmetrical die, it is argued that since "there is no reason" to suppose that the appearance of any of the six faces is any more likely than another, we must assign equal probabilities to all the faces. The probabilities of complex events (for example, that at least one appearance of either 1 or 4 will occur in three successive throws) can be then computed according to the calculus of probabilities (also a purely logical procedure).

The "logical" assignment of probabilities raises the problem of listing the basic "equiprobable" events. In the case of the die, such events readily suggest themselves. But not all situations are so simple. A classical paradox illustrates the difficulty. Suppose Robinson Crusoe catches two turtles on the beach and contemplates the chances that he can start a turtle farm. (Assume that he cannot determine the sex of turtles by inspection.) He could assume that the three equiprobable possibilities are (1) two males; (2) two females; and (3) male and female. According to this assumption, his chances are 33⅓ per cent. But he could assume with equal reason that there are four equiprobable cases: (1) male, male; (2) male, female; (3) female, male; (4) female, female. In this case his chances are 50 per cent.

The more nearly correct probability could be determined if Crusoe could get more evidence, for example, catch many pairs of turtles. But this would be an empirical, not a logical, determination of probability. It is clear that the assignment of a probability on "logical" grounds cannot also be "verified" logically. Such an assignment is made *arbitrarily*, depending on which events one has singled out as equiprobable. In some cases, to be sure, the choice of one set of equiprobable events seems obviously "natural" (as in the case of the symmetrical die), and so the assignment of numerical probabilities on logical grounds can be defended.

When the event under consideration is *unique*, and there is no natural list of equiprobable alternatives, there is no objective basis either on empirical or on logical grounds for assigning a numerical probability to it. An example of such an event is the outbreak of a thermonuclear war in a given time period. An assignment of a numerical probability to this event can be made only on intuitive grounds. This probability can represent a degree of belief of the person who assigns it, but there is no compelling reason to prefer one man's degree of belief to another's.

DECISIONS IN CONFLICT SITUATIONS

So far we have been dealing with problems in which the decision-maker needs to consider only his own preferences and the possible "states of nature." Whatever explicit assumption he makes about nature, the tacit assumption of a rational decision-maker is that nature is neutral with regard to his preferences and ambitions. She does not guide *her* choices by what he does, striving to frustrate (or to help) him. The situation changes drastically as soon as an *opponent* appears on the scene—to wit, another decision-maker whose interests are wholly or partially opposed to those of the first decision-maker and who is, moreover, also "rational."

The extension of decision theory to this situation (and more generally to situations with more than two "players," as the decision-makers are now called) is known as the theory of games.

A crucial difference between decision problems involving one decision-maker (sometimes called games against nature) and a bona fide two-person game is that in the latter the other player is not neutral. The decision-maker, who finds himself on one end of the decision process, as it were, cannot assume that the other end is determined by a "state of nature" and so depends on chance. In certain special cases, when the decision-maker knows that the interests of the other player are diametrically opposed to his own (the situation known as the zero-sum game),[b] the decision-maker can assume that the opponent will do his utmost to thwart him. The problem of assigning probabilities to the moves of the other does not arise in this context. In fact, in the so-called "games with perfect information," like chess, the moves of the other are in principle certain and would be actually certain if the game were played perfectly.[c] In a way, therefore, such games can be classed with decision problems under certainty, except that the outcomes are now arranged not in a one-dimensional array but in a two-dimensional one, since each outcome now depends on a *pair* of decisions (choices of action).

Such an array is called a strategy matrix. It is shown in game theory that the outcome of a play of any two-person game can be formalized as a single choice of a strategy[3] by each player. The rows and columns of the strategy matrix are accordingly the strategies available to the respective players; the entries are the outcomes.

We have seen that the problem of assigning probabilities to the possible states of nature (i.e., what is likely to happen and is not under the control of the decision-maker) does not arise in the theory of the two-person game. However, another problem of equal or greater difficulty does arise in prescriptive theory. The outcomes, we have seen, are the entries in the strategy matrix. The decision-maker must assign at least a preference ordering to these outcomes. He can in principle assign his own preferences by "introspective scanning." But how about the preferences of the other? In formal theory this is not a problem, because both players' utilities are presumed given. But it is a serious problem in prescriptive theory, because what the "best" strategy is depends on what strategy the other will choose, and this, in turn, depends on his preference order of the outcomes. Without knowledge of the others' preferences, the decision-maker does not know what game he is playing and so cannot choose the "best" strategy, no matter how rational he is and how rational he can assume his opponent to be.

If the game is known to be zero-sum, this difficulty is obviated. By defini-

[b] The name "zero-sum" derives from the circumstance that in such games, whatever the outcome, the sum of the payoffs (in utility units) to the two players is zero. Thus whatever one wins, the other necessarily loses. The situation is the same if the sum of the payoffs is any amount, provided it is the same for all outcomes. Thus constant-sum games are not essentially distinguishable from zero-sum games. "Zero-sum" is the more customary designation and will be used here.

[c] More precisely, the moves are certain to be selected from a *set* of best moves, but the certainty of the outcome is not affected thereby. The structure of games of perfect information is such that once the rules have been stated, the outcome of the game is determined. For example, the outcome of a perfectly played game of tic-tac-toe is always a draw. Variations in the outcomes of chess games are due entirely to the fact that chess is not played perfectly. If it were, then either White would always win, or Black would always win, or every game would end in a draw (we still do not know which).

tion, the utilities assigned to the opponent are one's own utilities with the opposite sign. However, even in this situation, two cases can be distinguished —games with saddle points and games without. A saddle point is an outcome that is both the worst for self *in its row* and the best for the opponent *in its column*.[d] All games of perfect information have such outcomes. In this case, an intuitively acceptable "best" strategy choice can be prescribed. This is the row (column) that contains a saddle point. This choice is best, because neither player can do better for himself *under the constraints of the situation* (namely, the partial control exercised by the opponent).

There are, however, also games without saddle points. Here there is no best single strategy for either player. But game theory shows that each player can choose a "mixed" strategy, which is best in a certain sense. A mixed strategy is a decision to choose each of the available strategies with a certain *probability*. It is best in the sense that it maximizes the *expected* utility gain for each player under the same constraints noted above.[e]

Thus the prescriptive problem is solved in the context of the two-person, zero-sum game. In real life, however, the problem remains of determining whether the game being played is indeed a zero-sum game. More generally, before a decision is calculated, the decision-maker must ascertain what the situation is. If the situation can be represented as a game, he must ascertain the other's utilities of outcomes. This problem falls outside the scope of both formal and prescriptive theory. It belongs to descriptive theory, which, in turn, is anchored in the behavioral sciences, whose methods depart widely from those characteristic of formal and prescriptive theories of rational decision.

LIMITS OF PRESCRIPTIVE THEORY IN CONFLICT SITUATIONS

So far, the limitations of rational decision theory we have discussed were *cognitive* ones. If probabilities could somehow be determined (in a one-person game), and if the utilities of outcomes, one's own and the opponent's (in a two-person, zero-sum game) could be correctly ascribed, the methods of prescriptive theory could determine a rational decision.

Once the limits of the two-person, zero-sum game have been transgressed, game theory cannot be unambiguously prescriptive even if the cognitive problem is solved. Examples of games without intuitively acceptable solutions are numerous; they appear already in the fundamental treatise on games,[4] together with the recognition of the limitations of the theory of games as a prescriptive theory. (The theory never claimed descriptive status.) We shall next examine two of the best known such examples.

---

[d] By convention "self" in a two-person game chooses a row of the strategy matrix; the opponent chooses a column.

[e] See the final remarks of footnote [a].

Prisoner's Dilemma[5]

In this nonzero-sum game,[f] each player has a choice of two strategies— C (co-operating) and D (defecting). The choice of C by both (CC) results in positive payoffs to both. The choice of D by both (DD) results in negative payoffs to both. However, a *single* defector gets a larger gain than that won by each of two co-operators, and a single co-operator suffers a loss larger than that suffered by each of two defectors. It follows that the temptation to defect is re-enforced by the fear of being the single co-operator. On the other hand, if both players defect, both lose, whereas they might both have won had they co-operated. Hence the dilemma. The game is illustrated in Figure 11-1.

	C	D
C	1, 1	−2, 2
D	2, −2	−1, −1

FIGURE 11-1. Prisoner's Dilemma[g]

Switching Sides

Another example of a game that poses a dilemma for a prescriptive theory involves three players who are to divide a dollar by a majority vote. The game allows bargaining, coalitions, and side payments (bribes). If A and B tentatively agree to take fifty cents each (freezing C out), C may offer one of them (for example, B), a better deal. Suppose C offers B sixty cents, if B deserts A. The 60-40 split is clearly to the advantage of both B and C, compared to the previous arrangement. Nevertheless, if B accepts C's offer, he is in danger of losing everything, since in that case it will be of advantage to both A and C to freeze B out and split 50-50. But if this happens, we are back where we started. No matter what arrangement is proposed, it is always possible for *two* of the players to think of a better arrangement (for them); and being a majority, they can defeat the previous proposal. There is no *stable* solution. Hence no solution can be prescribed *without appealing to principles outside of the theory of games.*

Social Norms

Some of these principles have been mentioned already by Morgenstern and Von Neumann, who speak of "social norms" governing bargaining pro-

[f] In a nonzero-sum game, the sums of the payoffs are not constant. Hence some payoffs may be better for *both* players than others.

[g] The first of each pair of pay-offs is to the row chooser.

cedures. The application of social norms involves either traditional or moral considerations and falls outside the scope of strategic thinking. A social-norm solution is not an "optimum within the constraints imposed," because the social norm is not a "rule of the game," and hence is not one of the original constraints.

For instance, if A, B, and C decide to take thirty-three cents each and to donate one cent to charity, it is clear that each of the three pairs is actually refraining from "optimizing," since any pair could get the whole dollar. Rather, the players are acting in accordance with some equity principle, not defensible on strategic grounds.

Similar considerations apply to the Prisoner's Dilemma. Suppose the players come from a society in which the following behavior norm (Kant's ethical formula) has become internalized: "When faced with a choice of action, choose the one that would benefit you if every one chose the same way." Two players subscribing to this principle will choose CC even in the absence of formal collusion. Now it is fallacious to argue that these players are also "optimizing rationally" because they have arrived at the best outcome on the basis of their knowledge of how people in their society behave. *On the basis of this knowledge,* a player who has not internalized the norm still might decide to defect and get the biggest payoff as the single defector. *This* would be the "rational" strategic choice. But then we are forced to the conclusion that two "rational" players (choosing DD) will do worse than two "irrational" ones (choosing CC). The hard fact remains that there is no solution of the Prisoner's Dilemma that is both strategic and intuitively acceptable. We can only conclude that decisions based on strategic thinking fail to "optimize" not because of cognitive errors, but because of the very nature of strategic thinking itself.[h]

THE LURE OF STRATEGIC THINKING

What is the attraction of strategic thinking? What makes it the predominant mode in decision-making purporting to be "rational"? To understand the prestige of strategic thinking, we should first look at its successes, not at its failures. We must look also at the success of the entire orientation into which

[h] Some game theoreticians argue that if "social norms" influence decisions, then the utilities associated with adhering to such norms should be included in calculating the entries in the strategy matrix. Thus our two "socialized" individuals should not be considered to be playing a Prisoner's Dilemma game. From the point of view of formal theory, this is correct, and we have seen that such an interpretation amounts to defining utilities tautologically (cf. footnote [a]). It is clear, however, that this conception of utility is useless in many decision problems, for it is doubtful whether a single utility measure exists for anything that may happen. Typically decision difficulties arise when one does not know how to compare utilities of outcomes, for example, the utility with a possible disutility of misplaced distrust (Othello's tragedy). Real-life situations structured like the Prisoner's Dilemma are genuine dilemmas.

the mode represented by strategic thinking naturally fits. This is the "scientific" or "rational," orientation. Specifically,

(1) Rational thinking is realistic. It takes into account verifiable facts. It guards against mistaking our wishes for facts. It separates questions about *what is* from questions about *what ought to be*.

(2) Rational thinking is deductive. It uses all the available techniques of reasoning, including calculations and mathematical inference.

(3) Rational thinking is predictive and therefore productive. On the basis of established facts, reasonable valid inductions, and rigorous deductions, rational thinking provides us with the most reliable estimates and expectations of future events, thereby giving us a measure of control over our environment.

(4) Rational thinking is unencumbered not only by sentiments (in which we usually find strong admixtures of wishful thinking), but also by awe of authority, by superstitious and neurotic fears, and other compulsions. It is therefore essentially free and courageous thinking.

(5) Rational thinking is indicative of sanity, because mentally disturbed people are the ones who violate the principles of rational thinking most conspicuously.

Since the strategic mode derives from a dispassionate pursuit of rational considerations, it appears akin to the scientific mode and so shares in the superlative prestige which scientific thinking enjoys. In short, strategic thinking appears today as thinking in the problem-solving mode, therefore as *mature* thinking.

The problem-solving orientation is usually juxtaposed to more archaic orientations when cultures are compared or to less mature ones when personalities are compared. Examples of the former are the "traditional" decision modes of preliterate societies; examples of the latter are the neurotic reactions of compulsive individuals in the face of difficulties. The Nazi slogan "The true German thinks with his blood" is a characteristic example of a regression affecting a whole nation.

Similar comparisons are used to bolster the strategic mode in matters of international policy. "Realistic" is the label most frequently attached to strategic thinking in this context. The implication is that the alternative is the "idealistic" (that is "unrealistic") mode, dominated by sentiment or wishful fantasy, neglectful of realities, devoid of technical knowledge, and generally irresponsible. In international affairs, the "realist" is scornful both of the ravings of the hate groups and of the pleadings of the pacifists. His own voice appears as the voice of reason, the voice of science in an area where dispassionate scientific standards are especially difficult to apply. In short, the "realist's" accusation against the "idealist," who is presumably dominated by hate or love impulses, is that the idealist, unwilling or unable to conduct an objective analysis, ignores problems instead of facing them. One of the idealist's cardinal sins, according to the realist, is oversimplification. The accusation is not unfounded. But it can be turned with equal force against the theorizing realist.

The tendency to simplify is endemic to all theorizing, because the aim of theory is to pose and solve tractable problems. The most successful scientific theories are those that have identified those features of phenomena that turned out to be both essential and tractable. The theoretician is thus understandably biased to seek out tractable problems, hoping to come to grips with the salient features of the phenomenon he is investigating. This bias underlies the unwillingness to restructure theoretical approaches that have been "paying off."

While we cannot claim that strategic thinking has been particularly successful in international affairs (in the absence of either meaningful comparisons or criteria of success), the forces of intellectual inertia in this area are nevertheless very strong. These forces may derive from persisting traditions or from a natural selection of power-oriented personalities into influential political positions. They may also derive from the close link between political and military problems in our era or, specifically in the United States, from the dominant role of the business orientation in policy-forming bodies. (Rational business decisions in a private-enterprise society are predominantly strategic.) The forces of intellectual inertia exert a pressure to cast the problems of foreign policy into strictly strategic terms. Foreign policy becomes intellectually indistinguishable from military policy, which, by its very nature, is essentially strategic. The paradigm of a policy "problem" becomes: (1) the setting of goals, which are expressed predominantly in terms of power relations; (2) an appraisal of means—that is, predominantly of power resources; (3) an appraisal of the opponent's goals and means (conceived in similar terms), and (4) the design of some optimization procedure under the given constraints—that is, allocating power resources and implementing power policies in pursuit of our goals.

Given this framework, there is a strong tendency to *select* problems that can be made to seem tractable. This tendency is clearly discernible in those who think professionally about foreign and military policy, those who are given credence by virtue of their claims to pertinent expertise. The nature of this expertise is determined by the nature of the problems singled out for attention—that is, strategic problems. The cycle is thus closed: The problems determine the selection of the experts, and the experts determine the selection of the problems.

The underlying intellectual framework in which policy decisions are made remains based on the "theory of rational decision." This is particularly true in the context of conflict, where power relations are the most clearly perceived variables. If a recommended decision is supported by calculations involving the accepted "realities" (which may be tangible, like weapons, or intangible, like some vaguely perceived interplays of pressure), and if the projected goals of a policy and the means at the disposal of the decision-maker are expressed in power terms, the recommendations are considered seriously (whether they are accepted or rejected). If, on the other hand, the goals, the means, the estimates, the motives are made in terms other than the accepted currencies, the recommendations are not taken seriously. They appear to be not merely poor recommendations, but irrelevant to the problems.

Calculation (explicit or implicit) is the dominant mode in strategic thinking. Being also the explicit deductive tool of the exact sciences, calculation confers the prestige of science on strategic thinking in international affairs. As strategists, we are most comfortable in the role of engineers or of operations researchers. We would like to regard the independent variables (the payoffs and constraints) as given so we can get on with the job to which our expertise is geared. The facetious sign said to adorn an office at the RAND Corporation speaks for our cynical recognition of this bias. "DON'T THINK," the sign reads, "COMPUTE!"

THE DRIVE TO SIMPLIFICATION

Let us now see what "givens" must be fed into the machinery of rational decision, particularly in the context of international conflict.

In the simplest case, where actions are assumed to lead to unique outcomes, all that is needed is a preference ordering of the outcomes. If this can be done without ambivalence, the problem is solved. But human experience indicates that unambivalent ordering can be effected only in very special circumstances—for example, where some quantity of which one cannot have too much can be singled out. Such quantities readily suggest themselves in the familiar contexts of business, technology, sports, and so forth. More profit, greater efficiency, higher scores can always be assumed as preferred. Where outcomes are complex, preference orderings are by no means obvious, since undesirable side effects often ride on desirable goals. In *principle,* as strategists, we are not supposed to weigh one against the other. This is the business of the decision-maker. He is supposed to have done this weighing in advance so as to present the strategist with an ordering. However, the very presence of the strategist (who may himself be the decision-maker in certain cases) creates a pressure to formulate the problem so that it can be solved. This pressure tends to focus attention on comparable variables and to call attention away from noncomparable ones. Accordingly, the pressure is to structure situations in the language of one-dimensional value scales.

Dramatic illustrations of this mentality are provided by the arguments offered by strategists in support of large-scale civil defense measures. Typically, such decision problems are formulated in terms of simple arithmetic. If a civil defense program can assure a reduction of immediate fatalities in a thermonuclear attack from 100 million to 50 million, the result is held to be without question an argument in favor of the program. It is admitted that the "gain" should be weighed against other considerations, for example, the money costs of the program. Or, in response to vigorous protests against this too obvious oversimplification, it is also admitted that the gain should be weighed against the possibility of increased likelihood of war. But these are characteristically presented as separate problems—that is, problems of estimating and comparing costs or the respective likelihoods of war. *Aside* from "costs" it seems to the computing strategist that the choice between 100 million and 50 million casualties is a perfectly obvious one.

Without challenging this particular judgment, I should like to challenge the principle that such choices can be made on quantitative bases alone. Assume the following farfetched but not unthinkable situation. The United States is currently suffering 40,000 traffic fatalities per year. Assume an invention that could reduce fatalities to 20,000 per year, of which 10,000 would die on the highways, and 10,000 more would die in some unspecified but painless manner (in connection with the operation of the invention). The identities of these 10,000 would be determined by lot and announced twenty-four hours before their deaths. My guess would be that this "improvement" would not be acceptable to the majority of Americans. The example may seem fantastic, but a somewhat analogous situation is said to have occurred during World War II. At a certain bomber plane base in the South Pacific, it was known that a pilot had a 25 per cent chance of surviving his tour of duty (thirty missions). A computation was made showing that the chance could be raised to 50 per cent if one-way missions were flown. A selection procedure could be instituted in which each pilot had even odds to draw a black or a white ball. If he drew a white ball, he would be rotated to the States. If he drew a black one, he would have to go on a one-way mission. Neither the commanders nor the pilots ever considered this alternative seriously.

It can be argued that the crucial feature in these examples is the foreknowledge of the doomed individuals. Certain death may be harder to accept than the original situation, even if the odds of dying are reduced. However, in the following example, this feature does not occur. In a conversation shortly after the end of World War II, Zhukov and Eisenhower were reported to have compared Soviet and American infantry tactics. According to Zhukov, Soviet infantry advances through a mine field "as if it were not there." American practice involves extensive preliminary mine-clearing operations. Zhukov is said to have argued that the Soviet tactics meant fewer total casualties. Whether Eisenhower was convinced of this or not, Soviet tactics seemed to him unacceptably callous.

Many more examples can be marshaled to show that the utility of saved human lives or the disutility of lost ones is not calculated primarily in numbers. The magnitude of effort to save five trapped miners exceeds by far the magnitude of effort that could be, but is not, undertaken to save many more lives in less dramatic circumstances. We are horrified when people burn in plane crashes, but are not so much affected when they burn in their own homes. Miscarriages of justice leading to the execution of innocent persons arouse indignation entirely out of proportion to the number of lives lost. In our roles as strategists we often phrase our arguments to imply that any but quantitative comparisons of lives lost or endangered are "irrational." Thus we dismiss the preoccupation with nuclear testing fall-out on the grounds that the number of lives endangered and the genetic hazards are small compared with natural hazards (cosmic radiation, X rays). "War is terrible," writes Herman Kahn, "but so is peace."

In pointing out seemingly "irrational" preference orderings ("irrational" because they cannot be neatly reduced to numerical terms), we depart from the role that, in other contexts, we rigorously defend—the role of ethically neutral scientists who presumably seek the most efficient means to each *given* goal. But we can never avoid postulating certain preferences (goals) and eschewing others. Whatever the source of this bias, it is consistent with the inclination to simplify the "givens." The bias inhibits examination of preference orderings that may be actually operating in the population.[i]

Compared with the simple, quantitative utility assignments postulated in strategy problems, the values held by real people often seem to violate the axioms of rational decision. They seem at times inconsistent, at times intransitive, at times anti-instrumental. It may be that, by a proper redefinition of context, the observed value preferences can be shown to be rational in the framework of some consistent value system. But this investigation is beyond the competence of the strategists and therefore beyond their inclination to pursue it.

The most obvious shortcoming of strategic thinking appears when decisions must be made under uncertainty. Here the drive to simplify leads to a reduction of the problem to a more definite one: that of decision under risk where the probabilities of outcomes are known. Recall that the solution of a risky choice problem consists of maximizing expected utility. The determination of the maximizing strategy is possible only if both the utilities and the probabilities of outcomes are known. We have already discussed our propensity to simplify the assignment of utilities. In addition to the same propensity, another one is revealed in the context of uncertain outcomes—the propensity to assign probabilities to unique events, for example, to an outbreak of thermonuclear war. Obviously, such assignments cannot be made on empirical

---

[i] Herman Kahn (See Reference 1) bases his estimate of ten to sixty million "acceptable" deaths in a thermonuclear war on a "poll." It should be unnecessary to point out the superficiality of such a procedure. Given different phrasings of questions, different descriptions of possible outcomes, different lists of alternatives, the results of such polls might be quite different and inconsistent. It is naïve in the extreme to interpret such results as indicators of value preferences. The procedure can be explained only by the investigator's impatience to get on with the problems which really interest him, namely the strategic problems.

grounds, since one cannot speak of a "frequency" of such wars. Nor can such assignments be made on logical grounds because no universe of equiprobable events is available as a starting point. It follows that such assignments can be made only on intuitive grounds. The "probabilities" represent no more than degrees of belief for which, in the case of a thermonuclear war, no basis in experience exists. Nor can such estimates ever be verified. A nuclear war either will occur or it will not. *Neither* event will provide evidence either for or against a degree of belief. There is therefore nothing (not even a concern for future vindication) to prevent the advocate of a policy from assigning probabilities to events at pleasure, in particular, in a way that makes the recommended policy the optimizing one.

The simplifying assumptions inherent in strategic thinking not only reduce uncertainty choices to risky ones, but also reduce two-person games to one-person games. It is by no means our contention that international conflicts can be exhaustively studied as two-person games. Still, we should expect that a two-person game model more closely approximates a conflict situation than a simple optimization problem (game against nature). Nevertheless, policy recommendations are frequently made in the latter context. This simplification is especially evident in civil defense planning, in which nuclear wars are implicitly identified with natural disasters of various magnitudes instead of with *responses* of an opponent who has taken our plans into account.

From the point of view of strategic calculations, games-against-nature models are preferable to two-person game models. In the latter, not only must one's own utilities be assigned, but also the opponent's must be estimated. Further, two-person game models with saddle points are preferable to those without saddle points. In the latter, not only preference orderings (one's own and the opponent's) but also numerical utilities are required. Moreover, the solution of a two-person, zero-sum game without a saddle point is a "mixed strategy solution." Translated into a recommendation, such a solution might read: "Spin a roulette wheel. If 1 through 10 comes up, build ICBM's; if 11 through 18 comes up, concentrate on medium-range missiles; otherwise strengthen conventional forces." It would take considerable effort to convince a decision-maker ignorant of game theory that such a recommendation might really represent a "rational" decision in a situation that can be represented as a zero-sum game without a saddle point.

Finally and most significantly, situations that should be represented as non-zero-sum games are frequently cast (tacitly) into zero-sum models.

MISREPRESENTATION OF CONFLICT SITUATIONS

When a nonzero-sum game is represented as a zero-sum game, the problem is not merely oversimplified but actually misrepresented. The zero-sum game has a unique solution, at least in formal theory, but many nonzero-sum games have not, at least not in the conventional framework of optimization procedures. Nonzero-sum games, as we have seen, introduce *perforce* concepts alien to rational decision theory. These concepts include negotiation, social norms, even "trust"—that is, recognition that the opponent is not entirely an enemy in the sense that his interests partially coincide with one's own. The Prisoner's Dilemma is a case in point. If collusion is allowed, the dilemma disappears, since the mutually beneficial outcome CC (cf. Figure 11-1) can be agreed upon. In the context of the balance of terror, this outcome can be taken to represent bilateral disarmament; the other outcomes represent unilateral disarmament (CD and DC) and status quo (DD). Admittedly, this model is as much an oversimplification as any of the models proposed by the strategists. However, the model does capture the essential nonzero-sum feature of the situation. The strategists' arguments against disarmament, on the other hand, reveal their zero-sum bias in the way they circumscribe their repertoire of assumptions. For example, their refusal to consider "trust" seriously in the formulation of strategy reflects a tendency to keep the image of the enemy as the opponent in a zero-sum game. Whatever the enemy gains, we necessarily lose. In a zero-sum game, it is sufficient to examine only one set of payoffs (one's own). The Prisoner's Dilemma then appears as in Figure 11-2.

	C	D
C	1	−2
D	2	−1

FIGURE 11-2. "Self's" Payoffs in the Prisoner's Dilemma

This is a zero-sum game with a saddle point, DD. It leads to the outcome that harms both players.

An explicit criticism of this tendency to cast conflict situations into zero-sum games was made by T. C. Schelling. Schelling's critique focused on the absence of psychological components in game theory. Undoubtedly Schelling had in mind not the formal (i.e., mathematical) game theory, but rather the sort of theory one could use in application, either descriptively or prescriptively. His failure to make this point explicit stimulated vigorous rebuttals from game theoreticians, who demonstrated that Schelling's critical appraisal was irrelevant to formal game theory. Since Schelling and the game theoreticians were talking about different things, the rebuttals also missed their mark. It will be instructive to examine and to analyze a sample of Schelling's suggestions for modifying and extending game theory because of the way they reveal the limitations of strategic thinking.

Consider the following nonzero-sum game (Figure 11-3).

	B_1	B_2
A_1	1, 2	0, 0
A_2	0, 0	2, 1

FIGURE 11-3. The Battle of the Sexes[6]

From the point of view of formal game theory, this game has no "solution." Neither player can guarantee himself a maximum payoff under the constraints of the situation. For example, if both players randomize their choices each gets an expected payoff of ¾. But this is not the best that either can do. In a negotiated settlement, either of the players can guarantee himself 1 if he is willing to let the other have 2. The question is: Who gets the bigger payoff? This question is relegated to negotiation, which is beyond the scope of game theory.

Theories of negotiation, arbitration, bargaining, and so forth have enjoyed a vigorous development since game theory appeared on the scene. These theories were doubtless inspired by the problems posed in nonzero-sum games and, to a large extent, by the relevance of these procedures to corresponding conflict situations. In particular, there have been attempts to construct formal bargaining theories in the spirit of rigor that characterizes the mathematical theory of games. (Compare the works of Braithwaite, Nash, Raiffa.) In formal bargaining theory, the solution of the Battle of the Sexes game awards 1½ to each of the players. The solution is intuitively acceptable because of the perfect symmetry of the situation: the bargaining positions of the two players are exactly the same. Thus a certain equity principle (analogous to a social norm) is introduced into bargaining theory. This equity principle can be extended to asymmetrical games, in which the bargaining positions of the players are not the same. In that case, the equity principle is supposed somehow to reflect the difference in the bargaining positions—for example, the threat opportunities open to each player (emphasized by "power-oriented" investigators) or the possibility of increasing substantially the utility payoff to one of the players at only a slight expense to the other (emphasized by "ethically oriented" authors).

These are, no doubt, psychological components. A particular psychological component, closely related to that of "threat credibility," is pre-emption. The concept of pre-emption destroys the symmetry of the Battle of the Sexes game. Suppose that in the process of negotiation, A "pre-empts" by announcing that he will choose Row 2 regardless of what B does. If B believes him, argue the proponents of pre-emption, he has no choice but to choose Column 2. The resulting payoffs are 2 to A and 1 to B, and "equity" based on symmetry goes by the wayside.

Now from the point of view of formal game theory, this solution is irrelevant to the game as it is represented in the strategy matrix. The matrix of strategies is a formal representation of a game in which all the allowed moves have *already* been defined in terms of strategies which must be chosen *simultaneously* and *independently*. If we assume that one player can choose a strategy and announce his choice to the other, this means that a different game is being examined. In the "pre-empted" Battle of the Sexes game the strategies would be schematically presented thus:

A's Strategies	B's Strategies
A_1: Choose Row 1	B_1: Choose Column 1, whatever A does
A_2: Choose Row 2	B_2: Choose Column 2, whatever A does
	B_3: Choose strategy analogous to A's
	B_4: Choose strategy opposite to A's

The resulting (2 x 4) game is then the following:

	B_1	B_2	B_3	B_4
A_1	1, 2	0, 0	1, 2	0, 0
A_2	0, 0	2, 1	2, 1	0, 0

We see that B_3 dominates B's other three strategies. That is to say, by choosing B_3, B can do at least as well (and possibly better) than by choosing any of the other three strategies. Thus there is no need to consider the other three (*N.B.*: within the framework of rational decision theory!). The game now reduces to the following:

	B
A_1	1, 2
A_2	2, 1

Only A has a choice, so the "game" has disappeared in any significant sense. We are back to the most primitive decision problem: a single decision-maker choosing under certainty.

So it appears that the introduction of pre-emption simply trivializes the game (when pre-emption is examined in the framework of formal game theory). In justice to the strategists, we should point out that they do not view pre-emption in this simple-minded way. They seem well aware of the real psychological problems involved in pre-emption. At least they allude to these problems when they refer to the "credible threat" with the emphasis on "credible." A dramatic model of the credible-threat situation is shown in Figure 11-4.

	SWERVE	STAND FIRM
Swerve	1, 1	−2, 2
Stand Firm	2, −2	−100, −100

FIGURE 11-4. The Game of Chicken

"Chicken" differs from Prisoner's Dilemma in that neither strategy dominates the other for either player. As in the case of Prisoner's Dilemma, game
theory cannot prescribe definitively here. A pre-emption by A would be the
announcement, "I choose Row 2, regardless!" (Or, in the case of the two
cars speeding toward each other, an announcement to drive straight ahead,
regardless.) Now the real game of Chicken (like the game of Brinksmanship
in international relations) is played in real time. Suppose the driver of one
car signals his "pre-emption" to the other. Unless one is committed to the
assumption that "our side always wins," one is forced to concede the possibility of counter-pre-emption in the remaining time. One might, if one
wished, construct a game in which both pre-emptions are announced and in
which the choices open to each player are now to believe or not to believe
the other's determination. The probability that the opponent means business
increases with the shortening distance between the two cars. This complicates
the game but does not change its character. A further complication can be
added by allowing "communications of the second order": that is, an announcement to the effect that one does not believe the other's intentions and
a reply to the effect that he in turn does not believe that the other does not
believe, and so on.

MISLEADING CONCEPTIONS OF "REALISM"

Now it would seem that posing a psychological problem to strategists would
either lead them to instigate psychological investigations or to examine current psychological knowledge for possible guidance. However, to the extent
that we have become engrossed in strategic thinking, we tend to shy away
from either seeking or making use of psychological knowledge. The reason
is easy to discern. Psychology studies man, his real behavior, his motiva-
tions, and underlying values. As strategists, we study (or purport to study)
the logic of conflict in which the values are given "utilities." We are most
comfortable in situations in which the constraints are imposed either by
neutral nature or by a *deus ex machina*, the enemy. In both cases, the constraints are fixed. Those imposed by nature can be studied with reasonable
assurance that the very act of studying them will not change them. Those
imposed by the enemy are circumscribed by power, which is always seen as
directed against one's own power. Once the conflict is formulated strategically,

it is not necessary to ask what the enemy *wants* to do, but only what the enemy *can* do. If he can blackmail us, he will. If he can do us in, he will. A genuinely psychological approach is a threat to the strategic view of conflict. This is why psychological problems are as a rule bypassed in strategically-oriented writings. These writings give hardly any thought to the actual psychological or cultural constraints imposed on decision-makers in real society, let alone to the value systems of these societies.

The strategist's idea of making a conflict more realistic is simply to make strategic considerations more complex. We have accordingly accumulated a vast collection of Rube Goldbergian contraptions, whose paramount attractiveness to virtuoso strategists is "ingenuity." In spite of our hopeless entanglements in this monstrous maze, most of us are quick to accuse those who would reformulate the issues and problems in human terms of muddleheadedness and naïveté. We have translated the game of strategy (where men may engage in ruthlessness and cunning to their heart's content *because* it is only a game) into a plan of genocidal orgies, and we call the resulting nightmare "realism." (In a pure power conflict, it is always "realistic" to expect the worst from the other, who is always the "enemy.") But even this tacit assumption is abandoned when we must make a strategy appear reasonable. At crucial points, the enemy is usually pictured as rational, that is, trying to maximize expected returns on the basis of utilities and probability estimates ascribed to him. This seems far from "expecting the worst." In the balance of terror, an irrational enemy may be far more dangerous than a rational one. But it suits us to assume the nuclear-age analogue of the Marquis of Queensberry rules.

The "realism" inherent in strategic thinking appears to be a curious mixture of cynicism and naïveté. One looks in vain for the sort of realism that preserves a connection, or at least a distinction, between data and assumptions, between facts and inferences. This lack is especially glaring in the failure to face the fundamental distinction between natural and behavioral science. As a rule, the assumptions made in natural science do not affect the material under study; in behavioral science they do. If strategic thinking is to be realistic, it must deal with human behavior and must recognize this peculiar feature of assumptions about human behavior. This is particularly true of the assumption inherent in decision problems. We have seen that the calculation of expected gain involves the assignment of utilities and probabilities to events. Typically, the events are unique, and consequently, only subjective probabilities can be assigned to them. But such a probability is in no way a property of the events. It is an *attitude* of the one who assigns the probability. Even more obviously, the utility of an event is an attitude. So are the estimates of others' assignments of utilities and probabilities. Thus the solution of a decision problem of this sort depends primarily not on an act of cognition, but rather on a choice of attitudes. The situation that results from such a formulation of a decision problem is a situation of *our own making*. That is, in "solving" such a problem we do not *discover* a portion of reality and act upon knowledge so obtained; we *make* a portion of reality. The enemy may be cunning and ruthless, but we have played an important part in making him so (just as he has helped to make us cunning and ruthless). This principle of self-fulfilling assumption in human affairs has been pointed out so frequently that it is embarrassing to be obliged to restate it. Nevertheless, the fact remains that, although many strategists mention this principle as a serious difficulty in international relations, they have neither incorporated it into their theories nor refuted its relevance. In strategic thinking, the constraints remain fixed; in real life they are fluid and essentially affected by the operating assumptions of the decision-maker.

SUMMARY

We have listed what seem to us some gross inadequacies of strategic thinking, having in mind at all times the context of international conflict, in which the inadequacies become, in our opinion, most flagrant and most dangerous. To begin with, we have described the tendency in strategic thinking to oversimplify problems in order to make them more tractable by methods of rational decision. Indeed, we have pointed out that when thinking strategically we often bypass the difficult problems of assigning utilities according to actually prevalent values (one's own and those of others) when simple numerical criteria are available; that we "objectify" subjective probabilities; that we leave the "rational opponent" out of the picture when the problem seems more tractable as a game against nature; that we tend to depict (usually tacitly) nonzero-sum games as zero-sum games. We could go on to touch on other questionable simplifications—for example, in the Nth-nation problem in nuclear deterrence, which is usually neglected in our preoccupation with bilateral deterrence.

We have said also that the psychological components of decision-making, being elusive, tend to be de-emphasized or left out altogether from strategic considerations.

Finally, we have pointed out that strategic thinking tends to ignore the dynamics of human interaction. In order to be solved, a strategic problem, once formulated, has to stay put. But *the formulation of the problem itself* is an "event" in the context of conflict, which may radically change the situation. Typically, the self-fulfilling assumption, although frequently mentioned in the writings of the strategists, does not function as a substantial factor in their formulations.

We might surmise on the basis of what has just been said that our critique of strategic thinking rests primarily on a contention that it is not sufficiently sophisticated, with the implication that strategic thinking could be "improved" by further development: One could be more careful in estimating probabilities and utilities, one's own and the opponent's in foreseeing possible deviation from rational behavior; one could introduce "dynamics" into the game matrices by making the payoffs variable instead of constant, and so on.

I have no quarrel with these conclusions in principle. But it was not the purpose of my argument to elicit such conclusions. I do not believe that the formulation of problems in the strategic mode can be made sufficiently realistic sufficiently soon to warrant the giant investment of effort required. Moreover, such an investment of effort would not be made in a vacuum but in the present atmosphere of global conflict. The pressures inherent in strategic thinking would therefore continue to operate and to drive our conceptions of the conflict into the same dangerous channels.

The main trouble with strategic thinking is that its power can be applied (if at all) only in the solution of problems, not in their formulation. But it appears (once we free ourselves from the compulsion to solve ready-made problems) that one of the most important problems of our age is to formulate our problems. Not "How can we get what we want?" but "What do we want?" is often the important question. We take for granted that we want to "win" the hot war if it occurs, and at any rate to win the cold one. Everyone knows what it means to win a basketball game. It is even fairly clear what it meant to win or lose past wars. We go on calling thermonuclear war "war," in spite of the fact that the actual events it comprises may have no resemblance whatsoever to the events we have known as "war." Because we call a thermonuclear war "war," we think we know or can imagine what it means to "win it." One simple-minded definition was actually offered: The winner of the war will be the one who writes the peace treaty. Is this what we want, "to write the peace treaty"? What does it mean to win the Cold War in terms of actual events, not phrases? Do we want to win it? How do we know we do? How do the Russians know that they want (if they do) a "Communist government" in every country? What kind of a government would it be in fact, not in cliché-ridden description?

One hundred and fifty years ago all Republicans were Democrats and vice versa. Republicans identified democracy with the republican form of government, which, in turn was pictured primarily as a government without a hereditary monarchy. Is it true today that all monarchies are less democratic than all republics? If not, why not? What reason is there to suppose that in another generation or so (history moves much more rapidly in our days) all free enterprise countries will be more democratic than all Communist countries or, for that matter, the other way around? Three hundred years ago the two "Isms," locked in mortal combat, were Catholicism and Protestantism. One thousand years ago they were Christianity and Islam. Who won? And how do these struggles appear to us now?

These questions are of much more fundamental importance to humanity than the strategic ones, to which by far the greater effort (in terms of money and talent) is presently directed. Nor is it simply a question of priorities, that is of assigning more effort in one direction or less in the other. Strategic and human ways of thinking do not merely compete for money and talent. They compete for the mind and soul of man.

NOTES

1. Herman Kahn, *On Thermonuclear War* (Princeton, N.J.: Princeton University Press, 1960).
2. For thorough and illuminating discussions of these matters, see L. J. Savage, *The Foundations of Statistics* (New York: John Wiley & Sons, 1954).
3. For a rigorous definition of strategy, see for example, R. D. Luce and H. Raiffa, *Games and Decisions* (New York: John Wiley & Sons, 1957).
4. John von Neumann and Oskar Morgenstern, *Theory of Games and Economic Behavior* (Princeton, N.J.: Princeton University Press, 1955, rev. ed.)
5. Game theoreticians have adorned certain games with nicknames which stem from anecdotes used to illustrate their structure. For the stories of the "Prisoner's Dilemma" and the "Battle of the Sexes," see Luce and Raiffa, *op. cit.* "Chicken" is described in Quincy Wright, William M. Evan, and Morton Deutsch, eds., *Preventing World War III: Some Proposals* (New York: Simon & Schuster, 1962), p. 253.
6. Cf. Luce and Raiffa, *op. cit.*, p. 90.

12

LESTER GRINSPOON

Interpersonal Constraints and the Decision-Maker

Today computers, operations research, systems analysis, organization theories, game theory, sampling, simulation, scenarios, and other techniques are being used to help corporate, military, government, and other decision-makers to be more "rational and objective." Although improvements have been made in all these theories and techniques, even the most optimistic decision theorist recognizes that exact understanding of how decisions are made remains obscure. This obscurity is owing in large part to the fact that the theories and techniques, drawn from many disciplines, deal primarily with external influences on a decision-maker. They do not define the extent to which and the ways in which a man's inner life contributes to the decisions he makes. "The heart," as Pascal said, "has its reasons which reason knows not of."

Much of man's inner life exists in the unconscious, of which he ordinarily has no awareness. This is a basic finding of psychoanalysis, which has also shown how important and pervasive the unconscious influences on behavior can be. Decision-makers are not exempt from these influences. Since the unconscious does not distinguish between personal and professional concerns, there is little doubt that unconscious elements contribute in some measure to every decision. But that contribution is unknown to the decision-maker or, as a matter of fact, to anyone else. There is a serious question as to whether it can be known in a useful way. To date, psychoanalysis is the only systematic way of acquiring the kind of insight that one needs to become aware of unconscious influences. While making these influences explicit is part of the psychoanalytic process, their interpretation by some other person, outside of the psychoanalytic relationship, may at best be of little consequence, at worst unfortunate.

Ideally, should the important decision-maker, as such, undertake analysis? One suspects that the action-oriented decision-maker would not be especially interested in an experience so profoundly introspective as psychoanalysis. He might be so inclined if substantial evidence existed that such an endeavor would help him to make "better" decisions. But to know that the unconscious exerts important influences on decisions does not necessarily mean that an awareness of the inner as well as the outer reality will affect the way in which these influences determine decisions. Ernest Jones writes:

> An impartial observer cannot fail to be struck by the disconcerting fact that analysed people, including psycho-analysts, differ surprisingly little from unanalysed people in the use made of their intelligence. Their greater tolerance in sexual and religious spheres is usually the only mark of a change in the use of the intellect. In other spheres they seem to form their judgements, or rather to maintain their previous convictions and attitudes, on very much the same lines of rationalised prejudices as unanalysed people do.[1]

Thus, while we acknowledge their existence in and importance to the decision-maker, what can or should be done about the unconscious determinants of decisions must at this time remain an open question.

CONSTRAINTS ON RELATIONSHIPS WITH OTHERS

While we cannot—and perhaps do not even wish to—make explicit the unconscious influences, there are other aspects of the decision-maker's emotional life which should be considered. Of particular concern are the consequences of the altered nature of his relationships with other people once he has achieved a highly responsible office. The very nature of a top decision-maker's office invariably imposes severe constraints on his interpersonal relations. This in turn affects such aspects of his inner life as his self-image, his ability to test the reality of facets of his environment, and the degree to which he feels alone.

The paths which men climb on their way to positions of power and responsibility are usually rigorous and competitive, and those who reach pinnacles of power are highly selected. Men who seek, and especially those who succeed in attaining, important decision-making positions may very well have character traits, emotional needs, and personal histories which distinguish them from others. Still, we have no reason to assume that the decision-maker, as such, has less need of a variety of human relationships. The importance of such contacts and relationships with other people may in fact increase at the very time that the decision-maker's role imposes peculiar restraints upon them.

THE PROBLEM OF ISOLATION

Recently, Clarence B. Randall, formerly Chairman of the Board of Inland Steel Company, described some of the ways executive responsibility breeds isolation.[2] He described the executive who becomes increasingly successful and decreasingly anonymous. He starts out as an ordinary commuter, moves first into the exclusive car at the rear of the train, and then into a chauffeured limousine. When he travels long distances, he no longer has the chance contact with his seatmate on a commercial plane; he now travels in a private plane with members of his staff. Before he enjoyed luncheon conversation with a variety of acquaintances at the nearest restaurant; now his luncheons are both private and prearranged. He has lost control over his appointment book so that to whom he talks, about what, and for how long are largely determined by business considerations. His social life has become increasingly constricted; here, too, the chance for unanticipated contacts with people of differing views and backgrounds has been minimized.

As the decision-maker moves up the ladder of power and responsibility, he becomes increasingly isolated, a prisoner to his office, while those whose job it is to serve and protect the office become his guards. Randall emphasized his belief that he had become "divorced from the tumult of outside thought" and he suggests that such isolation may be dangerous, not only for the man involved, but also for the organization he serves. The Versailles Court, established to insulate Louis XIV and his successors from all contact with their subjects, succeeded so well that it unquestionably laid the foundations for the French Revolution.[3] In modern times, President Wilson, during his illness following World War I, became extremely isolated, which prevented him from being attuned to the atmosphere in the Senate, and may have played a large role in the tragic failure to ratify the Treaty of Versailles.[4] Dean Acheson is also concerned with isolation when he says of the sources of policy:

> When this upsurgence of information, ideas, and suggestions is vigorous, appreciated, and encouraged, strong, imaginative, and effective policies are most apt to result. When the whole function of determining what is what, and what to do about it, is gathered into one hand, or into a small group at the top, the resulting action may or may not be strong, but it is likely to be ill-adapted to reality and self-defeating.[5]

THE ROLE OF SUBORDINATES

More specifically, the danger here may lie in the fact that blinders have been put on the decision-maker which prevent him from seeing not just parts of external reality, but aspects of himself as well. There are subtle ways in which an office may impose constraints on the relationships of its occupant. It is not simply that he is denied access to many people; he is forced to depend largely on a certain small group. This most often consists of subordinates who defer to him and who are careful about how and over what issues, if any, they disagree with him. The seriousness of this problem is roughly related to the degree of power and responsibility his office commands. It may be insignificant for the man who has one or two assistants and a secretary. But it should be a matter of concern to the general, the assistant secretary, the bureau head—to the man who has achieved a position in which almost all of his human transactions are with people who see their vital interests as best served by pleasing and impressing him.

To suggest that all who surround such a figure are sycophants overstates the case. Some have become so identified with the decision-maker that theirs is a kind of self-flattery; others have a deep sense of love for the man and wish to spare him anything they think might hurt him; still others may be struggling with competitive feelings toward him and for this reason may need to be especially agreeable, even flattering. Speaker of the House Sam Rayburn reported his first interview with the newly sworn-in president, Harry S. Truman, as follows:

> I wanted to help the fellow, so I went down there and said to him: "You don't have anything in the world that I want . . . I have come down here to talk about you. I have been watching this White House for many years. I know some of the hazards here and I want to tell you what your biggest hazard is in this White House. You have a lot of people around you here. Some of them . . . are going to try to do to you what they have tried to do to every President since I have been here. They are going to try to build a fence around you and in building that fence around you they will be keeping the very people away from seeing you that you should see. That is my first bit of advice.
>
> ". . . The next one is the special interest fellow and the sycophant. If some old boy from Missouri comes out here, he transacts his business and he has a ticket on that 6:30 B & O going back to Missouri, and he telephones down here and says he wants to pay his respects to the President. They will say, 'Why you can't see him for two or three days.' He gets on the train and goes on back. But the special interest fellow will come like the king of old. He would stand in the snow a week because the king had to see the Pope before he could navigate, and I said that fellow will stay around here for a month and will come in here sliding on his vest and, sycophantic, will say that you are the greatest man that ever lived in order to make time with you; and you know and I know that it just ain't so."[6]

There is a process of selection for those who surround the executive figure, one in which he himself, directly or indirectly, plays no small part. Men do not generally surround themselves with those who seem critical. Woodrow

Wilson, as described by Alexander and Juliette George, probably represents an extreme.

> All of Wilson's close friends—the men, the women, the professors, the politicians, the socialites—shared one characteristic: they were, or at least had to seem to him to be, *uncritical* admirers of the man and of everything he did. Intellectual disagreement or the feeling that a friend disapproved of some project he had in hand aroused intolerable anxieties. . . .[7]

It is not, however, entirely the fault of the incumbent. Indeed, the office itself, especially if it has prestige, tradition, and a public image, may have little tolerance for candor. Furthermore, the office guardians might experience considerable discomfort if such candor aroused their own ambivalent feelings about the chief.

Dangerous Effects on Decision-making

When a man becomes surrounded by people who do not, for one reason or another, accurately and truthfully reflect the impact of his ideas, his feelings, in short his person, upon them, he is in grave danger of having a false view of himself. The reactions of other people provide a most important reflection of the man but if the mirror is distorted, the image is not only worthless, but harmful.

When a man wishes to test an idea, he commonly chooses to discuss it with others who will examine it critically. If he is interested in as objective an opinion as possible, he avoids those who cannot be disinterested where he is concerned. The question arises whether a top decision-maker who has lost some or all of his anonymity can readily find such people.

In ancient times a king might dispose of a messenger who bore him news he did not wish to hear. Today the bearer of bad tidings is not consciously dealt with as though he were also their cause. Nevertheless, the information a decision-maker gets may be influenced, consciously or unconsciously, by what his subordinates imagine he does or does not wish to hear. The German ambassador to St. Petersburg in 1917 "doctored" his reports to Berlin in the direction of what he believed his superiors wished to receive; in his own diary he recorded what he really thought.[8] Conversely, when the make-up and relationship of a subordinate to his chief may be such that the underlying wish is to defy or anger the chief, distortion in the opposite direction may occur.

When the decision-maker seeks an opinion, it may be influenced, again consciously or unconsciously, by the subordinate's implicit judgment of the extent to which the question is open for consideration. This judgment may, in large part, be determined by prior expressions of the decision-maker's views, which will often be taken as givens not subject to re-examination; or, it may be based on a casual remark by the decision-maker, which is then treated as gospel. Its derivation may be more subtle: the subordinate may arrive at a judgment intuitively, from his total experience with the decision-maker. By whatever means his assessment is achieved, the subordinate's opinion—or recommendation, or "position paper"—is likely to approximate the views the decision-maker had already entertained.

The decision-maker's belief that the opinions of his subordinate were independently arrived at may result in reinforcement of his initial, casual, even impulsive thoughts about a subject which, if not originally fixed, will become increasingly so with such buttressing. This phenomenon comes to resemble a positive feedback system: the more the decision-maker limits the area open for discussion, the less likely are subordinates to explore beyond that area, and the more likely are they to reinforce a view which becomes increasingly limited and fixed. The part this kind of process may have played in leading President Wilson seriously to consider war against Mexico is described in Lincoln Steffens' autobiography. The receipt of information and opinions from a trusted friend completely outside of the establishment may have been crucial in Wilson's deciding against war.[9]

LONELINESS AS A CONCOMITANT OF HIGH OFFICE

Another consequence of increasing power and responsibility for the individual who possesses it is a growing sense of loneliness. As a man becomes more and more isolated from those with whom he used to be able to share his burdens, he is bound to experience an enhanced sense of aloneness. As Shakespeare's Henry V muses:

> What infinite heart's-ease
> Must kings neglect, that private men enjoy![10]

Moreover, many of his burdens take the form of important decisions, and the extent to which they ultimately can or should be shared is questionable. What opportunity, then, does the decision-maker have for relieving this sense of loneliness? Presumably he has his wife, perhaps other members of his family, and hopefully, a trusted friend or two. Yet, even here there may be obstacles in the path of understanding. Historically, a man's wife or his friend understood the technical aspects of his work almost as well as he did simply because there was little or no technology. Today a vast technology has accrued which no outsider can comprehend. Furthermore, governmental decisions increasingly involve information which cannot be shared legally or morally. Generally speaking, the higher the office, the more difficult its burdens are to share.

Woodrow Wilson emphasized the importance of being able to talk freely to a friend when he told Colonel House, "You are the only one in the world to whom I can open my mind freely and it does me good to say even foolish

13

ROGER FISHER

Defects in the Governmental Decision Process

Those of us who are disappointed with the direction in which the world seems headed often criticize our government for making a "bad" decision. It may be, of course, that few if any decisions are bad, that those in office, having more information at their command than their critics, are steadily making wise decisions, and that the United States is doing the best that can possibly be done. But those of us who are unprepared to accept this conclusion must ask ourselves why it is that sometimes better decisions are not made. The men who run the government are neither bad nor stupid. Far from it. With so many able and well-intentioned people in office, why aren't things better? If the avoidance of nuclear war depends upon our having a government staffed with men who are more intelligent or better-intentioned than those now there the chance of peace is indeed slim. If we hope to improve the quality of decisions we will have to look elsewhere.

My experience with the government—as an employee, as a consultant and as a lawyer dealing with it—suggests that hope for some improvement may lie in institutional changes in the process by which governmental decisions are reached. A first step toward such changes is to locate present defects in the governmental decision process. This brief paper is a preliminary diagnosis. It is an attempt to identify some institutional features which may be causing good people to reach bad decisions.

LACK OF ATTENTION TO FUNDAMENTALS

A government today is swamped with cables coming in from all parts of the world raising issues which must be decided immediately. Officials who are busily chopping at the trees lose sight of the forest. Long-range goals and the fundamental interests of the country and the world tend to be lost sight of by overworked officials responsible for attaining short-range goals and protecting day-to-day interests. The official who is trying to win a vote in the United Nations on a particular resolution is likely to forget the importance of developing a United Nations which has the confidence of other countries— an organization in which the United States does not always win. Those responsible for conducting a military engagement, should it occur, tend to think, as did General MacArthur in Korea, that the purpose of war is military victory. A hectic government office with ringing telephones and a constant clamor for immediate decisions is not a good place for backing off, thinking deeply, and placing a present decision into the context of well-considered, long-range goals. The burden of present work often results in both a failure to clarify fundamental goals and a failure to take them adequately into account.

SHORTAGE OF ORIGINAL SUGGESTIONS

The work of government officials also tends to limit the time in which they ask themselves such questions as "What might we be doing now which no one has suggested?" An in-box full of matters to be dealt with leaves an official unlikely to produce original suggestions for affirmative action which might lessen or avoid problems in the future, or to study situations which do not require immediate attention. In the present world, the State Department resembles the accident ward of an emergency hospital—not a place conducive to the invention of safety devices or precautionary measures, or to the successful practice of preventive medicine.

Perhaps the Guantanamo Naval Base in Cuba should be turned over to the Organization of American States for a medical research center on tropical diseases. Perhaps the Panama Canal should be given to the United Nations to provide for its continuing revenue to set a precedent and to avoid political problems in the future.[a] An acceptable fall-out shelter program might be worked out on an international basis with Soviet officials or through the United Nations. Should we invite Soviet astronauts to visit this country? Busy officials do not stop to produce such suggestions. This is true partly because

---

[a] These two sentences were written in 1962, at a time when neither Guantanamo nor Panama was in the news. In 1964, a better example would be proposed action with respect to Okinawa or other "left-over" islands in the Pacific.

People close to a decision-maker may, whether they are aware of it or not, be of great help to him simply by being available for listening and sharing. Robert J. Donovan said of President Eisenhower:

> His intimates are his sounding boards almost as much as they are his advisers. His brother Milton usually offers advice only in a few particular fields, but he listens to the President and lets him work his thoughts out on him. Sometimes when Milton is in Washington, the two will sit together in the President's bedroom for hours while the President grinds out his ideas on different subjects.[16]

But the intimates of a decision-maker can do more than this if they are skillful enough to be able to point out to the person of high office what may be obvious to others. For example, they might say, "But you're very angry now," or "Every time you suffer some sort of defeat you tend to do such and such," or "You're very flattered by these people." The decision-maker may feel angry, hurt, vindictive, threatened, elated, invincible and so forth—feelings which exert important influences on his behavior. These influences are preconscious and are to be distinguished from those previously referred to as unconscious. They are preconscious because, while a man is unaware of them at the time he takes the action they are influencing, they are capable of becoming part of his awareness through introspection or through being brought to his attention by others. Thus one important way in which they differ from unconscious influences is that they can readily and meaningfully be made explicit. Intimates of decision-makers are in a position to call them to his attention. A close associate of President Truman's might, for example, have pointed out that he was excited and elated over the success of the Hiroshima bomb at the time he was making the decision to go ahead with the second bomb.[17] This would not necessarily have influenced the decision, but it would have made the information available so that it could be considered and weighed along with other factors.

Decision-makers may or may not be fortunate in their capacity for insight and self-awareness, but all important decision-makers are unfortunate in that the conditions of their lives are so altered that some of the ordinary orienting influences, particularly contacts with others, do not function in the same way they do for less pivotal people. What can the decision-maker do to correct the kind of distortion which his high office introduces into his view of the world and of himself? What can he do to encourage people at all levels honestly to disagree with him and to propose ideas which they think may be unpopular with him? How can he be sure that when he is behaving unreasonably someone will call this to his attention? These and other questions emphasize the serious problems which are raised when those functions ordinarily served by unfettered interpersonal relations are impeded. It is clear that this is a dangerous dilemma for both the individual and the institution he serves. What is not evident is how individual decision-makers and large institutions can systematically compensate for these most important constraints on interpersonal relationships.

NOTES

1. Ernest Jones, *Papers on Psychoanalysis* (Boston: Beacon Press, 1948), p. 207.
2. Clarence B. Randall, "Business, Too, Has Its Ivory Towers," *New York Times Magazine*, July 8, 1962.
3. W. H. Lewis, *The Splendid Century* (New York: William Sloane Associates, 1953).
4. Thomas A. Bailey, *Woodrow Wilson and the Great Betrayal* (New York: The Mac-Millan Company, 1945).
5. Don K. Price, ed., *The Secretary of State* (Englewood Cliffs, N.J.: Prentice-Hall, 1960), p. 41.
6. C. Dwight Dorough, *Mr. Sam: A Biography of Samuel T. Rayburn, Speaker of the House* (New York: Random House, 1962), p. 367.
7. Alexander L. George and Juliette L. George, *Woodrow Wilson and Colonel House: A Personality Study* (New York: The John Day Co., 1956), p. 31.
8. Robert C. North *et al., A Handbook for Content Analysis: With Applications to International Crisis* (Evanston, Ill.: Northwestern University Press, 1963), Appendix B.
9. Lincoln Steffens, *The Autobiography of Lincoln Steffens* (New York: Harcourt, Brace & Co., 1931), pp. 735–740.
10. William Shakespeare, "Henry V," in William A. Nelson and Charles F. Hill, eds., *The Complete Plays and Poems of William Shakespeare* (Boston: Houghton Mifflin Company, 1942), IV, i, lines 253–254.
11. *The Diaries and Letters of Colonel Edward M. House,* a collection of the Sterling Memorial Library, Yale University, 1/13/15.
12. Charles Seymour, *The Intimate Papers of Colonel E. M. House* (Boston: Houghton Mifflin Company, 1928), Vol. I, p. 116.
13. *The New York Times,* May 31, 1959, p. 1.
14. *The New York Times,* June 27, 1959, p. 1.
15. Walter Millis, *The Forrestal Diaries* (New York: The Viking Press, 1951), p. 547.
16. Robert J. Donovan, *Eisenhower: The Inside Story* (New York: Harper & Brothers, 1956), p. 197.
17. Harry S. Truman, *Memoirs,* Vol. I, *Year of Decision* (New York: Doubleday, 1955), pp. 421–423.

things and get them out of my system."[11] He later added ". . . you are the only one to whom I can make an entire clearance of mind."[12]

The man in high office, because he is socially constrained by his office, moves in narrower circles than his less highly placed colleagues. He meets more people perhaps, but he learns to know fewer intimately, with the result that there are fewer in whom he can confide. The problem of finding people he can trust is an especially difficult one. The word "trust" here signifies not only whether a man can be expected to keep a confidence but also whether he can be expected to be candid. We cannot overlook the possibility that for some men, positions of power tend to dampen interest in or even tolerance for candor in others.

Because his office makes it difficult for a decision-maker to establish a close, give-and-take relationship with another person, he may come to over-value such a relationship once he has established it, with the result that he delegates duties improperly and attributes virtues incorrectly. Furthermore, when the relationship comes to an end, its loss may be especially difficult for the decision-maker, whose paths to other people are limited.

THE PROBLEM OF MENTAL ILLNESS

Mental illness, when it strikes the decision-maker—as it does with anyone else—may vary greatly in both duration and severity. Although laymen usually have little difficulty in recognizing severe mental illness, the untrained observer often dismisses as minor aberrancies or of no consequence cognitive and behavioral manifestations of early or mild mental illness. It may be especially difficult for the subordinate, who does not want to believe that anything is wrong with his chief, to see a significant pattern in the changes in his behavior. Beyond the difficulty of recognition, the even more perplexing problem arises of what to do once a person of high office is considered to be suffering from a mental disturbance. Although most people usually seek medical help on their own initiative, those with mental illness frequently do not. Most often those close to the mentally ill person convince him to seek help or seek help for him. But some of those close to a decision-maker may fear the consequences for his career that acknowledgment of his need for psychiatric help might produce. Others may fear his response to the suggestion that he seek help. In general, the earlier mental illness is recognized and treated, the more susceptible it is to control.

In the case of the person of high office, special obstacles impede early recognition and treatment.

This was certainly the case in Louisiana when Governor Earl K. Long became mentally ill in 1959. Because he was above committal in Louisiana, he was taken against his will to another state for commitment.[13] After returning to Louisiana, he won his freedom from the mental hospital by removing the superintendent and replacing him with a political friend who then declared the governor sane and free. Still ill, he then proceeded to purge those who had anything to do with his confinement.[14] In the case of James D. Forrestal, the first Secretary of Defense, there is some evidence to suggest that he was becoming ill late in 1948. By January 1949, it was noticed that he was having difficulty concentrating, that he was becoming less and less able to make decisions, and that after he did make a decision, he often wished to reconsider it. All this, however, was attributed to fatigue. Two months later, he was asked to resign, and within a few days he was admitted to a naval hospital with an acute depression. Less than two months later, he committed suicide.[15]

COMPENSATING FOR CONSTRAINTS

We have described how a man, as he moves into posts of ever-increasing importance in business or government, becomes increasingly isolated and lonely; he is surrounded by an aura of his own importance, sagacity, and omnipotence which is reflected by those about him. Paradoxically enough, as his decisions increasingly affect a greater number of people, he becomes more isolated from them, and as he becomes increasingly well-known, he grows lonelier. Furthermore, the decision-maker, for whom it is increasingly important to learn the part which his own weaknesses, idiosyncrasies, and feelings are playing in his decisions may become increasingly ignorant of it. Despite all that an institution may do to protect his physical health and well-being, to facilitate his communication and transportation, to apprise him of current and technological developments, it creates an unhealthy situation with regard to some vital interpersonal functions.

On whom can the decision-maker who bears such enormous responsibility unburden himself? With whom can he frankly discuss the personal aspects of a problem? Who can afford to disagree with him? Who can allow him to give vent to his feelings? Who can directly or indirectly indicate to him his excesses or his weaknesses? These and other questions suggest functions for which high executive offices do not provide, and indeed strongly tend to exclude.

Some of these functions are left to chance, and a man may or may not have the good fortune of having a wife or other family members or a few close friends who are able and willing to help him. The decision-maker surrounds himself with sales, marketing, public opinion, legal, military, or other advisers whose job it is to call to his attention those data which are relevant to the decisions he must make. He has available to him people who are experts in dealing with all kinds of information. When it comes to assessing the influences which arise within himself, he must depend on his own insight or his good fortune in having people who can help him.

they are busy and partly because such ideas are likely to fall within another official's domain. The governmental decision process tends to produce an inadequate supply of stimulating new ideas.

INADEQUATE CONSIDERATION OF THE
IMPROBABLE ALTERNATIVE

On every issue—whether it is raised by an original suggestion for affirmative action or by the necessity of responding to a situation—a course of action that superficially seems to be unwise probably will not receive careful consideration for a number of reasons.

An official is not expected to advance energetically and forcefully arguments for an action which he himself does not endorse. Officials are expected to believe in what they say. There is, apparently, difficulty enough in resolving the diverse views already existing among various government officials. No official is expected to compound the confusion by playing the devil's advocate and urging still another point of view—which no one really supports and which he himself would not adopt if he were president.

Every official is expected, to some extent, to play at being president. He is expected to take into account all the "fudge" factors—all the political considerations which might make unwise a course of action which otherwise appears desirable. A subordinate is likely to recommend the course of action which he believes his superior wants to hear. Beyond this, there is a constraint resulting from the tendency to identify an individual with the position he advances. A subordinate may be considered wrong or stupid if he advances a proposal which is rejected. And apart from the caution which may cause him to temper his views, a subordinate's role is usually perceived as that of a judge and not an advocate. He is not supposed to advance all the arguments in favor of or opposed to a position, but rather, in his wisdom, to give his advice.

The executive branch of government is not systematically designed to produce the considerations in favor of competing alternatives, as does a court of law. There, counsel is expected to advance arguments in favor of a position which he may not personally support. He is not to act as judge but as advocate. This process tends to assure that both sides of an issue are fully explored. In a government office, on the contrary, a decision tends to be reached on the basis of a kind of Gallup poll among the concerned officials. If, on the available evidence, a course of action appears to be the one to undertake, no one is expected to devote his time to developing evidence to prove the contrary. The alternative that looks on the surface improbable is rarely explored.

Most often, the course of action that seems to be superficially unwise will still seem so after further examination. Nine times out of ten, the course of action which all officials conclude to adopt on brief examination will be the one they would adopt anyway—even if there were an official designated to develop all the opposing considerations or the considerations in favor of an alternative action. But one time out of ten, the alternative that looks improbable on the surface may, upon full investigation, turn out to be better than others. The man who at first is thought by all to be guilty sometimes turns out to be innocent. If lawyers only worked for positions which they, as judges, would support, there would be more judicial mistakes than there are now. We may surmise that the fact that government officials are generally expected to work for only those positions which they, as president, would support tends to cause some administrative mistakes.

EFFECT OF A DECISION UPON THE DECISION-MAKER

One of the most distorting forces affecting the judgment of an official is the fact that since he is personally involved in the process of decision-making, he will feel some effects of the decision. A professor, for example, standing at his distant vantage point, can consider what a wise national decision would be. He suffers from a number of disadvantages—lack of responsibility, information, and experience—but his judgment on a particular issue has the advantage of being all but unaffected by personal involvement. His job, and such power and influence as he may have, are rarely at stake. Quite likely a decision on national policy will affect him only as it affects the nation as a whole. The outside critic will not suffer if the decision is unpopular, nor will he be rewarded if the decision is enthusiastically received.

The governmental decision-maker, however, must consider the effect of a decision on his personal future. A decision in the best interests of the country might also result in his being fired, or not being re-elected, or damaging his reputation, or adversely affecting his career. For such reasons, a governmental decision-maker feels constrained by public opinion. He may also be induced by public opinion to do things for the sake of popularity which he would not objectively consider to be in the national interest. Certain publics are much more important than others. A man likes to be commended by those whose views he encounters, by his immediate colleagues, and by certain sections of the press. Men are pleased to be praised by those whose views they respect. All such personal considerations tend to distort a decision-maker's judgment as to what is in the national interest.

EFFECT OF ONE DECISION ON THE ABILITY
TO MAKE ANOTHER

One decision may have an effect on another because of the interrelation of subject matter. In addition, issues decided by a government are interrelated because the people making the decision are working together on a number

14

ELLIOT G. MISHLER

The Peace Movement and
the Foreign Policy Process

The most important and the most difficult question that must be asked about the campaigns and organizations loosely comprising the peace movement in the United States is whether or not they have had significant effects on the government's foreign policy. Peace-action groups vary considerably in structure, programs, philosophies, and political goals. However, their shared ultimate aim is to reduce the risk of thermonuclear war; they hope to achieve this by bringing about changes in the current policies and postures of the American and Soviet governments. Individual and collective efforts should be judged primarily by this criterion. If we attempt to make such an assessment, however, we discover that existing information about the influence on foreign policy of peace efforts is fragmentary and largely limited to anecdotes and gossip. Judgments vary regarding the value of these efforts. Some observers believe their over-all influence has been minimal. Boulding, for example, comments: "On the whole . . . the peace movement has been small in numbers and sectarian in outlook. It has kept alive the hope of peace and it has provided a constant challenge to the blind acceptance of war as an institution. It has not, however, made much contribution to developing the institutions of peace, and it has not had much impact on the course of world events."[1]

It would be difficult to validate or invalidate this critical, sweeping judgment. Not only do we lack reliable knowledge about the ways in which particular proposals and campaigns have affected policy decisions, neither criteria nor procedures have been formulated that would permit a useful assessment of this or alternative views. While the peace movement has not

PART V

Influencing National Action

of different matters. If the president offends Congress by one decision, he may incapacitate himself from making several other decisions. It may not be possible to use personal political stock over and over again. To gain one point, it may be necessary to yield on a wholly unrelated issue. Thus a decision-maker may determine that the national interest requires a bad decision on one issue in order to make possible a good decision on another issue. The only common factor may be that some of the same people are involved in the decision process.

INSTITUTIONAL INERTIA

A government cannot reconsider every question every day. To be effective, a government must proceed in an orderly way and act consistently over a period of time. Institutional inertia is one of the strengths of government, but it also tends to preclude reconsideration of issues that ought to be reconsidered. It tends to cause things to be done today the way they were done yesterday, even though the passage of time has changed the circumstances.

To some extent, this commitment to a position previously taken is a personal commitment of the officials in office. A new administration feels free to act more boldly during its first year in office than it does later. The longer officials have done something in a particular way, the greater is their resistance to change.

A GOVERNMENT CANNOT UNDERTAKE PRIVATE ACTION

A final constraint on the governmental decision process is that it cannot make nongovernmental decisions. Since a government can only act officially, its decisions all suffer from the fact that they were made by the government. When governments face each other in an international conflict situation, it might be wise to ask private individuals to take steps which would change the context of the conflict or direct attention elsewhere. It might be wise to ask private individuals to initiate spontaneous action not suggested or directed by the government. An unofficial conference called by private citizens from different countries might usefully change the atmosphere; or academic institutions might usefully make suggestions to foreign governments fearful of becoming involved with Western governments. On other occasions it might be wise for newspapers, for example, to refrain on their own from publishing certain reports. The governmental decision process cannot produce such private decisions.

Trial balloons and planted stories suggest that government officials often try to act unofficially. No doubt they sometimes succeed. But in general, a government carries its official capacity with it as a turtle carries its shell. When the wisest national action is action by private individuals, the government cannot undertake it.

CONCLUSION

The above limitations on governmental decision-making are recognized to a greater or lesser degree by officials within the government. A typical response might be, "We understand the problem, it is not terribly serious, and what can be done about it is being done." Government officials are not unique in being fatalistic about defects and inadequacies in the world around us. All of us accept many situations on the assumption that nothing can be done about them. The amount that can be done, however, is not a fixed quantity to be obtained by scientific deduction. It is a function of many variables, including how hard one tries and how much one assumes he can do. If one assumes that he can do little or nothing, it is likely to be a self-fulfilling prophecy. In a large bureaucracy, in which institutional changes are bound to be difficult, it is easy to reach the conclusion that nothing can be done. The more widely that assumption is held, the more likely it is to be correct.

Finally, even if one assumes that nothing can be done by the government to overcome the institutional defects considered, outside critics may be able to compensate for the limitations. Emphasizing the importance of long-range fundamentals, providing original suggestions, and advancing arguments in favor of an improbable alternative are all feasible and appropriate activities for private individuals and organizations. This diagnosis suggests that those seeking to influence the government—a problem considered in the succeeding papers in this volume—will be more effective through such activities than by disagreeing with competent government officials on matters where the relevant considerations have been thoroughly reviewed and the decisions already made.

developed a unified program or aroused wide public support for its proposals, peace activities have become a visible and recognizable part of the political scene. The participants at least have some expectation that they may be able to influence the course of world events.

Conflicting assessments regarding the effectiveness of peace groups are also reflected in inconsistent and *ad hoc* advice. Calls for strikes and public demonstrations are countered by a recommendation to social scientists that if they wish to be "seriously influential" they should retire to think in the "solitude of their studies" instead of "organizing lobbies or pressure groups or marches on Washington."[2] There are differing beliefs about the relative usefulness of newspaper advertisements, letter-writing campaigns, appearances before Congressional committees, and political peace candidacies. Feelings differ about the advisability of enlisting mass support and participation or trying to attract such special groups as Negroes, university professors, or trade union leaders. There are different levels of concern about respectability.

This paper attempts an examination of how the efforts of peace groups may influence foreign policy. The focus is analytic, not evaluative. Evidence is not available to permit a responsible evaluation of the relative effectiveness of the diverse forms of action in which individuals and groups have engaged in the cause of peace. Our specific objective is to locate critical issues and variables in the influence process. The most important questions are: What is the process by which foreign policy decisions are reached? How and where may influence be brought to bear on this process? How are the efforts of peace groups and their political resources related to the possibilities and requirements for effective influence?

THE FOREIGN POLICY PROCESS: TARGET OF INFLUENCE

It is useful to look first at how foreign policy is made. Knowledge from the behavioral sciences on the processes of influence can be meaningful only if we understand the concrete social-political contexts within which these processes operate. If foreign policy reflects primarily the unresolved and unconscious psychic conflicts of the president and the secretary of state, then psychiatric theory might prove a powerful source of suggestion for effective influence. If the rigidities of a bureaucratic Department of State are critical features in foreign-policy formation, then it might be more instructive to turn to sociological analyses of such organizations. If foreign policy is made through discussions among a small group of policy-makers, then the experimental studies of interpersonal processes in such groups could be helpful. These alternatives are caricatures of an extremely complex process; but they show why one must investigate the nature of the foreign policy process before deciding how it may be influenced.

Political scientists, for example, Lasswell and Robinson, who have been concerned with the policy-making process, have described four stages: (1) the emergence of an occasion for decision, (2) the definition of the issues involved, (3) the consideration of alternative courses of action, (4) and the policy decision. This formulation of the policy process is not an empirical description of how decisions are actually made. It is an idealized picture of decision-making. It emphasizes rationality and suggests much more independence and separation among the several stages than it is reasonable to expect in practice. However, some simplifying model of this complex process is necessary, and while this particular model has serious limitations, it has the advantage of directing our attention to the fact that the policy process extends over time and that a policy decision is the final product of a series of stages. Most importantly, this view of foreign policy formation alerts us to the possibility that the requirements for effective influence may vary at different stages of the process.

Some of the various requirements for influence at different stages will be explored below. Here, we may note briefly that at early stages in the policy process the power to influence policy depends on control and manipulation of the situation confronting the decision-maker; at later stages it depends on the ability to affect the negative and positive consequences of alternative courses of action.

STAGES IN FOREIGN POLICY DECISION-MAKING:
FOCI FOR INFLUENCE

Institutional policies, in much the same way as individual attitudes, serve not only to guide action but also to organize events and experiences selectively. If a policy is stable, then we assume it reflects some balance of forces within the organization that formulated it: tension and conflict have been brought within manageable limits and maintaining the policy results in adequate rewards or benefits. This is in part what the behavioral scientist means when he talks of individual attitudes, social norms, and institutional policies as functional. They are "functional" in maintaining the person, society, or organization in its present state.

The intuitive definition of influence refers to the capacity to affect the policies, behavior, values, or attitudes of others. In a formal analysis of the problem, one theorist, James March, suggests that we know whether or not influence has taken place by an alteration in the course of events that would have been expected had the influence attempt not been made.

One important implication of these ideas is that effective influence does not depend solely, or even primarily, on the capacity to launch direct attacks on policies themselves. These attacks constitute one form of influence attempt; there are many other ways in which to influence policy by changing its functional significance through a change in the balance of underlying forces. An influence attempt occurs in a context where many forces are operating. The potential for influence depends on the capacity to influence these forces either directly or by bringing about changes in the situation so that the present balance is less functional for the system than it has been. The power to influence policy may reflect any of a number of different values or resources that the agent of influence may have under his control.

THE OCCASION FOR DECISION

Consider what seems to be required for effective influence at the first stage of the policy process—the point where occasions for decision arise. The determinants of influence are factors that provide control over the timing and nature of events confronting decision-makers. The influencing agent must be able to affect the specific events that will come to the attention of specific decision-makers at specific times. It is apparent that private citizens, organized or unorganized, are severely limited in their capacity to exert influence of this kind with regard to international relations.

Many situations requiring policy decisions develop without the possibility of intervention by organized or unorganized publics. The most important of these result from the actions of foreign governments: for example, the construction of the wall dividing East from West Berlin. Many other situations emerge with little advance warning and with an urgency that seems to demand an immediate response from decision-makers. In international crises, even the role of Congress appears to be severely limited. Thus, Robinson has found that of 22 foreign policy decisions between 1933 and 1961, Congressional participation and influence was lower in the five that involved a possible commitment to hostilities.

Whether or not an event is interpreted as a problem requiring decision often depends on how policy-makers wish to deal with it. The expropriation of American business property by a Brazilian governor, for example, can be ignored, treated as legitimate as long as proper payment is made, or handled as a major international incident. Some issues, particularly those involving military strategy, never come into public view before the final decision is made; for example, the decision to drop the first atomic bomb on Hiroshima, to send technicians to Vietnam, or to impose a quarantine on Cuba.

Despite these serious limitations, are there ways in which the peace movement can create occasions for decision? Here, it is important to distinguish between events that require relevant policy decisions and events that simply require governmental intervention. In this connection it is instructive to contrast the potential influence of a nongovernmental group on a domestic issue and on an international issue at this stage. On the domestic scene, special interest groups can exercise considerable control over the timing and substance of an event. A domestic organization can campaign for civil rights by insisting on the right of Negroes to ride interstate buses. If demonstrators are forcibly removed and imprisoned on charges of violating local ordinances, the Federal government is presented with an occasion for decision: its intervention in any form is an act of policy that bears directly on civil rights. On the other hand, if a peace group protests the resumption of atmospheric nuclear testing by picketing the White House, the president's response to the picket line, whether positive or negative, is not in itself a policy decision about nuclear testing. Nor would the banning of a peace demonstration by local authorities be in itself an act of policy.

The technique of freedom riders suggests one way of creating suitable occasions for foreign policy decision: the situation should involve other governments or their citizens, because only in acting toward them must our government engage in a direct act of policy. An illustration of the effective use of this tactic was the initiation of the Pugwash conferences between American and Soviet scientists. The State Department had to decide whether to grant or to deny visas to Soviet scientists who accepted invitations. The act of approval represented one part of our foreign policy vis-à-vis the Soviet Union. Lord Russell's suggestion that neutral nations sail ships to the Christmas Island bomb-testing area poses another situation that would require action at the international level—action very different in kind from that involved in dealing with American citizens who board Polaris submarines, or refuse to seek shelter during air-raid drills.

Some degree of control over how and when an occasion arises for policy decision provides powerful leverage for influencing the policy process. Our analysis suggests that there are serious limitations on the potential influence of peace groups at this stage. Important mechanisms of control are not in their hands.

DEFINITION OF ISSUES

Controlling occasions for decision may serve to limit but it does not determine how policy-makers will define the major issues in a situation. This second phase of the policy process is particularly critical, since judgments here profoundly affect the range of policy alternatives that will be given serious consideration. In some ways, the problem of influence is much more complicated in the second than in the first stage. Each policy-maker's view reflects his particular responsibilities, his assessment of the current political situation, his policy aims, and his personal values and beliefs. The situation is compounded further by the formal and informal organizational ties among the individuals who must arrive at a collective definition of the issues at stake. All of these factors predispose policy-makers to perceive and respond to new situations in certain ways. Whether or not the situation is viewed as a threat to national security or to basic values is a particularly critical question. These predispositions of policy-makers are not subject to the direct control of peace groups. But indirect ways of exerting influence can be effective.

One form of indirect influence lies in anticipating situations that may arise and attempting, in advance of their actual occurrence, to fix their meaning so that one definition rather than another seems natural and most appropriate when the event does occur. An example is the health-hazard issue. It was an important part of the debate on the resumption of atmospheric nuclear testing in 1961. In earlier testing series, this issue did not play an important public role. The public campaigns of SANE and groups of nongovernmental scientists seem to have led many persons to see the problem of radioactive fall-out as a major issue when the Soviets resumed testing. While members of the administration apparently did not consider fall-out an important variable in reaching their decision to resume testing, they had to deal explicitly with the health hazard issue in defending their decision to citizens here and abroad.

The potential effectiveness of this tactic appears to depend more on limitations in the governmental decision-making process than on the objective strength of peace groups or the persuasive logic of their position. The pressures of immediate events and the short-term orientation of policy-makers, concerned with surviving from one international crisis to the next, limit the focus of policy-makers to current problems and to known issues (see Fisher, "Defects in the Governmental Decision Process," in this volume). This provides an opportunity for private groups and individuals to anticipate problems and to suggest how they should be defined as policy issues before they have entered the decision-maker's field of awareness.

Affecting public opinion is another way of exerting influence at this stage of the policy process. "Public opinion" is an elusive area and, while reference is often made to its importance, few systematic studies of its impact are available. A recent review reports:

". . . the actual role of public opinion in the making of foreign policy decisions in the United States or elsewhere is something of an enigma. . . . [There are] contrasting descriptions or hypotheses, one of which suggests that public opinion may be a kind of tyrant with respect to the deliberations of the policy maker and the other which asserts that public opinion is virtually no factor at all in major decisions."[3]

There is no need to labor the difficulties of discovering whether and how public opinion influences general or specific policies. However, there are grounds for expecting that policy is affected by decision-makers' responses to expressions of public opinion. First, policy-makers believe that their roles carry the obligation to be responsive to public opinion (this applies particularly to elected representatives). It has been suggested by some political scientists[4] that leaders are responsive to public views because they have internalized the democratic ethic with regard to responsible, representative government. This factor appears to be equally important in the area of foreign policy. Leaders may also believe that the state of public opinion limits the types of action that can be taken. Roosevelt apparently felt, prior to our entry into World War II, that there were limits to the help he could offer England and France because the public was not prepared to go further. Many politicians today seem to feel that our government cannot support the admission of Communist China to the United Nations because it is strongly opposed by a considerable section of the American public.

In general, while some of these processes may be distinguished, our knowledge is limited about the specific ways in which policy-makers are influenced by shifts in public opinion and in the political "mood" or climate of the country. There can be little doubt that a strong peace movement would have a generally positive effect on foreign policy. But we do not know how strong it must be to exert a significant effect on critical issues.

We have discussed this stage of the policy process as if influence can be brought to bear on decision-makers before they have defined the issues involved. This is, in part, a limitation of depicting policy-making as a sequence of discrete stages. The act of definition of the issue, as we noted earlier, is bound up with whether an event is to be treated as an occasion for decision. The situation also changes and develops as various alternatives are considered. The more typical case is likely to be one in which the situation has been defined in a way incompatible with the aims of peace groups. This markedly increases the difficulties of exerting influence. Existing definitions are resistant to change. One might speak of them as "overdetermined." They permit the policy-maker to make sense out of the flow of events and crises he must handle. They also permit him to carry out his job within an organization that supports some definitions rather than others through its values, aims, and policies. When complex events are defined in this way—that is, relying more on shared norms and social reinforcement than on "objective" information—the definitions tend to be self-confirming; new events and new bits of information are transformed to reconfirm the initial definition. Dissonant information will not be sought actively and may be denied or ignored when it appears. An example of such an "overdetermined" view is our definition of any action by the Cuban government as an indication of the threat of Soviet Communism in this hemisphere.

It is difficult to see how views that are so functional for the system can be changed without a radical alteration of over-all policy goals or changes in the basic values governing policy. The weight of factors internal to the policy-making organization is likely to be far greater than influence which can be exerted by individuals outside the system. One source of potential influence for peace groups at this stage lies in identification, in the public mind, with ultimate human values. If the peace movement stands for such values, this "virtue," rather than practical power, may induce policy-makers to give serious attention to a point of view that will introduce dissonance into the situation.

ALTERNATIVES AND DECISIONS

When we turn to the later stages of the policy process—where alternatives are considered and decisions made—the possibilities of influence seem to depend on direct access to the decision-making system. One traditional route to the system leads through various forms of political pressure—that is, the use of the "levers" of political power. In general, peace groups are at a marked disadvantage in manipulating these levers. They do not represent large constituencies and the potential campaign funds available to them are relatively trivial compared to the funds controlled by other organizations and lobbies.

In the absence of real political power, access to the system for the purpose of proposing new alternatives or introducing information that might affect the value of other alternatives rests to some extent on the levels of disagreement, ambiguity, or difficulty experienced by policy-makers in attempting to arrive at a decision. When decision-makers cannot reach a viable consensus or compromise, this is likely to increase their receptivity to outside suggestions. It is to the general interest of the peace movement to support centers of dissent and diversity within the policy-making group, to enlarge the number of governmental units and agencies involved in decisions, and to increase the amount of time in which major decisions are reached.

As we have already noted, there is little that the peace movement can do to affect the international situation directly. Domestically, resistance and opposition to a particular decision can be expressed in the various ways open to political pressure groups. But one must ask the basic question: Why are these expressions sometimes effective and sometimes not? Why, for example, did opposition to the administration's fall-out shelter program in 1962 force alteration of plans? Why did equally strong opposition to the resumption of nuclear testing succeed at most in delaying the decision? We do not mean to equate these situations, but we suggest that the possibility of effective influence at the point of choice depends in part on how other groups in the general population are reacting to the situation. Fall-out shelters required individual action that aroused rather than dispelled anxiety, and despite the efforts of the mass-circulation publications the proposal did not gain widespread support. The resumption of nuclear testing in response to the Soviet testing series was firm action by the government, a response in kind to a foreign danger and an act that could count on general acceptance and public support.

CONCLUSION

By focusing on the complexity of the policy process, this paper has tended to emphasize obstacles and limitations peace groups encounter in their attempt to influence foreign policy. The aim of this analysis was not to add yet another obstacle to action or to suggest that conceptual exercises be substituted for action programs. We have raised questions about the influence process in the hope that continued examination of the problems involved will help the various parts of the peace movement to become more efficient and effective. This is not to suggest that the peace movement sit on its hands until it understands how, when, and where it is most effective.

There is no reason why some analysis of the process and an evaluation of actual influence should not be included as a part of action programs. The scarcity of systematic evidence on the problems we have discussed makes obvious the need for more evaluative research on the nature and effectiveness of peace campaigns and proposals. The limited usefulness of behavioral science studies also suggests the need for additional research on influence and policy formation in the field of international relations.

Finally, the present lack of evidence precludes valid comparisons of the relative merits of different types of peace activity. The level of public interest and support that may be enlisted in particular campaigns will continue to depend on other factors than any demonstrated value in influencing foreign policy. People will either join picket lines, or carry placards in demonstrations, or write policy papers, or do research because they are willing and able to do so and not because there is evidence that any of these activities is more effective than the others.

NOTES

1. Kenneth E. Boulding, *Conflict and Defense* (New York: Harper & Brothers, 1961), p. 333.
2. Arthur Schlesinger, Jr., letter to Dr. E. Hollander, published in SPSSI Newsletter (Ann Arbor: U. of Michigan Institute of Social Research, June 1962), p. 7.
3. James A. Robinson, *Congress and Foreign Policy Making* (Homewood, Ill.: Dorsey Press, 1962), Ch. 2.
4. Richard C. Snyder and James A. Robinson, *National and International Decision Making* (New York: Institute for International Order, Program of Research No. 4, 1961), p. 62.
5. Robert A. Dahl, *Who Governs?* (New Haven: Yale University Press, 1961).

15

JAMES A. ROBINSON

The Social Scientist and Congress

Social scientists may be excused if they feel that they are beginning to approach the centers of political decision-making. In recent years, they have undertaken new activities which give evidence that many scholars are trying to unite basic social studies with personal concern for public and international affairs. *The Journal of Conflict Resolution* has been founded; an advisory council to the President's Committee on Science has been created; government agencies are supporting and using social science research; such private societies as the American Academy of Arts and Sciences have convened special institutes on key problems of international affairs; such professional associations as the American Sociological Association and the American Psychological Association have established new committees on international affairs.

Much of this new effort has been directed at the Executive branch of the United States government. That is an appropriate target, for the Executive is the primary source of policy innovation in modern governments. Congress may also be a promising target. Two aspects of modern social science seem to me especially useful to the legislative branch, more useful in fact than legislators have recognized.[1] I refer to the techniques for surveying public opinion and to organizational theory. These two subjects deserve the attention of Congress because they correspond to two problems of special concern to congressmen: gauging constituent views and interests and overseeing the internal organization of the Executive branch.

OPINION SURVEYS

Members of Congress enjoy a variety of sources of data about their constituencies. They are themselves residents of their districts, have often grown
up there, have business and family interests, have numerous personal acquaintances, receive stacks of mail daily, make periodic personal visits to all parts
of the district, scan local newspapers, and so on. Despite all these sources of
information, politicians confront the same problems which public opinion
analysts face. They know from personal experience that their districts contain many kinds of interest, some of which differ from their own. Their
personal visits may systematically if unintentionally miss segments of the
population. Mail is biased in favor of people who write letters, and these
people may or may not be a good sample of the district. Newspapers are
selective in what they report. In short, there are many appropriate reasons
for a member of Congress to distrust his own perception of public opinion.

To offset these disadvantages, some congressmen have resorted to sending
mail questionnaires to samples of their constituents. A number of recent
papers have described Congressional polling techniques and the extent of
their use.[2] Their conclusions may be summarized as follows:

(1) Polls are relied on less than alternative sources of information about
constituencies, including personal visits, mail, newspaper editorials, and
contacts with party organizations.

(2) Almost all Congressional polls are mail questionnaires.

(3) Almost all Congressional polling is confined to members of the
House of Representatives.

(4) Between 20 and 35 per cent of the members of the House in the 85th
Congress (1958–59) used polls on some occasions.

(5) Between the 80th (1947–1948) and the 85th Congresses, the number
of congressmen using polls increased from about 28 to 163.

(6) Younger members tend to poll more than older.

(7) Representatives from competitive districts tend to poll more than
those from "safe" districts.

(8) New Congressmen tend to poll more than veteran ones.

(9) Republicans tend to poll more than Democrats.

In interviews with seventy-five Members of Congress in 1959, my colleagues and I asked which sources of information they relied on most in
making their decisions about foreign policy. We gave each congressman a
list of possible sources and asked him to rank the three that were most
important to him. The rank order was as follows:

(1) Hearings;

(2) Newspapers;

(3) Committee briefings by the Department of State;

(4) Other members of Congress;

(5) Travel;

(6) Private consultations with the Department of State;

(7) Publications of the Department of State;

(8) Social functions.

It had not occurred to me, either on the basis of my prior experience on the Hill or from the literature on Congress, to put polls of constituent opinion on this list. When we asked each congressman for any other sources which we had overlooked, none mentioned public opinion polls.

Although Congressional use of polls is not extensive, what is the quality of these polls when they are used? Space permits only gross characterization. For the most part, Congressional polls do not meet the elementary canons of survey research. Their samples are often not carefully drawn, and the universe of respondents is hardly ever known. Only Oregon and North Dakota provide candidates and officials with a complete list of registered voters. Representatives from other states rely on telephone books, city directories, and similar sources for lists of constituents from which to sample. These lists are probably adequate for superficial efforts to describe constituency opinion. When, for example, opinion in a sample is divided 8–2 against a particular proposed policy, a representative may have some confidence that this is the *direction* of opinion in his district, even if he allows for considerable sampling error about its actual *distribution*. However, for issues of high saliency on which the constituency may be closely divided, such instruments can hardly be expected to represent the district accurately.

Perhaps more to be criticized than the sampling technique is the wording of the questions. Many are loaded—"Do you favor paying off our huge national debt?"—and others are so ambiguously worded that it is difficult to interpret the results. Few congressmen obtain such data about the respondent as occupation and party affiliation, which would help to characterize the sample and to make cross-tabulations about opinions of subgroups within the constituency possible. Some members send questionnaires to every known address in the district as a kind of self-advertisement, rather than as a bonafide device to elicit constituency opinion.

This is not the place to enter into the question of whether congressmen should emulate the independence of view advocated by Edmund Burke or whether they should be weather vanes of constituent opinion. Perhaps the Burkean dilemma can be resolved by assuming that representatives should reflect constituency *values*, but not necessarily current opinions. A Congress which tried to represent opinion on specific issues would have to change its decisions often. On the other hand, it is a different matter for legislators to try to represent constituent values, that is, the enduring, long-term goal preferences or orientations. Because these are less subject to change (except through shifts in population), a representative might be expected to keep reasonably within the bounds of his constituency majority. To know these values or at least to corroborate his common-sense impressions, he would find the survey technique useful and probably more helpful and reliable than polling opinions on specific policies. Knowledge of the value profiles of the country might well help Congress to regain its lost influence as the chief instrument for representing and allocating social values.

My impression is that polls are respected by congressmen. The reason why more representatives do not use them is not because of disbelief in their accuracy, but because polls, are expensive, require some expertise in preparing reliable questionnaires, or are unnecessary because the member comes from a safe district. Although the distrust of polls associated with errors in the 1948 presidential campaign has been overcome, there is still considerable distrust of other kinds of social science which might be relevant to congressmen. I have in mind, for example, social science studies of organizational decision-making.

ORGANIZATIONAL BEHAVIOR

Since World War II, Congress has authorized two Hoover Commissions to study the organization of the Executive branch, and committees of Congress have conducted studies of particular agencies or departments, the most notable being those of the Senate Committee on Foreign Relations and the Senate Subcommittee on National Policy Machinery.

Each of these efforts—the Hoover Commissions, the Foreign Relations Committee studies, and the National Policy Machinery Subcommittee— ignored most of the advanced scholarly work in public administration and organizational theory. Herbert Simon has noted the first Hoover Commission's reliance on the nineteenth-century distinction between policy and administration, in spite of the thorough critique of the distinction by scholars of administration and the almost complete disappearance of the distinction in the advanced literature on organizations.[3] Although the Hoover Commission studies, like those of the Senate committees, were based on a large number of interviews with experienced people in public life, they were not the kind of interviews to which the serious student of organizations is accustomed. Questions were not necessarily comparable across respondents; interviewer neutrality was often not preserved; systematic analysis of data was usually not conducted and indeed could not be conducted, given the nature of the data gathered.[4] In all these recent studies of executive organization, there has been an almost total reliance on the "wisdom" of veteran and experienced public officials. No one would deny that such experience is a valuable source of knowledge about the political process, but social scientists are accustomed to recognizing the distinction between experience and experiment. They are also aware that the man who is ablest at running an organization may not be best at designing one.[5]

Despite my criticisms of the methodology of these studies,[6] I regard such opportunities as potentially the most fruitful points of contact between social science and Congress. It is with respect to the organization of policy-making within the Executive branch and, to a lesser extent, within Congress itself that social scientists might best help Congress.

Let me develop the argument this way. I think that there is overwhelming evidence to support the proposition that Congress is declining (and has been for some time) in influence vis-à-vis the Executive. This point I have tried to document elsewhere.[7] To the extent that Congress often defeats the Executive, it does so by reacting to an Executive proposal, rather than initiating policy. Congress amends, vetoes, and legitimates Executive-initiated policies, but Congress rarely initiates policies over the objection of the Executive. One of the places in which Congress has retained some of its former powers vis-à-vis the Executive is with regard to *the organization of the process for making policy* within the Executive.[8] Such studies and recommendations as those made by the Jackson Subcommittee on National Policy Machinery can exercise considerable influence on the way in which policy is made by the Executive. Although the relationship is not one-to-one, we generally assume that process affects substance of policy. If Congress would take advantage of this special source of influence over the Executive, it might do much to help improve policy-making machinery throughout the government. In working out such a task, Congress would find a large body of extant research and a considerable number of social scientists skilled in the necessary theory and techniques.

Take, for example, the problem of planning by the Executive. It is a common lament among the Executive departments that their personnel simply does not have enough time to plan ahead, to see the forest instead of the trees. Congressmen often agree with these complaints as they review Executive decisions and see the consequences of failure to look ahead and to consider the long-range implications of short-term decisions. Why should not Congress lift its objectives from criticizing day-to-day decisions, on which it often has little information, to the larger job of finding organizational devices that require the Executive to plan ahead and represent the kind of values Congress favors? Congress could be at once innovative and constructive, not simply reactive and critical. Congress could be influential where its strength is greatest—in overseeing the organization of the Executive.

Congress has not by any means taken full advantage of social science resources for surveying public values and for organizing governmental decision processes. I suggest that social science knowledge and social scientists would be useful to Congress in the representation of values and in making constructive as well as influential contributions to public policy. Social scientists with those skills and a desire to contribute them to political use have their opportunity. If the mountain will not come to Mahomet, let Mahomet go to the mountain. A more modern version might be: every social scientist has a congressman.

NOTES

1. In this essay I do not consider the potential social science contribution to debates on the content of political issues, but rather the process of deciding issues. Most of the volume in which this paper appears is devoted to the application of social and behavioral science theories to the substantive conduct of international conflict. In recent years, several social scientists have produced books or articles which bring the expertise or special insight of their research to bear on the merits or substance of issues. Examples include Morton Deutsch, "Psychological Alternatives to War," in Quincy Wright, William M. Evan, and Morton Deutsch, eds., *Preventing World War III: Some Proposals* (New York: Simon & Schuster, 1962); Amitai Etzioni, *The Hard Way to Peace* (New York: Collier Books, 1962); Harold Guetzkow, *Multiple Loyalties: Theoretical Approach to a Problem in International Organization* (Princeton, N.J.: Center for Research on World Political Institutions, 1955); and *idem*, "Isolation and Collaboration: A Partial Theory of Inter-nation Relations," *Journal of Conflict Resolution*, I (1957), 48–68.
2. John W. Smith, "Mailed Congressional Public Opinion Polls," unpublished paper, Department of Political Science, University of Michigan, 1961; Eugene A. Sekulow, "The Congressmen Ask the People," Ph.D. dissertation, The Johns Hopkins University, 1960; Carl Hawver, "The Congressman and His Public Opinion Poll," *Public Opinion Quarterly*, XVIII (1954), 123–129; Martin Kriesberg, "What Congressmen and Administrators Think of Polls," *Public Opinion Quarterly*, IX (1945), 333–337.
3. "Recent Advances in Organization Theory," *Research Frontiers in Politics and Government* (Washington, D.C.: The Brookings Institution, 1955), pp. 23–44.
4. An exception to this characterization of Hoover Commission studies is one by Harold Guetzkow, "Interagency Committee Usage," *Public Administration Review*, X (1950), 190–196.
5. Herbert A. Simon, *The New Science of Management Decision* (New York: Harper & Brothers, 1960), p. 5.
6. See my *Congress and Foreign Policy-Making* (Homewood, Ill.: The Dorsey Press, 1962), pp. 203–208.
7. *Loc. cit.*
8. *Ibid.*, pp. 105–106, 114–115.

16

LESTER GRINSPOON

The Truth Is Not Enough

It has been said that the truth is a scarce commodity, and yet the supply always exceeds the demand. As nearly as we can determine, the truth about the state of the world is that the very existence of a whole civilization, and perhaps more, is threatened. Yet, it does not appear that most people, including decision-makers and the public, have wholly grasped this fact. If they believed that their lives and those of their loved ones were threatened, we would expect them to be seething with concern and activity.

One authoritative survey which sought reasons for unhappiness in the United States reported:

> Problems that have a community or national or world locus are mentioned by only 13 percent of the population. Within this broader category, 4 percent of our respondents expressed unhappiness over problems of world tension and the possibility of war, a figure which may seem small in the era of the hydrogen bomb and the cold war.[1]

How do we explain this? Are we to believe that the facts are not available and that the mass media have conspired to hide the truth? This is a tempting explanation, but it cannot be reconciled with the fact that there are people without any special resources who fully appreciate the present situation.

It is not easy, even in a democracy, to be well-informed. Beyond motivation, enlightenment demands time and effort and is limited by intelligence and imagination. For one reason or another, all the known facts about a situation may not be available to the public. Much of what appears in the mass media has undergone some process of selection, and frequently some degree of distortion. Undiluted technical information is meaningless to most people and its interpretation by experts often leads to ambiguity. Still, the gross facts of the Cold War and the nature of modern weapons are not beyond the grasp of most people. A realistic appreciation of the present danger does not require a great deal of intelligence, technical knowledge, or political sophistication.

There have been many instances in history and literature in which only a few individuals have correctly perceived a danger to which they then tried to arouse others. For the Jews in Germany during the thirties, the handwriting was on the wall; there were those few who understood it and tried to awaken others. Laocoön, in Virgil's *Aeneid,* tried to warn his people of the danger which should have been obvious to all.

Similarly today, a handful of concerned individuals find themselves vainly trying to awaken people to grave and impending dangers. Albert Einstein attempted to sound the alarm in 1946 that "The unleashed power of the atom has changed everything save our modes of thinking and we thus drift toward unparalleled catastrophe."[2] Yet, sounding the alarm has often proved insufficient. In May 1960, for example, a great sea wave hit the Hawaiian city of Hilo. It killed sixty-one persons and injured several hundreds more despite ten hours of warning. Ninety-five per cent of those threatened by the wave heard the warning and all but 6 per cent indicated that they understood what the warning meant. Despite this, of those who heard the warning only 41 per cent evacuated the threatened area while 59 per cent did not.[3]

This paper raises the question of why people seem not to listen and respond to the alarm. If we wish to be effective in *producing* useful action, we must understand why warnings are ignored. Only then can we hope to sound the alarm more effectively. We shall first attempt to explain why people keep certain truths at bay and to specify the mental mechanisms by which this is accomplished. We shall then consider what happens when people are suddenly made aware of alarming facts with which they have no way of coping; and finally whether there are less frightening and more effective ways of confronting people with unwelcomed truths.

WHY TRUTH IS UNACCEPTABLE

The truth about the nature and risk of thermonuclear war is available; the reason why it is not embraced is that it is not acceptable. People cannot risk being overwhelmed by the anxiety which might accompany a full cognitive and affective grasp of the present world situation and its implications for the future. It serves a man no useful purpose to accept this truth if doing so leads only to very disquieting feelings—feelings which interfere with his capacity to be productive, to enjoy life, and to maintain his mental equilibrium.

This remarkable ability to avoid the acceptance of compelling facts suggests that the individual is employing active psychological processes which protect him from uncomfortable feelings. These conscious and unconscious mechanisms involved in maintaining men's internal peace are protective and adaptive. They are employed by that agency of the mind known as the ego. They defend and protect the individual against intrapsychic, obnoxious mental elements; and while we sometimes speak of them as though they were protecting directly against external noxious stimuli, they do so only secondarily insofar as these latter are translated by the individual into internal noxious elements.

The Mechanism of Denial

Of the psychological mechanisms which protect men from anxiety, denial is one of the most primitive and at the same time one of the most important. People are using this mechanism when they manage to ignore or dismiss internal or external events, the perception of which is painful. Common examples are the avoidance of contemplating one's inevitable death or the reluctance to acknowledge the presence of a fatal disease. Daniel Defoe chronicled the widespread denial used by the people of London in 1664; they would not accept the fact that increased bills for burials in parishes at one end of town signified a revisitation of the plague.[4] In modern times, we recall people's striking lack of awareness of the existence of concentration camps in their immediate vicinity.

Despite the magnitude, the imminence, the ever-present danger of nuclear accident and conflict, such a calamity is particularly easy to deny because of two distinct characteristics. First, the distance between the weapons and the potential victims is so great that the threat seems remote. Technological advances have increased the range of weapons and contributed to an increased psychological distance (despite the fact that delivery time is decreased). Second, the nature of the act of destruction, simply pushing a button, is so far removed from conventional physical aggression that it, too, contributes to psychological distance.

Denial, like other mechanisms to be discussed, has most important adaptive functions. Its use is not necessarily pathological. Without it, we would be much less likely to travel in airplanes, undergo surgery, eat meat, or to carry out countless other acts of daily life.

The Defense of Isolation

Archibald MacLeish points to the separation of fact from feeling as characteristic of our society. He says:

> . . . knowledge without feeling is not knowledge, and can only lead to public irresponsibility and indifference, conceivably to ruin. . . . [When]

the fact is dissociated from the feel of the fact . . . that people, that civilization is in danger.[5]

MacLeish is speaking of isolation, another mechanism men use to defend
themselves against feelings which may be painful. When a man can acknowledge the fact that a continued arms race could lead to a nuclear war—which
might mean death for himself, his family, and millions of his countrymen—
without experiencing any more effect than he would when contemplating the
effects of DDT on a population of fruit flies, then he is probably making
use of the defense of isolation. People can speak quite facilely about
death resulting from nuclear war because they are speaking of death as
something quite apart (isolated) from the feelings associated with the concept
of total annihilation. It becomes an abstraction, something which has no real
connection with themselves. One might speculate, somewhat fancifully, that
this defense of isolation is becoming institutionalized by our rapidly developing reliance on computers and cybernation. Isolation also has adaptive
functions. It enables men to do many things which they might otherwise
not do. For example, the use of isolation is essential to the doctor who must
see a corpse as a subject of study in the pathology laboratory.

Displacement as a Defense

Displacement is another important mental mechanism which people employ
to defend themselves against distressing facts. They unconsciously transfer
effect from its real object, in this case the threat of nuclear war, to substitute objects. The superpatriot's concern about "the enemy" may, among
other things, represent displaced anxiety about war.

Through displacement, people can attach emotion to substitute objects which
allow for its discharge. A case in point may be the fluoridation issue. People
are surprisingly complacent about the possible consequences of exposure to
Strontium 90 and other harmful radionucleides, despite medical warnings
about both short- and long-term effects. Contrast this general complacency
about Strontium 90 with the strong public reaction against fluoridation in
some communities. In Wellesley, Massachusetts, a suburban middle-class
community, fluoridation was voted down almost two-to-one in 1961, in spite
of overwhelming recommendations to the contrary by dental and public
health authorities. Much public interest and emotion was aroused by both
sides in the dispute. The argument against fluoridation was that individuals
should not be required to ingest any artifact, no matter how beneficial. The
objection was to exposing persons en masse to an agent over which they had
no control. The equally vociferous arguments in favor of fluoridation held
that the risks were nonexistent or exceedingly small and were greatly outweighed by the benefits to be derived.

It is possible that some of the concern, both for and against fluoridation,
is displaced feeling about fallout. Notice the similarities between fluoridation

of a community's water supply and the contamination of its atmosphere with Strontium 90. Neither substance can be felt, seen, heard, tested, or smelled. In both instances people are faced with an imperceptible substance, the ingestion of which they cannot avoid. One might add that if the fluoridation proponents had as appealing a name for the additive as "sunshine units" is for Strontium 90, they, too, might allay some of the anxiety that leads to opposition.

The mechanism of displacement works both ways. Not only is anxiety about the possibility of war displaced, but the possibility of war itself may serve as a substitute object for the anxiety of personal internal conflicts. Many people actively engaged in war-peace issues may be dealing with their internal conflicts by substituting remote international conflicts for them. Here, involvement may be largely determined by displacement. On the other hand, because the possibility of World War III may by displacement be made the external substitute for a fantasy of destruction against internal objects, it must be denied to prevent the anxiety associated with the achievement of the aims of the fantasy. Thus, one would expect individuals in whom displacement is operating in this manner to express little interest in the international conflict.

Rationalization, Intellectualization, and Dogmatism

A ubiquitous defense, rationalization, accounts for such common attitudes as, "It's so terrible it'll never be used," "No one's mad enough to start an H-bomb war," "I'm sure the president (premier) and all those generals know more about it than we do," "Perhaps it's God's will. . . ." Such rationalizations protect the individual from a genuine engagement with indisputable facts.

Intellectualization is another mechanism, used by both those engaged in preparing for war and those involved in peace research. An individual appears to have an excellent understanding of the facts, and his grasp of technical aspects may be impressive. All of this knowledge, however, keeps him quite distant from the psychological and political actualities. Doctors in their shop talk make frequent use of intellectualization; so do strategic thinkers.

Another way in which people defend themselves from truths which threaten them with unmanageable anxiety is the defense of dogmatism. Essential to this mechanism is an airtight system of beliefs which provides all the answers and does away with uncertainty and anxiety. New facts, however much they have to be distorted, are merely integrated into the system.

This is by no means an exhaustive treatment of the mental mechanisms individuals use to defend themselves against intolerable feelings stimulated by disturbing truths. There are others, and while all of them are defense mechanisms, their adaptive function should be emphasized too. They are important means by which people orient themselves to their daily tasks and protect themselves from whatever threatens to upset their routine. In the same way that they make it possible for motorists to drive on highways without overwhelming anxiety in the face of nearly 40,000 traffic deaths and 1,500,000 injuries yearly,[6] so they make it possible for people to go about their daily lives as though the threat of thermonuclear, chemical, and bacteriological warfare did not exist.

DISTURBING EFFECTS OF TRUTH

It has been argued that solutions to the dangerous problems which beset the world would be found more readily if whole populations really appreciated the nature of the present risks. Proponents of this view suggest that ways must be found to make people aware, such as showing during prime television time movies of twenty megaton bursts. The consequences of such an endeavor might, however, be disastrous. For if such a scheme were successful, defense mechanisms would be overwhelmed and people would be burdened with feelings with which they might have no way of coping constructively. Contrary to expectations, they might seize upon activities which could result in increased world tension. In fact, there is some experimental evidence which shows that fear-bearing communications decrease the ability of the recipient to respond adaptively to important facts.[7]

An anecdote may help to illustrate some aspects of this problem. Not long ago the author and a companion were attempting to spot and fish for striped bass from an airplane. The technique consists of flying low to find schools of bass close enough to the beach to be within surf casting range, then landing on the beach and fishing in the surf. An ideal beach for bass fishing located at the tip of a twelve-mile spit of sand can be reached only by special means of transportation. On this particular day we scoured the area to find that the only signs of life were two fishermen and, 500 yards north of them, two skate, an undesirable fish. Wishing to be helpful, we decided to land and tell the two fishermen that they were wasting their time, that there were no striped bass for miles around. That they were not pleased to hear this was not too surprising, but that they were annoyed and angry with us, was. After a little reflection, we realized what we had done. These fishermen had gone to considerable trouble, including at the very least a half day's travel, to get to the isolated spot where the bass fishing was reputed to be so good. In spite of the fact that they undoubtedly had not had a single strike all morning, they continued to maintain the pleasant fantasy that the ocean was full of striped bass which might strike their lures at any moment. We arrived with our lofty truth and in a moment pricked the bubble of their happy illusion and then flew off. The only thing they knew to do there was to fish, but suddenly there were no fish. Had we been able to offer them some alternative along with the fact that there were no fish, they might not have become angry. We might have, for example, invited them to fly with us or suggested where they might with more promise of success dig for quahogs. As it was, aside from the truth, we offered them nothing, and we observed from the air that they continued to fish, but now unhappily, in waters they knew to be barren. The truth alone had accomplished nothing more than to spoil their fun.

Just as the truth was not enough for the bass fishermen, so it is that people living in the thermonuclear age cannot really accept the facts of this moment in history *without a concomitant means or hope of altering them for the next.* The truth alone is not enough. A psychotherapist, for example, does not offer an interpretation his patient is not prepared to deal with. Furthermore, it is his responsibility to understand what the consequences of the interpretation will be, what it will mean to this particular patient in this particular relationship at this particular time. Similarly, the surgeon does not tell his patient he has cancer simply because he has it. Those who would have others know "the truth" must take into account what "the truth" would mean to them and how they would respond to it. The truth is relative in interpersonal affairs; it has meaning only in relation to people, and this meaning is often difficult to anticipate. The messenger of "truth" bears part of the responsibility for the results of his effort. Doing good can be initiated unilaterally, but it must be evaluated according to the total consequences. The responsible "do-gooder" will consider this in advance.

What happens when people's means of keeping facts at bay have been suddenly destroyed? For a while they may suffer anxious, depressed feelings, feelings which may be incapacitating. For some, these feelings may precipitate serious mental illness. However, most will either reconstitute their defense mechanisms, much as a self-sealing tire seals over after a puncture, or they will embrace some anxiety-relieving activity which they believe is capable of altering the unacceptable facts. Perhaps what most commonly takes place is a mixture of restitution of old defenses and adoption of new ideas and activities. New activities may be primarily intellectual or largely action-oriented. While they may be helpful and adaptive as far as the individual is concerned, they may be adaptive or maladaptive with regard to the development of a peaceful world.

Reactions to Unalloyed Truth

A case in point is the response to an article by this author and a colleague, which appeared in 1961.[8] It presented the world situation with its probability of nuclear war in much the same way that the reality of the fishing circumstances was presented to the striped bass fishermen. The authors received thirty-eight letters in response to this article, thirty-four of which expressed feelings about what the individual could or should do about the situation.[a] Thirteen of these responses involved some sort of constructive suggestion, such as working toward disarmament or the establishment of world law. The following quote illustrates this group of responses:

What is at stake is a large part of humanity, untold damage to values and civilization, unforeseeable genetic damage and quite unimaginable human suffering. . . . A greatly strengthened U.N. and enforceable universal disarmament together with a workable system of world law in those areas which common self interest now makes essential is certainly within the realm of the possible—and no lesser alternative will do.

However, there were twenty-one responses which were anything but constructive. One expressed complete hopelessness about the situation:

We are in a trap, from which there is no visible escape. I, for one, believe there will be a nuclear war and that where I live is a target area. I also believe there is nothing I can do about it.

One of the four who expressed interest in suicide kits wrote as follows:

. . . my wife and I, having read many more things on thermonuclear war than your article, have decided we definitely prefer for ourselves and our small son death to any struggle for survival during or after an H-bomb attack. . . . Can you tell me (1) where I might obtain [a suicide kit?] or (2) where I might get a pill that would without much pain induce death promptly, or (3) to what sort of person or agency I might in the D.C. area apply to obtain such or gain information about such?

Fifteen respondents expressed an interest in or plans for leaving the country. One of these responses follows:

Six weeks ago I returned to the United States after an extended stay abroad, determined to do "something" of meaningful consequence to abate and reverse the drift to destruction. Trying to determine what that "something" could be, I have during these past weeks spoken with government leaders, businessmen, publishers, and ordinary citizens, in Washington, New York, and Chicago. The sundry lot represented the full range of social and political backgrounds and beliefs. The consensus assumed a nuclear war to be entirely likely within the next ten years, but to my chagrin, there was almost complete indifference beyond the acceptance of the fact. The rationalizations took two main forms: "We are doing the best thing we can do" (better dead than Red) or, "There's nothing we can do!" There was

---

[a] As a stimulus, this article was biased because it specifically mentioned both fleeing and suicide kits as possible individual responses to the nuclear threat. It was published in a journal which reaches a limited and selective portion of the population. While fallout shelters were also mentioned in the article, it was published prior to the time they became a widely discussed national issue.

a minority third group either wanting to do or actually doing something, but often hopelessly vague or idealistic in terms of political realities and accomplishments, and, of course, always frustrated by the enormity of the task at hand. . . .

Now, my thinking has progressed to the pessimistic (or realistic) point, whereby the problem becomes one of mustering up the courage and fortitude to make the break to a far away land, and then, to decide where best to go in the Southern Hemisphere.

Thus, while some of these thirty-four responses may have been adaptive for the individual, almost two-thirds of them were clearly maladaptive with regard to altering the world situation.

CAN TRUTH BE MADE ACCEPTABLE?

There are existing models for making disturbing "truths" acceptable. One of them derives from the psychotherapy relationship. A patient or a group of patients can, on the strength of their relationship with the responsible and trusted therapist, accept from him "truths" which under any other circumstances they might not be able to deal with constructively. Another model might be a program or activity which promises to modify unacceptable facts. If people believe there is something they can do about an otherwise intolerable situation, they can come closer to a fuller appreciation of that situation. One can conceive of a model which represents a hybridization of the above two. In this case, a leader who commands the respect and trust of his people would not simply call attention to disturbing facts; he would provide the means, or at least a belief in the means, by which they could be altered. He would, so to speak, take with one hand and give with the other.

CONCLUSION

Most people are far from being meaningfully aware of the extraordinary facts of the present world situation. What would happen if they were suddenly and forcefully confronted with them in the absence of concomitant means of dealing with them? We would suggest that, as far as the individual is concerned, there are two possibilities. First, he would not be reached. He would deny, isolate, displace, rationalize, distort, and use every other possible means to preserve his internal peace. In fact, the more his peace is threatened, the more hypertrophied may these defenses become. Second, having been profoundly disturbed by a threatening confrontation, the individual would translate the resulting anxiety into some sort of activity program. Group dynamics, not considered here, adds another whole dimension to the problem. Still, with this kind of confrontation we cannot be sure whether the individual will be aroused to do something constructive or destructive with regard to the problems of the world, or whether he will just go fishing in barren waters.

NOTES

1. Gerald Gurin, Joseph Veroff, and Sheila Feld, *Americans View Their Mental Health* (New York: Basic Books, 1960), p. 28.
2. Albert Einstein, *New York Times*, May 25, 1946, p. 13.
3. Roy Lachman, Maurice Tatsuoka, and William J. Bonk, "Human Behavior during the Tsunami of May 1960," *Science*, CXXXIII (1961), pp. 1405–1409.
4. Daniel Defoe, *A Journal of the Plague Year and Other Pieces* (New York: Doubleday, Doran & Co., Inc., 1935).
5. Archibald MacLeish, "The Poet and the Press," *The Atlantic Monthly*, CCIII (1959), pp. 40–46.
6. J. I. Recht, *Accident Facts* (Chicago: National Safety Council, 1961), p. 12.
7. Irving L. Janis and Seymour Feshbach, "Effect of Fear-Arousing Communications," *Journal of Abnormal and Social Psychology*, XLVIII (1953), pp. 78–92; *idem*, "Personality Differences Associated with Responsiveness to Fear-Arousing Communications," *Journal of Personality*, XXIII (1954), p. 166. Also Janis, "Motivational Factors in the Resolution of Decisional Conflicts," *Nebraska Symposium on Motivation* (1959), pp. 198–231.
8. Lester Grinspoon, M.D., and E. James Lieberman, M.D., "Escape from the Bomb," *The New Republic*, CXLV (1961), pp. 10–15.

Index